MW00511092

The Immigration Battle in American Courts

This book assesses the role of the federal judiciary in immigration and the institutional evolution of the U.S. Supreme Court and of the U.S. Courts of Appeals. Neither court has played a static role across time. By the turn of the twentieth century, a division of labor had developed between the two courts whereby the Courts of Appeals retained their original function as error-correction courts, while the Supreme Court was reserved for the most important policy and political questions. Anna O. Law explores the consequences of this division for immigrant litigants, who are more likely to prevail in the Courts of Appeals because of advantageous institutional incentives that increase the likelihood of a favorable outcome. As this book proves, it is inaccurate to speak of an undifferentiated institution called "the federal courts" or "the judiciary," for such characterizations elide important differences in mission and function of the two highest courts in the federal judicial hierarchy.

Anna O. Law is an Assistant Professor at DePaul University. She previously served as a program analyst at the United States Commission on Immigration Reform, a bipartisan congressional blue-ribbon panel charged with making policy recommendations to Congress and the White House. She was also an expert commentator in an award-winning documentary about the Supreme Court that aired on PBS channels nationwide in 2007. Her articles have appeared in the *Journal of American Ethnic History* and the *Georgetown Immigration Law Journal*.

The Immigration Battle in American Courts

ANNA O. LAW

DePaul University

CAMBRIDGE UNIVERSITY PRESS
Cambridge, New York, Melbourne, Madrid, Cape Town,
Singapore, São Paulo, Delhi, Tokyo, Mexico City

Cambridge University Press
32 Avenue of the Americas, New York, NY 10013-2473, USA

www.cambridge.org
Information on this title: www.cambridge.org/9780521767088

First published 2010
Reprinted 2011

A catalog record for this publication is available from the British Library.

Library of Congress Cataloging in Publication Data

Law, Anna O., 1970–
   The immigration battle in American courts / Anna O. Law.
      p.   cm.
   Includes bibliographical references and index.
   ISBN 978-0-521-76708-8 (hardback)
      1. Emigration and immigration law – United States – History.
   2. United States. Supreme Court – History.   3. Appellate courts –
   United States – History.   4. Judgments – United States – History.   I. Title.
   KF4819.L39   2010
   342.7308′2–dc22   2010017721

ISBN 978-0-521-76708-8 Hardback

For my parents, Yuk Pang and Yip-Wang Law

Contents

List of Tables and Figures   *page* ix
Acknowledgments   xi

1   Introduction   1
2   How Do We Know What We Know? Data,
    Methods, and Initial Findings   19
3   The Rise of Two Courts with Differentiated Functions   54
4   Interstitial Policy Making in the U.S. Courts of Appeals   102
5   Institutional Growth and Innovation: The Ninth
    Circuit Court of Appeals and Immigration   144
6   Continuity Amid Change: The Federal Courts'
    Commitment to Due Process   188
7   Conclusion   231

Appendix A. Further Elaboration of Case Selection Methods   237
*Appendix B. Further Elaboration on the Search
for Modes of Legal Reasoning*   241
Appendix C. Numerical Codes for Modes of Legal Reasoning   245
Appendix D. Interview Questions   247
Index   249

Tables and Figures

TABLES

2.1 Definitions of Most Frequently Occurring Modes
of Legal Reasoning   *page* 47
3.1 Percentage of Immigration Appeals in the Courts
of Appeals by Origin   94
4.1 Analysis of Pairs of Cases that Reached the Supreme
Court, 1881–2002   142
5.1 Number of BIA Appeals Filed During 12-Month
Periods 2001–2006 and as Percentage of Total
Appeals Filed in Circuit   153
5.2 Immigration Cases in the Ninth Circuit and Nationwide,
1994–2005, for 12-Month Period Ending September 30
(Percentage of National Immigration Appeals)   154
5.3 Terminations of the Ninth Circuit's Immigration
Appeals by Calendar Year   159
6.1 Three Most Frequently Occurring Modes of Legal
Reasoning by Frequency, Percentage of Usage, and
Decade, 1881–2002   218

FIGURES

3.1 Frequency of Modes of Legal Reasoning in the
Third, Fifth, and Ninth Circuits, 1881–2002   84
3.2 Modes of Legal Reasoning by Court, 1881–2002   85
4.1 Use of Statutory Interpretation, 1881–2002   111
4.2 Immigration Caseload at Supreme Court and
U.S. Courts of Appeals, 1881–2002   115

4.3   Pro-Alien Rates by Circuit, 1881–2002   125
4.4   Use of Fact/Evidence, 1881–2002   131
6.1   Modes of Legal Reasoning in Courts of Appeals
      Cases in which the Alien Prevailed, 1881–2002   215

Acknowledgments

There is almost nothing remarkable about saying that one is an immigrant or a descendant of immigrants in the United States because so many can lay a claim to that legacy. Still, this is a deeply personal book. My great-grandfather, Hoy Hung, was the first Chinese silk merchant who traveled between China and Hawaii in the early 1900s to run his dry goods business. Because of his merchant status, he was exempt from the Chinese Exclusion Act, but not from harsh interrogations by immigration officials on each of his trips to Honolulu. My parents, Yip-Wang and Yuk Pang Law, and I are immigrants from Hong Kong. I have lived the immigrant experience myself in having to make requisite linguistic and cultural adjustments and adaptations to this country. For more than 30 years, my mother has been a social worker in Honolulu serving Chinese immigrants. Many of her clients have become family friends, and I have been able to observe the impact of immigration policies on actual people. My uncle, Alan Ma, is a prominent immigration attorney in Honolulu. It was perhaps inevitable that I would end up in this area of research.

This book is a major overhaul of my doctoral dissertation – so major that my dissertation advisor will not recognize it. It also marks the end of a journey that took much longer than I originally anticipated. Luckily I did not have to travel it alone. Scholarship is not produced in a vacuum, and I am grateful to and humbled by the number of friends and colleagues who helped me with this project. Larry Fuchs at Brandeis was the first to inspire me to think about the possibilities of using U.S. immigration policy as a lens to study a multitude of phenomena in American politics. Indeed he was the one who talked me into going to graduate school, a possibility that I had previously never even considered. James Hollifield and Dan Tichenor have, from my undergraduate years until the present, provided impeccable professional advice, guidance, and, what was most important, encouragement and friendship. Susan Martin, the executive director at the U.S. Commission on Immigration Reform, for whom I worked, also encouraged me to go back to graduate school. My time at the commission was invaluable in teaching me about the diverse policy and political considerations in this area of law. I am also very grateful to two American political development and law scholars, Paul Frymer and Mark Graber, who have gone out of their way to be encouraging and supportive of my professional development and overall well-being.

At the University of Texas at Austin, my committee members Gary Freeman and Alan Kessler were particularly helpful with feedback. Sandy Levinson, who was my dissertation supervisor, deserves a special accolade for his willingness to take on the project after seeing a germ of potential that was not evident even to me back then. When he first agreed to sign on to the project, he jokingly said that he had no idea what the role of a dissertation chair was supposed to be, given that he had not supervised one before. I knew better. I had already done my own "background check" and had read Sandy's preface to Robert McCloskey's *The American Supreme Court*, in which he wrote about his rewarding relationship with McCloskey, his own dissertation supervisor. I still felt keen pressure not to be Sandy's first, worst, and last advisee. He was a supportive dissertation advisor, even as he provided critiques and suggestions when necessary that pushed me to clarify concepts and ultimately to improve the final product. He made the dissertation process a very enjoyable one at a difficult time in my graduate career when I was running out of gas.

During the writing of this book, many friends and colleagues at DePaul, other universities, and organizations generously offered their time and assistance. I had particularly productive discussions about methodology and research design with Molly Andolina, Jake Bowers, Dave Klein, Jeff Ladewig, Mark Makenzie, Kevin Scott, Wayne Steger, Frank Thames, Margie Williams, and Cara Wong. Others read various iterations of chapters or book proposals and provided critical feedback. They include Alex Aleinikoff, David Barnum, Larry Bennett, Norm Finkelstein, Barry Friedman, Paul Frymer, Jim Hollifield, the Honorable "Judge H" of the Court of Appeals for the Ninth Circuit, Desmond King, Dave Klein, Steve Legomsky, Kevin Scott, and Dan Tichenor. I benefited from the outstanding assistance provided by my very capable undergraduate research assistants Trisha Chokshi, Victoria Dohnal, Tyler Norkus, Ryan Vanderbilt, and Nina Yabes. Karen Drummond, librarian at the Board of

Acknowledgments xiii

Immigration Appeals (BIA), provided some very important unpublished documents about the history of the BIA. Marion Smith and her staff at the Immigration and Naturalization Service (INS) archives helped me wade through a number of documents detailing the historical development of the INS. I extend a special thanks to the judges and central staff of the Court of Appeals for the Ninth Circuit who agreed to be interviewed for this project. Michael Heilman, retired member of the BIA, also graciously submitted to an interview. The interview data from the Ninth Circuit personnel and Heilman provided rare and invaluable insight into various processes that would not have been otherwise accessible.

I received funding at critical junctures of the project from a number of sources. Fellowships provided by the Social Science Research Council's International Migration Program and the Center for Comparative Immigration Studies at the University of California, San Diego, allowed me to finish the dissertation in a timely manner. At DePaul, the Undergraduate Research Assistants Program allowed me to incorporate undergraduates into my research. Several University Research Council fellowships funded research trips and a Competitive Research Leave allowed me to finish writing the bulk of the manuscript.

Allen McDuffee provided prudent copyediting and Mary Harper produced a fantastic and comprehensive index. Special thanks also to Lewis Bateman at Cambridge University Press, who provided patient advice and assistance in shepherding the project along and for taking a first-time author seriously. Kudos as well to Emily Spangler and my entire Cambridge production team that helped bring this book into being.

Finally, I wish to thank my friends and family, who had to endure several years of what must have seemed to be my interminable pacing, thinking aloud, complaining, and constant worrying about this book project. I am grateful for my parents' love and support. Look, Ma! I FINALLY finished it! I thank Lynn Arce, Rob Barr, Josh Becker, Junehee Chung, Brian Hayashibara, Jeff Ladewig, Janice Lee, Brenda Mak, Cathy May, my cat Moana, Christina Rivers, April Smith, Lavita Strickland LeGrys, Frank Thames, Sharon Vaughan, Kim Winegar, David Williams, and Cara Wong – all of whom contributed to the preservation of my sanity. I wrote 95 percent of this book at a coffee shop called Intelligentsia. Thank you to the Intelligentsia morning crew for keeping me happily caffeinated during this long project and for their frequent and concerned inquiries about my progress on this book.

Chicago, IL
2009

I

Introduction

The Statue of Liberty in New York Harbor has represented hope and freedom for many generations of immigrants. The image of Lady Justice, with her blindfold and scales, that is found in almost every courtroom of the United States has inspired many litigants' and jurists' hopes for an equitable meting out of justice. This book examines the intersection of two traditions in U.S. life and politics that are represented by those ubiquitous images: the country's legacy as a nation of immigrants and its commitment to provide equal treatment under the law. In this nation of immigrants, how have the two highest federal courts, the Supreme Court of the United States and the U.S. Courts of Appeals, treated aliens' petitions to enter or to remain in this country?[1]

The U.S. Supreme Court has a dubious track record when it comes to immigration. Historian Leonard Dinnerstein summarized the Court's behavior in immigration cases as follows: "In the land that proudly proclaims its immigration heritage, the Supreme Court, over the years, has consistently allowed Congress and the executive branch of the federal government the right to admit, exclude, or banish non-citizens on any basis they chose including race, sex, and ideology."[2] What explains this

---

[1] I am very aware that the term "alien" has a pejorative meaning attached to it. I use the term in this book only for the sake of consistency with the terminology used in government and legal documents. For better or worse, almost all U.S. government documents and federal legal opinions use this term. "Alien" is also a legal term of art that refers to one's legal immigration status and applies to those who have not obtained U.S. citizenship by birth on U.S. soil, through naturalization, or through derivative status through a relative.

[2] Leonard Dinnerstein, "The Supreme Court and the Rights of Aliens," reprinted from *This Constitution: A Bicentennial Chronicle*, published by Project '87 of the American

situation? For the Supreme Court to afford this degree of latitude and deference to the elected branches is unusual because the Court has in many other areas of law, such as criminal law, not hesitated to challenge or contradict the two other branches of government. The Supreme Court's perceived hostility toward aliens in exclusion and deportation cases is jarring when juxtaposed with the welcoming and hopeful symbolism of the images of the Statue of Liberty.

It would seem that it is not advantageous for aliens to follow through on the often-made, thoroughly American threat to "take their case all the way to the Supreme Court" if indeed that Court is hostile to aliens' immigration claims. But are the U.S. Courts of Appeals, the second highest level of appellate courts, any more welcoming of aliens' immigration claims than the Supreme Court? This question of whether the Supreme Court and the Courts of Appeals treat immigration cases in similar fashion is the empirical inquiry that drives this book. This investigation will also guide more than the theoretical examinations about the institutional development of these two courts over time. The purpose here is not to compare judicial decision making in immigration law with judicial decision making in another area of law. Rather, the goal is to examine vertically the different development paths followed by two different sorts of courts across time and in a single area of law.

As a political scientist, I study laws as products of political conflict mediated by institutional norms and structures. Legal institutions such as the Supreme Court and the Courts of Appeals, beyond being brick and mortar structures, can also be construed as institutions in the sense that they comprise stable sets of rules, procedures, and norms that are "regularities in political life [that] shape the expression and aggregation of political preferences."[3] Institutional settings and context directly influence judicial decision making by circumscribing the roles and missions of the institution, and "shap[ing] the interests, resources, and ultimately the conduct of political actors," including judges.[4] Similarly, American political development scholars Karen Orren and Stephen Skowronek have observed, "Institutions participate actively in politics: they shape interests and motives, configure social and economic relationships, promote as

Political Science Association and American Historical Association, Fall 1985 (available at www.apsa.com/imgtest/SupremeCourtAlienRight.pdf).
[3] Robert C. Lieberman, "Ideas, Institutions, and Political Order: Explaining Political Change," *American Political Science Review* 96, No. 4 (2003):697–712, 699.
[4] Rogers Smith, "Political Jurisprudence, The 'New Institutionalism,' and the Future of Public Law," *American Political Science Review*, 82, No. 1 (March 1988):89–108, 91.

well as inhibit political change."[5] Just as rules and conventions in a game such as baseball or football can circumscribe outcomes and shape the strategy of the players, the rules, procedures, norms, and structure of the federal judiciary (or of any government institution for that matter) shape how these institutions' occupants behave. A court's institutional setting signals how judges and justices should comport themselves and can limit those judges' and justices' perceptions of what is within the possible and proper range of actions when they decide cases.

I make three central arguments in this book. First, that the Supreme Court and the Courts of Appeals operate in decidedly different institutional contexts, and that each court's unique institutional context acts as a filtering mechanism that shapes the judges' perception of what they should be doing and how they should be doing it. Second, that the contexts of both courts have slowly changed over time and that neither the Supreme Court nor the circuit courts/U.S. Courts of Appeals have played a static role in the federal judicial system. Third, that the evolving institutional settings of the courts have consequences for the courts themselves, for the occupants of those institutions, and for the alien litigants who appear before the courts. Essentially, the evolved federal judiciary has taken a different form than the one envisioned by the founders, but this new form has simply redistributed the missions and duties of the judicial institution to its different segments. In the end, the federal judiciary may have wandered from the structural design intended by the founders, but the roles and missions that the founders wished the judiciary to serve in the political system are still being carried out.

Using the case study of judicial decision making in immigration cases, I explore the relationship between the U.S. Supreme Court and the U.S. Courts of Appeals' distinct institutional contexts and the judicial decision making processes on each court. Among the institutional attributes that constitute the setting of each court are the formal rules of operation and procedure, such as congressionally mandated acts prescribing the jurisdiction of federal courts over cases. Less formal rules of operation, as well as exogenous changes to the courts' institutional settings, will also be a focus of this study; Chapter 4 and 6 will show that changes occurring outside the federal courts can have ripple effects that eventually affect the courts themselves. Phenomena such as alien litigants' organized responses to legislative changes, or policy changes made by the elected branches to

---

[5] Karen Orren and Stephen Skowronek, *The Search for American Political Development* (New York: Cambridge University Press, 2004), 78.

ratchet up or relax immigration enforcement, may also affect the number and nature of cases reaching the federal courts.

In the literal sense, judicial decision making in immigration cases is an important subject of inquiry because, in exclusion and deportation cases, either a Court of Appeals or the Supreme Court is the final arbiter of the fate of the aliens in these legal proceedings. In these cases, the courts are deciding whether or not aliens can enter or remain in the United States, and, especially with political asylum cases, these decisions may have life or death consequences. In exclusion cases, the courts must decide whether the federal government and its regulatory agencies have properly prevented an alien from entering U.S. territory. In deportation cases, the courts must determine whether the federal government and its administrative agencies have properly expelled or removed an alien from U.S. territory.[6] Although Congress may pass laws stipulating how many aliens may enter the United States, for what purpose, and how long they may remain, it falls to the federal courts to interpret these laws and apply them to individuals. It is therefore vital that one understand the ways in which the U.S. Supreme Court and the U.S. Courts of Appeals adjudicate immigration appeals.

There is also a normative component to the question of how the Supreme Court and the Courts of Appeals treat aliens. The manner in which our legal institutions and their occupants treat aliens is an indicator of whether our institutions have lived up to their constitutionally prescribed roles and is ultimately a bellwether of the vitality of our democratic system. In this government of separated powers, the framers envisioned that the judicial branch would perform a very specific function. In *Federalist 78*, Alexander Hamilton worried that the judicial branch would be the weakest branch because it "has no influence over either the sword or the purse." At the same time, he and the other federalists believed that "the courts of justice" as an independent judiciary, separate from the legislative and executive branches, "are to be considered bulwarks of a limited Constitution against legislative encroachments."[7] The framers so desired an independent judiciary that they determined that judges should serve for life in order to insulate them from political retaliation and electoral pressures. This arrangement would allow judges to check the excesses and errors of the elected branches of government.

---

[6] After congressional reforms in 1996, the previously distinct legal categories of exclusion and deportation were collapsed into one legal action called "removal."

[7] Alexander Hamilton, Federalist Papers No. 78. *The Federalist Papers*, ed. Clinton Rossiter (New York: Penguin, 1961), 465, 471.

Concomitantly, Hamilton and the framers also suggested a normative role for the federal judiciary to play in the government system – to make tough and sometimes unpopular decisions that the elected branches of government might be unable or unwilling to make.

In American history, the origins and the functions of judicial review were never clearly understood; the proper role of the federal judiciary in the political system is still contested today.[8] One view of judicial review is that the federal judiciary exists to protect the rights of vulnerable groups who, because of the absence of political power, cannot protect themselves, and whom the elected branches may not be willing to protect. There is evidence that the Supreme Court has, at least in some instances, embraced its expected role to make politically unpopular decisions that may benefit minority groups in our society. As evidenced by the now famous Footnote Four of the Supreme Court case *United States v. Carolene Products* (1938), the Court was conscious of its unique status among the other branches of government and it specifically stated that it would subject policies directed at politically unpopular "discrete and insular minorities" to "more searching scrutiny."[9] Indeed, in other areas of law, such as criminal law and equal protection jurisprudence, the Court has frequently and sometimes forcefully asserted itself as the protector of such groups. For example, during the Warren Court years, the Supreme Court played an instrumental role in facilitating a rights revolution by granting rights and protections to women, racial minorities, and criminal defendants. But this situation begs the question of whether aliens count as a "discrete and insular minorit[y]." In analyzing the impact of the famous Footnote Four pronouncement, legal scholar John Hart Ely has noted that aliens are an "easy case" when determining who is deserving of judicial protection against discrimination. He writes, "Aliens cannot vote in any state, which means that any representation

[8] See, e.g., Barry Friedman, "The Importance of Being Positive: The Nature and Function of Judicial Review" (The William H. Taft Lecture in Constitutional Law), 72 *University of Cincinnati Law Review* 1257 (2004); Barry Friedman, "Dialogue and Judicial Review," 91 *Michigan Law Review* 577 (1993); Michael Klarman, *From Civil Rights to Jim Crow: The Supreme Court and the Struggle for Racial Equality* (Oxford: Oxford University Press, 2006); and Howard Gillman, *The Votes That Counted: How the Supreme Court Decided the 2000 Presidential Election* (Chicago: University of Chicago Press, 2003).

[9] *United States v. Carolene Products*, 304 U.S. 144 (1938). In the famous Footnote Four of this case, the Supreme Court articulates its view of the proper role of the institution as being one that acts as the guardian of politically weak "discrete and insular minorities." The Court understood its role as requiring the justices to submit policies that affect such minority groups to "more searching judicial inquiry."

they receive will be exclusively 'virtual.'"[10] Lacking suffrage, aliens have few avenues of recourse in the political system except the federal courts. But have the U.S. Supreme Court and U.S. Courts of Appeals come to the same conclusion as Ely, and even if they have, do they actually treat aliens as deserving of judicial protection against discrimination? One cannot answer this question without empirically assessing how the two courts treat immigration appeals.

Although their expectations of the role that the federal judiciary was to play in the American political system was clear, the framers were very vague as to what form the judiciary, and especially the lower federal courts, should take. All that Article III Section I of the Constitution states is that "The judicial power of the United States, shall be vested in one Supreme Court, and in such inferior courts as the Congress may from time to time ordain and establish." It was evident that there was to be one Supreme Court that would be the highest national court at the apex of the federal judiciary hierarchy, which would also complete the tripartite design of the federal government along with the Congress and the presidency. But what about the structure, size, and design of the lower federal courts, which were also known as the "inferior courts?" Both the Constitution and the *Federalist Papers* refer repeatedly to "the judiciary" or "the judicial branch," implying that the institution would be monolithic and consistent at all of its levels. Perhaps this is understandable given that the Constitution was drafted at a time when conceptualizations of the form and functions of the federal judicial system were vague and uncertain. As this book will show, in certain types of immigration cases, namely exclusion and deportation or removal cases, the Supreme Court appears not to have been the best friend of the hapless alien. Instead, it has often fallen to the U.S. Courts of Appeals to protect this politically vulnerable group from errors or abuses of power committed by the immigration bureaucracy. One way to make sense of this situation is to examine how the two courts treat aliens' appeals in light of their distinctive institutional contexts.

At first glance, it may seem odd to use immigration law as a lens to study judicial decision making because aliens, as outsiders in every sense of the word, are legally entitled to so few rights. This is especially true of challenges to their right to enter or to stay in the United States. As immigration law scholar Peter Schuck has written, "In a legal firmament

---

[10] John Hart Ely, *Democracy and Distrust: A Theory of Judicial Review* (Cambridge, MA: Harvard University Press, 1980), 160–61.

transformed by revolutions in due process and equal protection doctrine and by a new conception of judicial role, immigration law remains the realm in which government authority is at the zenith and individual entitlement is at the nadir."[11] Indeed, the scenario Schuck describes plays out at the Supreme Court level where, by virtue of its implications for and close connection to national security and national sovereignty, the Court has not only adopted a deferential attitude toward executive branch action on immigration but has also repeatedly recognized congressional plenary power over this subject. In this sense, judicial decision making in immigration law, particularly in exclusion and deportation decisions, is the hardest test case of the notion that the two courts are distinct. Schuck further noted, "In a constitutional system marked by an extraordinary degree of political, institutional and social fragmentation, manifestations of solidarity and nationhood can exercise a potent hold over the judicial, as well as the lay, imagination."[12] One would expect that all the federal courts would be marching in lock step in immigration law.

In addition, strong and unequivocal doctrinal directives issued by the Supreme Court characterize this area of law. Through a series of cases that cite congressional plenary power over immigration, the Supreme Court has repeatedly deferred to Congress and declined to closely scrutinize government actions for compliance with the Constitution. For instance, the Court wrote in *Oceanic Steam Navigation Company v. Stranahan* (1909), "Over no conceivable subject is the legislative power of Congress more complete."[13] Furthermore, the Court has also stated that in exclusion and deportation cases it will not require the government to provide due process protections that would be required in other areas of law, such as criminal law. The Court's infamous statement in *United States ex rel. Knauff v. Shaughnessy* (1950) is an example of its view of the extent of due process that should be provided: "Whatever the procedure authorized by Congress is, it is due process as far as an alien denied entry is concerned."[14]

One would think that these doctrinal directives would facilitate consistency in treatment of immigration cases throughout the federal court system. Given the hierarchical nature of the federal judiciary and the

[11] Peter Schuck, "The Transformation of Immigration Law," 84 *Columbia Law Review* 1 (1984).

[12] Ibid. at 17.

[13] 214 U.S. 320 at 339. The phrase was subsequently cited affirmatively in *Fiallo v. Bell* (1977), 430 U.S. 787 at 792 and other immigration cases.

[14] 338 U.S. 537 at 543.

long-established norm of *stare decisis* (following precedent), one would expect the U.S. Courts of Appeals simply to toe the line, apply the U.S. Supreme Court doctrine, and defer to congressional intent in the major-ity of cases. In exclusion and deportation cases, it would be unlikely for judges at any level of the federal judiciary to find in favor of the alien, and therefore alien victories in any level of the federal courts should be very rare. Moreover, one would not expect the lower federal courts to reach pro-alien outcomes that seemed to contravene established legal precedent or congressional intent. Instead, the data collected for this study show numerous and varied instances when judges of the Courts of Appeals engaged in seemingly purposive behavior to either shirk existing prec-edent or congressional intent in order to find in favor of the alien. Why are the U.S. Courts of Appeals behaving this way and what is motivating their behavior? The exclusion and deportation cases in this study, then, are not just discrete legal decisions about anonymous foreigners; the pro-cedures and processes by which the aliens' cases are adjudicated provide insight into the institutional incentives that shape and channel judicial decision making.

From an institutional development perspective, the federal courts in immigration law present a fascinating study of the effect of institutional context on decision making because this area of law embodies a ten-sion in the institutional expectations of the judges. One element of an institution's context is the role, mission, and purpose of that institution, which also prescribes expectations of how institutional occupants should behave. Martin Shapiro has taught us that the Supreme Court can play multiple roles in our political system, often in the same area of law.[15] Yet immigration cases illustrate a different permutation of institutional role. Aliens can be considered a politically unpopular "discrete and insular" minority group deserving of special protection by the federal courts. On the one hand, this protection calls upon judges, as members of an inde-pendent third branch of government, to check the abuses and excesses of the elected branches' exercise of government power over individuals. On the other hand, immigration as a policy area is similar to foreign policy, where the belief is that decisions should be confined to one body that can take decisive action. Because immigration decisions also have implica-tions for visions of national identity and sometimes national security, it is also a policy area where the nation should ideally speak with one voice

---

[15] Martin Shapiro, *Law and Politics in the Supreme Court: New Approaches to Political Jurisprudence* (London: The Free Press of Glencoe, 1964). See, especially, Chapter 5 on the Supreme Court's multiple roles in reapportionment law.

through one of the elected branches of government rather than through a cacophony of different voices from multiple government institutions and actors. This area of law therefore embodies the conflicting expectations of the federal courts to live up to their institutionally prescribed role as an independent adjudicator separate from the elected branches of government (its *Carolene Products* Footnote Four role) and its politically prescribed role to defer to the elected branches of government. Within immigration law, one finds a collision of the Supreme Court's dual role as a policy court and as a court of law.

Despite this enduring tension in the role of the Supreme Court in immigration cases, the role of the federal courts in immigration has been largely ignored by social scientists. This situation results from the prevailing assumption that the courts defer to Congress and to the executive branch on immigration issues. It is true that many of the Supreme Court's opinions cite the plenary power of Congress, as the Supreme Court in particular, and with few exceptions, refuses to scrutinize federal policy toward aliens for constitutional violations. In a long line of legal doctrine citing first national sovereignty and then congressional plenary power over immigration, the Supreme Court has consistently and systematically deferred to Congress in immigration appeals and declined to hold its actions to significant limitation.[16] Social scientists' research agendas, with few exceptions, focus overwhelmingly on the cultural, economic, and political impact of immigrants in American life, and on the demographic trends of immigrants – not on immigration law.[17] In

---

[16] See, e.g., the long line of plenary power cases that begin with the national sovereignty cases; these laid the foundation for the plenary power doctrine. This line of cases includes *Wong Wing v. United States* (1896), in which the Court wrote, "No limits can be put by the courts upon the power of Congress to protect, by summary methods, the country from the advent of aliens whose race or habits render them undesirable as citizens, or to expel such if they have already found their way into our land and unlawfully remain therein." 163 U.S. 228, 237. This theme can be found more recently in Justice Scalia's concurrence in *Miller v. Albright*, 523 U.S. 420, 456 (1997) and the majority opinion in *Zadvydas v. Davis*, U.S. 678, 695 (2001).

[17] However, two law professors (McClain and Haney-Lopez) and one historian (Salyer) have produced excellent studies on this very subject. Charles J. McClain, *In Search of Equality: The Chinese Struggle Against Discrimination in Nineteenth-Century America* (Berkeley: University of California Press, 1994); Lucy E. Salyer, *Laws Harsh as Tigers: Chinese Immigrants and the Shaping of Modern Immigration Law* (Chapel Hill: The University of Carolina Press,1995); and Ian Haney-Lopez, *White by Law: the Legal Construction of Race* (New York: New York University Press, 1995); although Haney-Lopez, too, is a law professor. Two more recent studies by David S. Law provide an example of research on immigration law that combines legal, empirical, and institutionally based analysis: "Strategic Judicial Lawmaking: Ideology, and Publication in

political science, there are many excellent and valuable studies on various aspects of immigration, but the subject of immigration law has been largely overlooked.[18] Instead, the study of immigration law has largely been the province of law professors such as T. Alexander Aleinikoff, Stephen Legomsky, David Martin, Hiroshi Motomura, Peter Schuck, and a growing group of legal scholars who publish primarily, although not exclusively, in American law reviews.[19] As legal scholars, their theoretical interests and methodological approaches are necessarily different from those of social scientists. Because of contrasting and distinct disciplinary conventions, law professors do not bring the same analytical frames to their analysis, such as a focus on institutional contexts and development that political scientists can bring.

Political science research on law and courts also has its blind spots. The subfields of public law and judicial politics engage in the study of law and courts, but the subfields still disproportionately focus on the Supreme Court to the exclusion of the lower courts.[20] Although there are now growing numbers of studies being done on the U.S. Courts of

the Ninth Circuit Asylum Cases," *University of Cincinnati Law Review* 73:817 (2005) and "Judicial Ideology and the Decision to Publish: Voting and Publication Patterns in the Ninth Circuit Asylum Cases," *Judicature* 89:212 (2006).

[18] Recent political science studies of immigration, including Daniel Tichenor, *Dividing Lines: The Politics of American Immigration Reform* (Princeton, NJ: Princeton University Press, 2001); Wayne Cornelius et al., *Controlling Immigration: A Global Perspective* (Stanford, CA: Stanford University Press, 2004); Peter Andreas, *Border Games: Policing the United States/Mexico Divide* (Ithaca, NY: Cornell University Press, 2001); Desmond King, *The Liberty of Strangers: The Making of the American Nation* (Oxford: Oxford University Press, 2004); and Aristide Zolberg, *A Nation By Design: Immigration Policy in the Fashioning of America* (New York: Harvard University Press, 2006), pay scant attention to the legal and judicial aspects of immigration policy in the United States.

[19] See, e.g., Stephen H. Legomsky, "Immigration Law and the Principle of Plenary Congressional Power," *The Supreme Court Review* 255 (1985); Hiroshi Motomura, "Immigration Law After a Century of Plenary Power: Phantom Constitutional Norms and Statutory Interpretation," 100 *Yale Law Journal* 545 (1990); Peter H. Schuck, "The Transformation of Immigration Law," *Columbia Law Review* 84:1 (1984); and Daniel Kanstroom, *Deportation Nation: Outsiders in American History* (Cambridge, MA: Harvard University Press, 2007). An example of several empirical studies undertaken by law professors include Stephen Legomsky, *Immigration and the Judiciary: Law and Politics in Britain and America* (New York: Oxford University Press, Clarendon, 1987); Peter Schuck and Theodore Hsien Wang, "Continuity and Change: Patterns of Litigation in Immigration, 1979–1990," 45 *Stanford Law Review* 115 (November 1992); and Jaya Ramji-Nogales, Andrew I. Schoenholtz, and Philip G. Schrag, "Refugee Roulette: Disparities in Asylum Adjudication," *Stanford Law Review* 295 (2007).

[20] A search for articles in political science journals in the JSTOR database with "Supreme Court" in the title, between the years 1980 and 2008, returned 168 articles. (This search

Appeals, the U.S. district courts, and state courts, few of these compare multiple levels of the federal judiciary, and even fewer studies do so over time in the fashion of a longitudinal study.

The dearth of immigration law research is surprising. From a political development perspective, immigration has played a major role in U.S. constitutional development; and as Chapter 5 will show, immigration has been an impetus for institutional change and innovation at the U.S. Court of Appeals for the Ninth Circuit. Moreover, such cases as *Chae Chan Ping v. United States* (1889) ("the Chinese exclusion case") and *Fong Yue Ting v. United States* (1893) (whether, as a matter of sovereignty, the U.S. government can expel someone from U.S. territory) are landmark cases not just in U.S. immigration law, but in U.S. constitutional law.[21] They have shaped the course of the development of U.S. constitutional law, by defining the limits of the idea of national sovereignty and the procedural safeguards available to some of the weakest members of our polity – aliens – those who are not U.S. citizens by birth or naturalization. These two Supreme Court cases and many others also represent the Court's attempts to balance its role as a policy/political court and its role as a court of law.

What is less obvious in the immigration story is how the U.S. Courts of Appeals have shaped the development of U.S. law. The findings in this project show that around the turn of the twentieth century, the Courts of Appeals adopted a dissimilar strategy from the Supreme Court in adjudicating immigration cases. The empirical data in this project suggest that there are some interesting phenomena being missed by a focus too

---

excluded articles about state supreme courts and supreme courts of other nations.) A similar JSTOR search for articles with "Circuit Courts," "Circuit Courts of Appeals," or "Courts of Appeals" in the title drew 32 articles. See also Barry Friedman, "Taking Law Seriously," 266 ("Many of the political science studies focus on the Supreme Court. But if constraint is the issue, all the important action might be going on in the lower courts ... Studying the lower courts is more difficult than studying the Supreme Court in no small part because there is less available data. But normative concerns, not difficulty with the data, ought to define the agenda of the scholar interested in judicial behavior"); and *Law and Courts – The Newsletter of the Law and Courts Section of the American Political Science Association*, 11 No. 3 (Summer 2001) (available at http://www.law.nyu.edu/lawcourts/pubs/newsletter/summer01.pdf). See especially Stephen Wasby's "Symposium: The Courts of Appeals, What Should Be Studied? An Introduction," 4, where he notes the move from a paucity of Courts of Appeals research to the present situation, which he characterizes this way: "One can say that there is now at least a 'small hardy band' of political scientists – indeed, more than just a small band – studying the U.S. courts of appeals and regularly writing about them" (4); and Martin Shapiro, *Law and Politics in the Supreme Court*, 3, 6.

[21] 130 U.S. 581 and 149 U.S. 698.

narrowly directed to the Supreme Court, and that the Courts of Appeals
and the Supreme Court are guided by diverse motivations and logics in
deciding these cases.

THE HISTORICAL INSTITUTIONALIST APPROACH
AND THE FEDERAL COURTS

This study follows four courts: the U.S. Supreme Court and the U.S.
Courts of Appeals for the Third, Fifth, and Ninth Circuits, over a broad
sweep of time, 1881–2002. The purpose is not merely to study the past
by incorporating historical data, but to emphasize the change over time
of institutional contexts.[22] This approach heeds Paul Pierson's admoni-
tion not to "reduce a moving picture to a snapshot" because by doing so,
we "run the risk of missing crucial aspects of the process through which
formal institutions take shape, as well as the ways in which they either
endure or change in social environments that are themselves constantly
changing."[23] Chapter 3 explains why the different parts of the same institution, the federal judiciary, are evolving along independent and temporally
specific paths. Orren and Skowronek have argued that "the institutions
of a polity are not created or recreated all at once, in accordance with
a single ordering principle; they are created instead at different times, in
light of different experiences, and often for quite contrary purposes."[24]
They term this phenomenon "intercurrence." Intercurrence as a political phenomenon, like federalism, is theoretical and very abstract, and
one may wonder about the real-world implications of this concept. This
book aims to animate the intercurrence concept and show how it affects
the litigants and the judges in these courts. Toward that end, it traces
and assesses the results within the federal judiciary where distinct parts
within the *same* institution develop intercurrence, complete with dissimilar systems of purposes, incentives, and motivations. It compares the U.S.

---

[22] Orren and Skowronek, *The Search for American Political Development*, 3.
[23] Paul Pierson, *Politics in Time: History, Institutions, and Social Science* (Princeton,
NJ: Princeton University Press, 2004), 104.
[24] Orren and Skowronek, *The Search for American Political Development*, 112.
See also Karen Orren and Stephen Skowronek, "The Study of American Political
Development," in Ira Katznelson and Helen V. Milner, eds., *Political Science: The
State of the Discipline* (New York: W.W. Norton and Company, 2003), 748; Karen
Orren and Stephen Skowronek, "Beyond the Iconography of Order: Notes for a 'New
Institutionalism,'" in Lawrence C. Dodd and Calvin Jillson, eds., *The Dynamics of
American Politics: Approaches & Interpretations* (Boulder, CO: Westview Press,
1994).

Supreme Court and the U.S. Courts of Appeals on different institutional dimensions and within one single policy area. The purpose is to better understand the decision making processes within each court.

This book also takes seriously the interaction between ideas and institutions, or, more precisely, between ideas and institutional settings or contexts. A court's institutional setting can shape the justices' and judges' consideration and selection of different kinds of legal reasoning. An analysis of the patterns in the modes of legal reasoning, or of the justifications that appear in legal opinions, is a first step in assessing the influence of the institutional setting of each court. The theoretical expectation is that as the Supreme Court gained more and more discretion over its docket through a series of acts of Congress, the Court has behaved more like a political/policy court, that is, a court that thinks in terms of grand ideas of jurisprudence and policy rather than focusing on the facts of the individual case, as a court of appeals devoted to the correction of errors might do. The contemporary U.S. Courts of Appeals evolved from courts that closely adhered to Supreme Court precedent to courts that have gained a degree of independence and insulation from the Supreme Court. Their autonomy came about by a combination of mushrooming caseloads and the high Court's increasingly narrow jurisdiction, which meant that the Court could no longer closely supervise and monitor the Courts of Appeals. The theoretical expectation here is that the Courts of Appeals will behave like courts most concerned with correcting errors, that is, will be courts that assiduously search for procedural violations in the decisions of lower courts, and that these courts will also reliably cite Supreme Court doctrine. Later in the development of the Courts of Appeals, one might expect to see these courts use more of the kinds of policy and political modes of legal reasoning favored by the Supreme Court. But if indeed the Courts of Appeals continue to act as subordinates or helpmates to the Supreme Court, then one will find frequent citations of Supreme Court doctrine.

Ultimately, this book tackles the dynamic effect of changing institutional settings on judicial decision making. Chapter 3 explains how a set of interrelated mechanisms that are extrajudicial in nature have affected the nature and magnitude of the caseloads of the U.S. Courts of Appeals. These factors include developments in immigration policy, including the strategies the U.S. government has used over time to enforce immigration policy and the manner of that enforcement generally; specific pieces of immigration legislation, and the responses of the aliens themselves to federal immigration laws. The interactions of these three factors have shaped the nature and the volume of the immigration appeals pouring into the federal courts.

Not only have the federal courts had to adjust to the changing character of immigration appeals over time, but, as illustrated in Chapter 5, these extrajudicial changes also have had profound and often uneven impacts on the U.S. Courts of Appeals system. The Ninth Circuit, for example, has had to experiment with new institutional practices and procedures to process what was first a steady rise in immigration appeals beginning in the mid-1980s, and then a sharp spike in immigration appeals in 2002 that was precipitated by a number of factors, including rule changes at the Board of Immigration Appeals (BIA). These innovations, necessitated by the surge of immigration appeals, have in turn altered the nature of judicial review by contributing to the "mission creep" of the Ninth Circuit Court of Appeals, which has moved away from its original error correction function and toward the discerning selection of cases practiced by a *certiorari* court, such as the U.S. Supreme Court.

One argument advanced in this book is that, although the modes of legal reasoning that appear in legal opinions are to some extent driven by the facts and nature of the cases, judges still have room to pursue a desired legal outcome. Sometimes it is the distinctive institutional setting of the court that either facilitates or discourages certain modes of legal reasoning that can lead to a judge's or a justice's desired outcome. For example, judges at all three levels of federal courts can selectively apply precedent, and U.S. Courts of Appeals judges can use creative statutory interpretation or discretion to elude existing doctrine or congressional intent. The factor that is common to all these kinds of purposive behavior in the courts is that institutional attributes provide incentives for judges to behave in certain ways. As Paul Frymer's excellent study on political parties has shown, institutional attributes can work in powerful ways to shape political parties' decision making processes, often in ways of which these institutional occupants may not even be aware.[25]

CONCLUSION

This book challenges the doctrinal and Supreme Court-centered research on immigration law and political science's public law/judicial politics

---

[25] Paul Frymer, *Uneasy Alliances: Race and Party Competition in America* (Princeton, NJ: Princeton University Press, 1999).

subfields. In addition, the book has several interrelated objectives. One objective is to use judicial decision making in immigration law as a lens to learn about the institutional development paths of the U.S. Supreme Court and the U.S. Courts of Appeals by exploring how the institutional settings and contexts of each court evolve over time and how these changes affect the justices' and judges' perceptions of their missions and purposes. As will become evident in the following chapters, it is not just that the U.S. Supreme Court may play different roles in different policy areas, but that the circuit courts/U.S. Courts of Appeals also play different roles from the Supreme Court within the same policy area. It is not just separate and distinct institutions that are intercurrent; different parts of the same institutions may also be intercurrent. The primary aim of the project is to demonstrate that it is more appropriate to treat the U.S. Supreme Court and the U.S. Courts of Appeals as analytically distinct systems rather than as static components of the federal judicial hierarchy. This study also explores the causes and implications of intercurrence within a single institution, the U.S. judiciary.

By tracing the evolution of the immigration issue, across time in the two courts, it can be seen that the Supreme Court evolved from an appellate court into a very different kind of court, one that made policies for the rest of the nation. The circuit courts/U.S. Courts of Appeals evolved from courts that were designed solely to alleviate the workload of the Supreme Court into appellate courts that were insulated from Supreme Court supervision and eventually became independent policy makers. By the turn of the twentieth century, the changing roles and missions of the courts over time had created a situation that could be characterized as a division of labor; each court had differentiated missions and functions. Driving the altered roles and missions of the two courts are the transformations in institutional contexts that have eventually led the two courts to diverge in their approaches to deciding cases. The implication for alien litigants is that they have met with more favorable treatment at the U.S. Courts of Appeals than at the highest court in the land.

In *Federalist 78*, Alexander Hamilton worried that the judicial branch would be the weakest and "least dangerous branch," that it would be susceptible to being overpowered, overrun, and overawed by the other two branches. At the same time, he and the other Federalists were philosophically committed to a government system of separate powers and they fervently hoped that the generically conceived "courts of justice" would function as an independent judiciary that would check and balance

the power of the elected branches of government. The behavior of the
Supreme Court in immigration, with its systematic deference to Congress
and to the executive branch, demonstrates that at least in some policy
areas, "insular minorities" cannot rely upon the protection of the high
court if that Court persists in deferring to the other branches. The irony
is that the higher up the judicial hierarchy an exclusion or deportation
case travels, the less likely it is that the alien will get a hearing where the
primary consideration is not about whether equity is being served in her
particular case. It matters little whether the aliens' cases that reach the
Supreme Court are meritorious or not; the point is that the Court will be
more concerned about the political and policy implications of its decision
than it is about the facts of the case the justices are deciding. As I argue
in the following pages, this situation is not because the Supreme Court
is more anti-alien or xenophobic than are the U.S. Courts of Appeals;
rather, the Supreme Court has institutional incentives to adjudicate cases
in ways that are not always beneficial to individual aliens whose cases
come before it. Conversely, the U.S. Courts of Appeals have different
institutional incentives, incentives that influence them to adjudicate cases
with consideration of the individual facts of each case, an approach that
works to benefit aliens. Therefore, the level of the federal judiciary at
which a judge sits greatly affects her approach to legal decision making. Institutional contexts, although not static, are stable regularities that
influence the behavior of institutional occupants, and as such must be a
subject of study in their own right.

CHAPTER ORGANIZATION

Chapter 2 has several objectives. First, the chapter introduces the federal
institutions of the immigration system that an alien's appeal must pass
through. Second, the chapter presents an analytical strategy that relies on
multiple methodologies. Ultimately, this multi-method approach presents
a fuller and more nuanced understanding of the judicial decision making
process.

Chapter 3 focuses on the evolving roles and missions of the U.S.
Supreme Court and the U.S. Courts of Appeals, beginning with the original framers' debates over the role of the federal judiciary in the new
country's political system. The chapter demonstrates that although the
development and growth of the federal judiciary wandered from the
framers' original conceptions, the structures nevertheless live up to their
hopes for the mission and function of the institution to protect citizens,

albeit with different structural forms. The chapter also uses the immigration example to show why caseloads have increased and how these pressures have further widened the mission and functions of the U.S. Supreme Court and the U.S. Courts of Appeals.

Chapter 4 defines the nature and institutional limits of purposive behavior at the U.S. Courts of Appeals. Although the nature and facts of each immigration appeal often drive the selection of the mode of legal reasoning in that case, some of these modes of legal reasoning embody inherent purposive potential in the sense that they provide judges and justices choices among different possible legal outcomes. The utility of each mode of legal reasoning is further enhanced by particular institutional attributes of each court. The chapter explores a number of strategies that U.S. Courts of Appeals judges may use to pursue policy preferences. It lays out the range of strategic options that is both encouraged and constrained by the particular institutional setting of the Courts of Appeals, which is distinct from the range of behaviors encouraged or constrained at the Supreme Court.

Chapter 5 is based on the in-person interviews conducted with eight Ninth Circuit judges and three central staff members. It investigates and assesses the impetuses and institutional innovations necessitated by the Ninth Circuit's skyrocketing caseload of immigration appeals since 2002. The chapter urges scholars who study institutional development to be sensitive to the effect of exogenous pressures on development within the same institution. One need not only distinguish between the U.S. Supreme Court and the U.S. Courts of Appeals when studying the judiciary, but one must also make finer distinctions among the different U.S. Courts of Appeals. As the case study of the Ninth Circuit and immigration illustrates, exogenous developments in immigration law and politics can unevenly affect the U.S. Courts of Appeals system, thereby producing targeted and isolated development and innovation.

The earlier chapters concentrate on factors driving institutional creation and changes; the goal of Chapter 6 is to highlight factors that may mitigate or weigh against institutional development and evolution. The chapter argues that the Supreme Court's and U.S. Courts of Appeals' commitments to procedural due process in immigration appeals illustrate that the idea of due process should be construed as an element of continuity in the middle of institutional development. The fact that due process is a viable and relevant constraint and consideration in judicial decision making in immigration appeals, an area of law where one should least expect to find legal protections of any kind for aliens, shows the deep entrenchment of this idea in the U.S. judicial mind. Although the roles and missions of the Supreme Court and the circuit courts/U.S. Courts of Appeals have evolved over time, there is a clear line of procedural due process cases paralleling the national sovereignty and plenary power doctrine cases that dominate this area of law.

2

How Do We Know What We Know?

Data, Methods, and Initial Findings

The answer to the question of whether there is any difference in the way the U.S. Courts of Appeals or the U.S. Supreme Court treat immigration cases is very much dependent on how one measures the result. How do we know what we know? One way to go about answering the question is to compare the rate at which aliens prevail in their legal challenges in each level of the courts. But to ask whether aliens typically win or lose at the Supreme Court or the Courts of Appeals is to focus only on the legal outcome of a case, and such a focus is highly misleading because it glosses over the motivations for the decision. One realizes what the judges and justices have decided without gaining much understanding of why they decided the way they did. Moreover, given the fact that the Supreme Court and Courts of Appeals use different case selection mechanisms, and have different degrees of control over their dockets, comparing the legal outcomes of the two courts is not very meaningful. This chapter proposes refocusing the inquiry to better understand how the Supreme Court and Courts of Appeals decide immigration cases in comparable ways in order to obtain a fuller assessment of what is happening to aliens' appeals in these two levels of the federal courts. The methodological approaches adopted are crucial, and for this reason the discussion of methodology in this chapter, and especially in the appendices, is fairly detailed.

Before one can begin to analyze how the Supreme Court and the Courts of Appeals treat immigration appeals, one must first understand the path by which immigration appeals reach the federal courts in the first place. The chapter opens with a description of the institutions of the immigration bureaucracy. It then moves to an analysis of the origins of the popular conception that the Supreme Court is inhospitable toward

alien claims. The second part of the chapter details the multi-method-
ological strategy of the study. The chapter concludes with some initial
appraisal of the data.

AN ALIEN'S PATH OF APPEAL

To understand how an alien's legal appeal ends up in the federal courts,
one must first be familiar with the myriad federal agencies that an alien
passes through before she even reaches the federal courts. The personnel
of these administrative agencies often frame the terms of analysis in each
case, which the federal courts must later review. The federal appellate
courts must also assess the accuracy of the adjudications and procedures
of these administrative bodies.

An alien's contact with the immigration bureaucracy typically
begins when the Department of Homeland Security (or, previously, the
Immigration and Nationalization Service) serves the alien with a written
notice to appear at an initial administrative hearing in immigration court
before an immigration judge. An alien can appeal the immigration judge's
decision to another administrative body, called the Board of Immigration
Appeals (BIA). An appeal of the BIA's decision can enter one of the different levels of the federal court system, depending on the type and nature
of the immigration case.

Throughout U.S. immigration history, the management of immigration
was placed in diverse federal agencies. The regulation of immigration by the
federal government began in 1891 when the office of the Superintendent
of Immigration was first housed in the Treasury Department. The Bureau
of Immigration was transferred to the Department of Commerce and
Labor in 1903 and then the Bureau of Immigration and Naturalization
was moved to the Department of Labor in 1913.[1] The Border Patrol
was created in 1924 as part of the Bureau of Immigration and the two
were consolidated into the Immigration and Naturalization Service (INS)
in 1933. In 1940 the INS was transferred to the Department of Justice
by a presidential executive order. The INS, headed by a commissioner,
operated for many years under the regulations in the Immigration and
Nationality Act that designated powers to the U.S. Attorney General.[2]
The INS, as it existed from 1940 to 2003, embodied the dual (some have

---

[1] T. Alexander Aleinikoff, David Martin, and Hiroshi Motomura, *Immigration and
Citizenship Process and Policy*, 6th ed. (St. Paul, MN: Thomson West Publishing,
2008), 268–69.
[2] Ibid.

argued contradictory) functions of enforcement of immigration laws and the dispensation of immigration benefits. The same agency whose agents apprehend illegal aliens for deportation also processes applications for family- and employment-based petitions and naturalizes aliens by granting U.S. citizenship. The INS's previous functions were divided among several agencies in 2003 by the Homeland Security Act, which represents the largest reorganization of government agencies since the New Deal era.[3] Congress took advantage of the large reorganization to divide the contradictory functions of the old INS. It did so by creating the Bureau of Citizenship and Immigration Services (BCIS) to handle the benefits side of immigration (family-based, employment-based, and nonimmigrant visa petitions, and naturalization). The enforcement functions of the old INS were placed in the Bureau of Customs and Border Protection (BCBP). The BCBP is intended to carry out the enforcement of immigration laws in the immediate areas around the nation's borders. The enforcement of immigration laws in the interior of the country is charged to the Bureau of Immigration and Customs Enforcement (BICE).[4]

The Immigration Judges

An alien who is apprehended or investigated by INS (and now DHS) and who is found to be deportable or removable begins his journey through the bureaucracy at an administrative hearing before an immigration judge. The alien can appeal the decision of the immigration judge to the BIA, and he or she is informed of this right of appeal, in writing, along with notice of the judge's decision. The government may also appeal an immigration judge's decision to the BIA.

There are currently 226 judges that staff the nation's 54 immigration courts. Today these judges' time is consumed with removal proceedings, where they must decide whether aliens qualify for a waiver that would prevent their deportation or removal. These judges must also decide whether to grant bonds for aliens in detention.[5] Historically, immigration

---

[3] Homeland Security Act, Public Law No. 107–296, 116 Stat. 2135. See also the links in the web site http://www.dhs.gov/xabout/structure/ to learn more about the different components of the immigration agencies that fall under the Department of Homeland Security.

[4] Aleinikoff, Martin, Motomura, *Immigration and Citizenship Process and Policy*, 268–75. There are many more federal agencies besides DHS that have a hand in immigration policy. To learn more about these other agencies, see pages 278–91 of Aleinikoff, Martin, and Motomura's textbook.

[5] Ibid. at 279–80.

judges, who were previously known as "special inquiry officers," had many other administrative duties. They were given their judge-like decision making role in 1956, a function that they continue to carry out today. Through the early 1980s, the immigration judges' ability to do their jobs was often dependent on the resources the local district director of the INS was willing to pass along. In 1983, immigration judges were placed under the jurisdiction of the Executive Office for Immigration Review (EOIR), which is part of the Department of Justice. The aim was to give the immigration judges more independence from the district directors and the INS's enforcement imperatives.[6] After the post 9/11 government agency reorganization that created the Department of Homeland Security (DHS), the immigration judges' corps remained in EOIR and the Department of Justice instead of being transferred to the Department of Homeland Security. In 2008, immigration judges heard 270,000 "removal matters," for a caseload of 1,200 cases per judge, per year.[7]

The Board of Immigration Appeals

The Board of Immigration Appeals is one of the key components of the immigration bureaucracy. This body has been referred to as "the Supreme Court of immigration law."[8] The BIA was preceded by the Board of Review, which was created in 1922 to "make recommendations to the Secretary of Labor."[9] The Board of Review remained a subdivision of the Department of Labor between 1922 and 1940; then Congress moved immigration regulation duties to the Department of Justice. The Board of Review was renamed the Board of Immigration Appeals on August

---

[6] Ibid.

[7] Transcript of "Immigration and the Courts" panel at the Brookings Institution, Washington, DC, February 20, 2009, 8 (transcript available at http://www.brookings.edu/events/2009/0220_immigration.aspx).

[8] T. Alexander Aleinikoff and David Martin, "Ashcroft's Immigration Threat," *Washington Post,* Feb. 26, 2002, A21. Aleinikoff and Martin, both immigration law professors, also served as general counsel at the Immigration and Naturalization Service during President Bill Clinton's administration.

[9] "A Study Conducted For: The American Bar Association, Commission on Immigration Policy, Practice, and Pro Bono, RE: Board of Immigration Appeals: Procedural Reforms to Improve Case Management," Dorsey and Whitney, LLP. http://www.dorsey.com/news/news_detail.aspx?FlashNavID=news_search&id=240514703 (accessed 6 Dec. 2006) (hereafter Dorsey Report), 8; and "Board of Immigration Appeals – History and Origin" (BIA History Report), unpublished manuscript on file with author and obtained from Karen Drummond, librarian of the Board of Immigration Appeals, Falls Church, VA: 1.

30, 1940, and was housed thereafter in the office of the U.S. Attorney General.[10] The BIA was given the authority to have final review of immigration cases "subject only to possible review by the Attorney General." In 1983, during a reorganization at the Department of Justice, the BIA was moved under the newly created Executive Office of Immigration Review.[11] As a report on file with the BIA librarian describes:

The Board of Immigration Appeals differs basically from its predecessor, the Board of Review. It is still not a statutory body but it has been given the responsibility and power to make final decisions. It is now responsible solely to the Attorney General. It has become completely independent of the Immigration and Naturalization Service, the body charged with investigation and prosecution in immigration matters and executing the decisions of the Board of Immigration Appeals.[12]

The BIA is the Attorney General's creation, and it is the Attorney General who defines and modifies the BIA's powers.[13] Although it is now a distinct entity from INS/DHS, the board and its members cannot act independently of the Attorney General of the United States.

As a practical matter, Philip G. Schrag has written that the BIA really exists "for one reason" and that is to correct the errors of other immigration officials, including immigration judges, who may "sometimes make mistakes – of law, of procedure, or of the application of law to fact."[14] Schrag adds that in light of the court stripping measures passed by Congress in 1996, the role of the BIA becomes all the more important. He writes, "This [error correction] function has become even more important since 1997, when new federal legislation curtailed aliens' rights to seek further review, in federal courts, of some Board decisions. The Board is now in some instances the *only* institution that can correct errors."[15] About 10 percent of immigration judges' decisions are appealed to the BIA. In 2008, the BIA adjudicated 23,000 cases.[16] The vast majority of the aliens' appeals terminate at the Board of Immigration Appeals because the expense required for further appeal to the federal courts is often too much for an alien and her family to bear.

---

[10] BIA History Report, 4, and 8 C.F.R. § 90.2.
[11] Dorsey Report, 8.
[12] BIA History Report, 5.
[13] Dorsey Report, 8.
[14] Philip G. Schrag, "The Summary Affirmances Proposal of the Board of Immigration Appeals," 12 *Georgetown Immigration Law Journal*, 531, 534 (1998).
[15] Ibid. at 534.
[16] The Brookings Institution, "Immigration and the Courts," 8–9.

Despite its very important role in the immigration system, the BIA has been a neglected agency, even in contemporary times; it is often given short shrift during the allocation of funding, personnel and other resources. One of the biggest challenges to this agency is the ever-expanding number of cases that are appealed to it. As the Department of Justice has increased the number of immigration judges nationwide, the number of appeals to the BIA has also increased. Yet, the agency has not received the resources to keep pace with its growing caseload. In fact, as detailed in Chapter 5, its personnel have been reduced even in the face of rising caseloads, resulting in consequences that emanate to the U.S. Courts of Appeals. Retired BIA Member Michael Heilman, who served on the BIA from 1986–2001, said, "As a general matter, the Department of Justice, and certainly the typical Attorney General, had no interest in immigration issues, unless they became newsworthy."[17] Not surprisingly, if a backlog grew and became an issue, "the Board tended to be seen as the source of the problem."[18] Perhaps because immigration for many years was viewed by politicians and policy makers not as a significantly high profile or important issue, or an issue with little political payoff, the administrative agencies, including the BIA and the immigration judges, received little credit for their work but plenty of blame when problems arose.

The Federal Courts

Theoretically, an alien or the government may appeal to the federal courts if they are unhappy with the decision of the Board of Immigration Appeals. In actuality, the cost of an appeal to the federal courts may be prohibitive. In 2008, the 12 U.S. Courts of Appeals together adjudicated 10,280 petitions.[19] Unlike in criminal proceedings, where a defendant is entitled to counsel at public expense, immigration proceedings are civil in

[17] Email communication with author, December 28, 2007. (Before he became a member of the BIA, Heilman served as a BIA staff attorney and later as associate general counsel at the INS and on appellate and Supreme Court cases involving the BIA.)
[18] Email communication with author, December 28, 2007. Heilman traces the BIA backlog to the generous practice, which came to an end as late as the 1980s, of allowing aliens to file a BIA appeal by simply completing a form in a cursory manner "with no legal issues identified" and without the formality and professionalism of a legal brief. This practice came to an end because of the tremendous pressure brought about by a flood of Central American asylum cases in the 1980s and the legal challenges resulting from the Immigration Reform and Control Act of 1986. Heilman explained that "In this curious practice lay the seeds of the backlog."
[19] "Workload of the Courts," *The Third Branch: Newsletter of the Federal Courts*, January 2009 (available at http://www.uscourts.gov/ttb/2009–01/article02.cfm).

nature and do not entitle the alien to counsel at public expense. Although a small number of *pro se* immigration appeals are filed to the federal courts, most of the appeals are from aliens who have hired counsel at their own expense or are being represented *pro bono* by nongovernmental or community-based organizations. Until 1961, no statute gave aliens the right to appeal their BIA decisions to the federal courts. Because aliens, before they are deported, must first be taken into custody, they could appeal to the federal district courts via the ancient writ of *habeas corpus*.[20]

With the adoption of the Administrative Procedure Act (APA) of 1946 came the general presumption of the right to appeal administrative agency decisions to the federal courts (unless precluded by statute or precedent). This move, combined with the passage of the Immigration and Nationality Act of 1952, provided "declaratory and injunctive relief" under the APA to aliens who were not in federal custody and detention to allow their appeal of exclusion and deportation orders to the federal courts from the BIA.[21]

Congress later restructured the appeals process in 1961 via amendments to the Immigration and Nationality Act and this is the procedure of review that lasted until 1996. The 1961 restructuring allowed review of exclusion cases through a writ of *habeas corpus* at the federal district courts. If dissatisfied, the alien could then appeal to the U.S. Courts of Appeals and then to the U.S. Supreme Court. Meanwhile, deportation cases, instead of being limited to the old procedure of *habeas corpus* review, could be appealed to the U.S. Courts of Appeals via a procedure called "petition for review."[22]

The path and structure of immigration appeals was completely revamped in 1996 with amendments to the Immigration and Nationality Act and changes made through the Antiterrorism and Effective Death Penalty Act (AEDPA) and the Illegal Immigration Reform and Immigrant Responsibility Act (IIRIRA); both acts passed in 1996.[23] The 1996 Act combined the earlier "deportation" and "exclusion" into one procedure called "removal." Orders of removal, like old deportation orders, could still be appealed to the federal courts, but the 1996 Act made several

[20] Aleinikoff, Martin, and Motomura, *Immigration and Citizenship Process and Policy*, 291–93.
[21] Ibid. at 291.
[22] Ibid. at 292–93.
[23] AEDPA is Pub. L. No. 104–132, 110 Stat. 1214; IIRIRA is Pub. L. N. 104–208, 110 Stat. 3009.

major changes. First, judicial review was eliminated for large classes of immigration cases, including deportation cases where an alien in the United States had committed a crime, and had been convicted of that crime; cases involving administrative exercises of discretion concerning grants of waivers; and cases where the Attorney General had exercised her discretion. These new changes are codified at 8 USCS § 1252.2. In cases where judicial review was still available, the 1996 Act prescribed deferential standards of review.[24]

Many of the provisions of the Immigration and Nationality Act of 1996, especially the court-stripping measures, continue to be challenged in the federal courts. In 2001, the Supreme Court confirmed that the legislative changes of 1996 did not preclude *habeas corpus* review for aliens in district courts if it involved "pure questions of law."[25] But the scope of habeas corpus review of the Courts of Appeals continues to be contested.[26] As detailed in Chapter 6, some judges and justices have sought to mitigate some of the harshness of the 1996 reforms by circumventing in various ways recent congressional attempts to limit judicial review in certain immigration cases. Partially as a response to the actions taken by the federal courts to preserve some jurisdiction over immigration appeals, Congress sought to clarify the extent of the availability of judicial review via the REAL ID Act in 2005.[27] Among other immigration-related provisions in this act, Congress noted that it did not intend the district courts to have habeas corpus review of immigration appeals; these appeals would be the sole province of the U.S. Courts of Appeals. The manner whereby the cumulative effect of these legislative changes, which were then exacerbated by other exogenous factors, led to a great increase in immigration cases heading to the U.S. Courts of Appeals will be discussed in Chapters 3 and 5.[28] The REAL ID Act also preserved the Courts of Appeals review over "'constitutional claims or questions of law', not withstanding virtually any other INA provision 'which limits or eliminates judicial review.'"[29] Most important for the purposes of the

---

[24] Aleinikoff, Martin, and Motomura, *Immigration and Citizenship Process and Policy*, 292.
[25] *United States v. St. Cyr*, 533 U.S. 289 (2001).
[26] Aleinikoff, Martin, and Motomura, *Immigration and Citizenship Process and Policy*, 293.
[27] REAL ID Act, Pub. L. 109–13.
[28] See also Lenni B. Benson, "Making Paper Dolls: How Restrictions on Judicial Review and the Administrative Process Increase Immigration Cases in Federal Courts," 51 *New York Law School Law Review* 37 (2006/07), esp. 42–3.
[29] Aleinikoff, Martin, Motomura, *Immigration and Citizenship Process and Policy*, 293.

argument in this book, the recent changes to the immigration laws ensure a primary and increasingly important role of the Courts of Appeals in adjudicating immigration appeals.

THE SPECIAL ROLE OF THE NINTH CIRCUIT IN IMMIGRATION APPEALS

As will be detailed in Chapter 5, the surge of immigration cases in the U.S. Courts of Appeals has been highly uneven, as primarily the Second and Ninth Circuits have had to bear the brunt of the increase. In fact, throughout U.S. immigration history, the Ninth Circuit has played a special role. Even before the creation of the U.S. Courts of Appeals system in 1891, the western federal district courts and circuit courts played a leading role in creating and enforcing U.S. immigration law. The reason for the pivotal position played by the federal district courts in California, Oregon, and Washington, prior to the creation of the Courts of Appeals system and later the Ninth Circuit Court of Appeals, was the jurisdiction of the courts that correspond to geographically determined state lines. California, Oregon, and Washington contain multiple international ports of entry, including those along the land border with Mexico and Canada. These states also host multiple, very busy international airports. Along the Mexican border with Arizona and California are heavily traveled land ports of entry, such as Nogales, Arizona, San Diego, San Ysidro, El Centro, and Calexico, California. Seattle and Blaine in Washington state are popular crossing points for those entering the United States by land from Canada. Within the Ninth Circuit's jurisdiction are the international airports in Honolulu, Los Angeles, San Francisco, Seattle, and Portland; these are often gateway cities for aliens, including millions of tourists from Asia and the Pacific Rim countries. Most important, these cities and states are not only initial entry ports for legal and illegal aliens, but many aliens also choose to settle and reside in these areas.

Immigration scholars know that immigration is largely a regional phenomenon. Aliens, both legal and illegal, have historically and continue today to reside and work in only a handful of states and metropolitan areas. They settle in the large metroplex areas of New York, Florida, Illinois, Texas, and California not only because of the availability of jobs, but because of the influence of migration networks that encourage the concentration of migration flows to selected destinations.[30] The location

---

[30] See, e.g., a report by demographer William Frey, "The United States Population: Where the Immigrants Are," http://usinfo.state.gov/journals/itsv/0699/ijse/frey.htm.

of immigration proceedings are based on the alien's place of residence, thus the large number of immigration appeals in the Second, Fifth, and Ninth Circuits, where disproportionate numbers of legal and illegal aliens reside.

Because of these factors, the Ninth Circuit in particular has from the earliest days of federal immigration policy played a central role. This circuit's influence in immigration law has increased over time with the larger and larger percentage of immigration appeals adjudicated today by that circuit. The most recent statistics show that the Ninth Circuit alone adjudicates a little more than 50 percent of all immigration appeals nationwide.[31] As one of the Ninth Circuit judges I interviewed stated, "The Ninth Circuit makes immigration law."[32]

The well-known image of the majestic Statue of Liberty in New York harbor welcoming millions of immigrants to this country orients the popular perception of the location of any immigration "gateway" toward the east coast. Yet, it was the federal courts in the western states that played a key role in federal immigration law. Even before the creation of the U.S. Courts of Appeals system in 1891, the federal district courts and circuit courts in the western states, especially those in California, Oregon, and Washington, were instrumental in shaping and enforcing U.S. immigration law and policy. Recall that there was no significant federal immigration policy to speak of or to enforce before the 1882 passage of the Chinese Exclusion Act.[33] But because of the focus of this law and the pattern of immigration to the United States, where Chinese and other immigrants began migrating to California with the discovery of gold, the federal district courts became the front line of enforcement of the Exclusion Act and its subsequent harsher amendments. The manner in which the courtrooms of U. S. District Judge Ogden Hoffman (Northern District of California), of U. S. circuit court Judge Lorenzo

---

[31] Judge Michael Daly Hawkins was quoted stating that immigration appeals constitute 48% of the Ninth Circuit's docket (Solomon Moore and Ann M. Simmons, "Immigration Appeals Crushing Federal Appellate Courts," *Los Angeles Times*, May 2, 2005, 1). By the time I interviewed the court staff on 6/11/07, they reported that the percentage had risen to a little more than 50%.

[32] Interview with Judge C, 6/13/07. I explain later in this chapter why the judges are cited anonymously.

[33] Before the Chinese Exclusion Act, there were the Alien and Sedition Acts of 1798, parts of which expired or were not renewed under the Jefferson administration. These laws, however, were passed at a time in U.S. political history when the ideas of judicial review and of applying to the federal courts for redress of an infringement of one's rights were not yet established.

Sawyer (Northern District of California), and to a lesser extent of U. S. District Judge Mathew Deady (District of Oregon) were transformed into "*habeas corpus* mills" as Chinese aliens, often represented by elite counsel, went to the federal courts by the thousands to challenge their detention and exclusion, is well documented.[34] Judge Hoffman's often-sympathetic treatment of the Chinese aliens probably worked to increase the flow of Chinese aliens to his court.[35]

With the creation of the Ninth Circuit Court of Appeals by the Evarts Act, the western federal courts continued to play a central role in creating immigration law. And although the Ninth Circuit's adjudication of immigration appeals became far less generous toward aliens' claims than Hoffman's court had been, the region now encompassed by the Ninth Circuit continues to play a prominent role in interpreting and enforcing federal immigration policy and law because of its geopolitical location. Historian David C. Frederick writes, "The Ninth Circuit may have had a greater impact on the enforcement of anti-Chinese legislation than any other court, arguably including the Supreme Court itself."[36] As will become apparent, this assessment still holds true for the contemporary Ninth Circuit Court of Appeals.

ANATOMY OF A "BAD REP" – THE ORIGINS OF THE SUPREME COURT'S ALLEGED HOSTILITY TOWARD ALIENS

The Ninth Circuit is synonymous with immigration policy, but what is the reputation of the Supreme Court on immigration? The origin of the Supreme Court's lack of receptiveness and even hostility to aliens' claims can be traced to a specific component of the plenary power doctrine and to the nature of immigration law. Stephen Legomsky has described immigration law as "a special subspecies," "a maverick," and a "wildcard" within the broader public law because the Supreme Court has, "declined to review federal immigration statutes for compliance with substantive

---

[34] See Christian Fritz, "A Nineteenth Century 'Habeas Corpus Mill': The Chinese Before the Federal Courts in California," 32 *American Journal of Legal History*, No. 4 (Oct. 1988); Christian Fritz, *Federal Justice – The California Court of Ogden Hoffman, 1851–1891* (Lincoln, NE: University of Nebraska Press, 1991); see especially "Chapter 7: The Chinese Before the Court." See also David C. Frederick, *Rugged Justice: The Ninth Circuit Court of Appeals and the American West, 1891–1941* (Berkeley, CA: University of California Press, 1994), especially Chapter 3 "Testing Tolerance: Chinese Exclusion and the Ninth Circuit."

[35] Frederick, *Rugged Justice*, 60.

[36] Frederick, *Rugged Justice*, 52.

constitutional constraints."[37] Peter Schuck writes, "Probably no other area of American law has been so radically insulated and divergent from those fundamental norms of constitutional right, administrative procedures, and the judicial role."[38] Immigration law is an area of public law in which, it appears, the normal rules do not apply.

The main reason immigration law is perceived as partitioned off from the rest of public law is the centrality of the plenary power mode of legal reasoning in this area of law. As T. Alexander Aleinikoff points out, the plenary power doctrine is actually composed of two analytically distinct ideas: "1) Congress received...all the power that a sovereign state may have to regulate the entry of aliens, and 2) the courts would not subject congressional choices to any limitations on federal power located elsewhere in the Constitution (such as in the First Amendment or the prohibition against retroactive legislation)."[39] The Supreme Court not only declined to hold Congress to constitutional and procedural standards, but for a time, it denied aliens' ability to appeal at all to the federal courts to fight their exclusion and deportation. Culminating in the case of *United States v. Ju Toy* (1905),[40] the Supreme Court changed course from its original position of permitting aliens to challenge their exclusion and deportation via writs of habeas corpus to adopting the position in *Ju Toy* that "due process of law does not necessarily require a judicial trial."[41] The *Ju Toy* case had a profoundly negative effect on aliens' claims because their cases were now adjudicated exclusively by executive branch administrative agencies, mainly the Bureau of Immigration, which was greatly influenced by nativist forces. As Lucy Salyer demonstrates, the *Ju Toy* decision, for all practical purposes, meant that from 1905 to 1924, there was a virtual removal of all immigration cases from federal judicial review and these cases were subject to the mercy of the Bureau of Immigration. That bureau was more concerned about the enforcement of Chinese and national origins-based exclusionist policy than it was with providing procedural protections and other legal niceties to ensure a fair process of adjudication for the aliens.[42]

---

[37] Stephen H. Legomsky, "Immigration Law and the Principle of Plenary Congressional Power," 84 *The Supreme Court Review* 255 (1984); and Stephen Legomsky, "Ten More Years of Plenary Power: Immigration, Congress, and the Court," 22 *Hastings Constitutional Law Quarterly* 925 (1995).

[38] Schuck, "The Transformation of Immigration Law," 1.

[39] T. Alexander Aleinikoff, *Semblances of Sovereignty: The Constitution, the State and American Citizenship* (Cambridge, MA : Harvard Univeristy Press, 2002), 16.

[40] 198 U.S. 253.

[41] Ibid.

[42] Salyer, *Law as Harsh as Tigers*, 117–216.

The Supreme Court's reputation of unfriendliness toward alien claims can be attributed to the latter notion that the Court has consistently adopted a very deferential approach toward congressional and administrative agency actions on immigration. Indeed the Court itself perpetuated the plenary power doctrine in the starkest and strongest language. In *Wong Wing v. United States* (1896), for example, the Court wrote, "No limits can be put by the courts upon the power of Congress to protect, by summary methods, the country from the advent of aliens whose race or habits render them undesirable as citizens, or to expel such if they have already found their way into our land and unlawfully remain therein."[43] Similarly, in *Miller v. Albright*, a case from the Court's 1999 term, Justice O'Conner makes the same point when she writes, "Judicial power in immigration and naturalization is extremely limited."[44] The foundational plenary power decisions of *Chae Chan Ping v. United States, Fong Yue Ting v. United States,* and *Nishimura Ekiu v. United States* created the idea that Legomsky and others have referred to as "immigration exceptionalism" – the notion that immigration law lies outside mainstream public law.[45] While the idea of plenary power insulated immigration from broader public law, immigration exceptionalism was furthered by cases such as *Ju Toy*, which extended the idea of congressional plenary power and the judicial deference to the determinations of administrative agencies supervised by the executive branch.

The Supreme Court gained its anti-alien reputation because it appears to have washed its hands of immigration questions and ceded power over the immigration issue to Congress and the executive branch, especially to executive branch administrative agency personnel. Citing congressional plenary power in this area of law and a concern for national sovereignty, the Supreme Court has systematically deferred to Congress on immigration matters and has "declined to review federal immigration statutes for compliance with substantive constitutional constraints."[46] It has done so despite the fact that the power to regulate immigration per se is not

---

[43] 163 U.S. 228, 237.

[44] 523 U.S. 420, 459.

[45] Stephen Legomsky, "Symposium: Restructuring Federal Courts: Immigration: Fear and Loathing in Congress and the Courts: Immigration and Judicial Review," 78 *Texas Law Review* 1615, 1616, 1619 (June 2000).

[46] Legomsky, "Immigration Law and the Principle of Congressional Plenary Power," 255. The closest reference to congressional power to regulate immigration is found in Article I, Section 8, Clause 4, which gives Congress the power to regulate naturalization. Nowhere in the U.S. Constitution is it explicitly stated that Congress has the power to regulate immigration policy more broadly.

a constitutionally enumerated power of Congress. Schuck describes the strange status of immigration law this way: "Probably no other area of American law has been so radically insulated and divergent from those fundamental norms of constitutional right, administrative procedures, and the judicial role."[47] Simply put, the United States' moniker as "a nation of immigrants," along with the ubiquitous Statue of Liberty as a symbol of welcome, when juxtaposed against the consistent refusal of the highest court in the land to hold congressional and executive agency actions to standard constitutional and procedural norms, is incongruous. It is no wonder that aliens and their advocates do not regard the Supreme Court as their friend or ally.

REFOCUSING THE INQUIRY

Although plenary power has been a recurring theme in immigration cases, it usually appears only in exclusion and non-asylum-based deportation cases. Yet there are many other types of immigration cases in which the government and the federal courts must make a decision about whether an alien may physically enter or remain in U.S. territory, or symbolically enter as a member of the national community. For this reason, the cases in the database created for this study include a wide range of immigration cases. Among them are exclusion cases, general deportation cases, asylum-based deportation cases, criminal deportation cases, naturalization and denaturalization cases, alienage cases, and cases in which an alien is arguing his or her right to reenter the United States after a previous deportation by challenging the circumstances of the first deportation. What all these types of cases have in common is that American political and legal institutions must render a decision about whether the person may literally or symbolically enter and remain in the U.S. community.

Deportation cases are not the only kind of immigration cases that reach the federal courts. Alienage and naturalization and denaturalization cases can also be construed as entry/exit cases in which the federal courts are making a decision not about whether to physically allow the alien to enter the polity, but whether to symbolically and legally allow them to enter and remain as a member of the national community. When one includes these cases along with the exclusion and deportation cases in which the alien obtained a victory, one can see that a focus on the smaller subset of cases in which the Court used the plenary power doctrine is

---

[47] Schuck, "The Transformation of Immigration Law," 1.

misleading and perpetuates the idea that the Supreme Court, regardless of the ideological tilt of the Court regime, is anti-alien. Perhaps because the number of immigration cases in the Courts of Appeals is so much larger than in the Supreme Court's or because of the geographical and ideological diversity of these courts, there has been no parallel attempt to draw general characterizations of the Courts of Appeals' system as a whole and its treatment of aliens, save some anecdotal evidence that the Ninth Circuit may be more liberal in its ideological tilt than other circuits.[48] The point is that the selection of case types matter in ascertaining the answer to how the U.S. Supreme Court and U.S. Courts of Appeals decide immigration cases.

Given the availability of Supreme Court and Courts of Appeals opinions, it is tempting to compare alien win/loss rates at the Supreme Court and the U.S. Courts of Appeals, but I refrain from doing so for several methodological reasons. First, the Supreme Court and the Courts of Appeals adjudicate very different pools of cases. Because the Supreme Court has the luxury of controlling its own docket, the Court picks and chooses among immigration cases. In contrast, the U.S. Courts of Appeals must adjudicate all immigration cases properly appealed to it. Also, the Supreme Court database of cases for this study contains only those cases that were granted *certiorari* by the Supreme Court and not the ones that were denied review. Because the docket control procedures of the Supreme Court are very different from those of the Courts of Appeals, there may be selection bias built into the Supreme Court pool of cases. It may be that there is something qualitatively different about the immigration cases that were granted review by the Court compared with the many other cases at the Courts of Appeals level that were either not appealed to the Supreme Court or not granted *certiorari*. However, these

---

[48] Solomon Moore and Ann M. Simmons, "Immigrant Pleas Crushing Federal Appellate Courts," *Los Angeles Times*, 2 May 2005, A1: "Some immigration attorneys acknowledge that the generally liberal reputation of the 9th Circuit and its willingness to challenge rulings by immigration judges and the BIA often influenced their decision to appeal to the court"; Bob Egelko, "Plan to Unify Immigrant Appeals: Sen. Specter's Provision to Centralize Jurisdiction Draws Fire," *San Francisco Chronicle*, 13 March 2006, A1: "But immigration lawyers and the American Civil Liberties Union say the plan is ill-conceived, dangerous and a thinly veiled attack on the Ninth U.S Circuit Court of Appeals in San Francisco, which now hears about half of the nation's immigration appeals"; Zachary Coile, "A Quiet Move in House to Split the 9th Circuit," *San Francisco Chronicle*, 30 Nov. 2005, A1:"Conservatives long have claimed that the Ninth Circuit is too liberal ... Critics of the legislation believe the issue is less about the efficiency of the court and more an ideological battle waged by lawmakers who dislike the court's decisions on issues ranging from medical marijuana to the Endangered Species Act."

differences (if they exist) are difficult to determine because the Court is notoriously unforthcoming with explanations of why it grants or denies *certiorari*. Thus, comparing the legal outcomes or dispositions of the U.S. Supreme Court and the U.S. Courts of Appeals would be highly ambiguous and, indeed, not particularly useful. One would be comparing apples and oranges.

The conventional wisdom that aliens do not meet with much success in Supreme Court litigation is not particularly illuminating, because ultimately the belief rests on the flawed assumption that legal dispositions from the U.S. Supreme Court and from the U.S. Courts of Appeals are comparable. A more fruitful approach is to understand the motivations and mechanisms that inform the legal decision making of the Supreme Court and Courts of Appeals. After all, the concern that is driving the questions about whether the Supreme Court is hostile or indifferent to aliens is a concern for the equitable treatment of alien claims by each tier of the federal judicial hierarchy.

THE BENEFITS OF MULTIPLE METHODOLOGIES

With the goal of moving the focus away from the disposition of the case, which does not reveal much about why judges and justices have decided the way they have, this book aims to understand the similarities and differences in the decision making processes of the U.S. Supreme Court and the U.S. Courts of Appeals and their personnel. In order to answer the research question of whether there are differences between the way the Supreme Court and Courts of Appeals justices and judges decide cases, this study drew on multiple methodologies, including creating an original database of cases that allowed cross-tabulated comparisons of the modes of legal reasoning; conducting interviews with Ninth Circuit judges and central staff; close readings and interpretative content analysis of some of the legal opinions; and doctrinal analysis – all with attention to the developmental trends in federal judicial history and immigration history.

Each one of the five distinct methodologies enabled a different layer of analysis and a distinctive way of approaching the research questions posed in this book. First, the quantitative cross tabulation analysis, made possible by a large N database, allowed the assessment of aggregate trends in both levels of the courts, and facilitated the tracing of changes that happen over time. In this way, I was able to empirically chart the moving picture story of the development of the courts. Second, the close readings or interpretative content and textual analysis of many of these legal opinions (see Chapter 4) revealed rhetorical turns that indicated shifts in the justices' and judges' intentions and analytical strategies within individual cases. Third, the doctrinal analysis undertaken in Chapter 6 was necessary because legal institutions operate by logics dissimilar to those of the elected branches of government; namely, legal institutions are bound by *stare decisis,* the following of precedent. Any institutional development analysis must be mindful of the doctrinal constraints of this body of law. Fourth, the addition of the interviews with the Ninth Circuit personnel allowed me to confirm or rule out judicial behaviors found in the legal opinions. More important, the qualitative interviews with key actors provided a deeper understanding of the institutional processes and even the individual thought processes of the judges. Finally, the strength of American political development research is its ability to contextualize political phenomenon by indicating the extent to which processes and mechanisms are historically contingent. The tracking of court histories of the U.S. Supreme Court and the U.S. Courts of Appeals, and attention to developments in U.S. immigration policy, set the background for the political development of the two courts. Of course any methodology has its limitations. It was my hope that in using a diversity of methods, the weaknesses of some methods would be balanced and offset by the strengths of other approaches. Ultimately, the combination of multiple methodologies not only allowed me to triangulate, cross check, and verify my findings, but it facilitated the construction of a far richer understanding of judicial decision making and institutional development.

THE COURTS AND CASES

One source of primary data for this book was an original database comprising 2,218 legal opinions on immigration, with 200 opinions from the Supreme Court, 13 opinions from the circuit courts (in existence before 1891), and 2,005 opinions from three U.S. Courts of Appeals. (This study does not include cases from the immigration courts or the BIA because these bodies are not constitutionally created Article III courts, nor are they appellate courts of general jurisdiction, as the Supreme Court and Courts of Appeals are; they are administrative units and are governed by an entirely different set of institutional contexts.) The majority of these opinions are published, although the database also includes 548 unpublished opinions, mostly from the Ninth Circuit. There are twelve U.S. Courts of Appeals and one Federal Circuit Court of Appeals that are organized geographically; the boundaries of each circuit correspond to state lines. My database includes cases from three of these Courts of Appeals: the Third Circuit (Pennsylvania, Delaware, New Jersey, Virgin Islands), Fifth Circuit (Texas, Louisiana, Mississippi), and the Ninth Circuit (California, Arizona, Alaska, Hawaii, Nevada, Guam, Oregon, Washington, Idaho, Montana, and the Northern Marianas Island). Together the Fifth and Ninth Circuits adjudicate the bulk of all immigration appeals in the United States. The Ninth Circuit alone adjudicates a little more than 50 percent of all immigration appeals nationwide; as of 2006, 40 percent of the Ninth Circuit's docket consisted of immigration appeals.[49] Although, beginning in the early 1990s, the Second Circuit also saw a huge spike in immigration appeals in both raw numbers and as a percentage of the docket, the Fifth Circuit adjudicates the second-largest number of immigration appeals nationwide, after the Ninth Circuit. For contrast, the Third Circuit was added to the study because of the relatively low but consistent level of its immigration caseload over time.

The opinions were collected using Lexis/Nexis and cover the years 1881–2002.[50] This broad time period encompasses variations in the country's mood toward immigrants, whether welcoming or restrictionist. The time period of this study begins near the passage of the Chinese Exclusion Act in 1882, which marked a long period of restrictionist sentiment in U.S. immigration history that lasted into the 1950s. The study ends at 2001, which demarcates the end of the Immigration and Naturalization Service era and the creation of the Department of Homeland Security. However, cases were also included from 2002 to assess whether the September 11, 2001, terror attacks had any discernible effect on the judicial decision making process in the relevant field of immigration appeals. Because the cases in this study involve only immigration entry/exit issues, the search terms would not have picked up any terrorism cases that arose out of the 9/11 terrorist attacks even if they had made it to the Courts of Appeals level, which they had not. My aim in adding the 2002 cases was to make sure that the catastrophic attacks in 2001 did not change everything about how judges and justices decided garden-variety immigration cases. I regard the terrorism cases, although they may have immigration elements, as an entirely distinct set of cases from the purely entry/exit decisions because the terrorist cases embody much stronger national security and criminal elements; therefore, those cases are not a part of this study.

[49] Egelko, "Plan to Unify Immigrant Appeals," A1.
[50] See Appendix A for a more detailed description of how the cases were collected.

The cases in the database created for this project involved nationals from 116 countries around the globe. Because I used the search terms "immigration" *and* "exclusion" *or* "deportation," the cases in the database are limited to immigration appeals that involve decisions about whether an alien may physically enter the United States or remain in U.S. territory. Migration specialists often term such entry/exit policy "immigration" policy rather than "immigrant" policy; the latter pertains to the treatment of immigrants once they are within U.S. borders and beyond the initial entry/exit decision. This database does not contain cases pertaining to the rights of aliens outside the entry/exit decision. Therefore, well-known immigrant cases, such as *Yick Wo v. Hopkins* (1886)[51] (discriminatory application of a neutral law against Chinese laundries); *Graham v. Richardson* (1971)[52] (whether aliens are entitled to welfare benefits); and *Plyler v. Doe* (1982)[53] (whether children of illegal aliens may be barred from public school) are not considered here. All of these cases, which involve the rights of aliens once they are within U.S. territory, are excluded from this study because these are analytically distinct from the entry/exit decisions. The "immigrant" cases, such as *Yick Wo, Plyler,* and *Graham v. Richardson,* involve entirely different lines of governing doctrine and legal considerations and their inclusion in this database would have clouded the overall analysis.

Among the Courts of Appeals cases, the vast majority of the cases, 61 percent, are general deportation cases in which the U.S. government seeks to deport, expel, or remove an alien who is already within U.S. territory. Aliens may be deported for a number of reasons. An alien who is discovered to be in the country illegally (by surreptitiously crossing a U.S. border, or overstaying a valid nonimmigrant visa, for example) can be deported. An alien who has been legally admitted to the United States and is a lawful permanent resident ("greencard" holder), but who has not yet become a citizen, can also be deported if he commits a crime.

The second largest group of cases in this study, 24 percent, is asylum cases. In an asylum case, an alien is fighting to stay in this country because she fears persecution if she must return to her home country. These cases routinely involved accounts of assault, torture, rape, murder, and many other forms of persecution. Although the outcome of any immigration case has a human consequence, in no instance is the importance of the

[51] 118 U.S. 356.
[52] 403 U.S. 365.
[53] 457 U.S. 202.

courts' role in deciding a person's fate so clear as it is in many of the asylum cases, where life and death can hang in the balance.

The third largest group is exclusion cases (4 percent). Unlike deportation, which involves the removal or expulsion of an alien already within U.S. territory, exclusion cases involve aliens seeking admission to the United States from outside U.S. soil.[54] The remainder of the cases are alien rights cases (3 percent), deportation cases specifically involving criminal aliens (3 percent), alienage cases (2 percent), and naturalization/denaturalization cases (2 percent). In alien rights cases, aliens challenge a government procedure or practice about some aspect of immigration law and enforcement. Other types of cases that are represented in this study but constitute less than 1 percent of those studied include alienage cases (in which a person is contesting his or her legal immigration status), and some cases where an alien was found in the United States after a previous deportation, but was challenging a current removal order based on the circumstances of the alien's previous entry.

THE INTERVIEWS

The database was supplemented with interviews with eight U.S. Courts of Appeals judges and three central staff members from the Ninth Circuit Court of Appeals.[55] Several considerations guided the recruitment of the judges. Like Supreme Court justices, these judges grant very few interviews; indeed many turned down my requests or did not respond at all. Therefore, my goal was to obtain as many interviews as I could without regard to random sampling procedures because interviews of these key actors are rare to begin with. Some of the judges were referred to me by the central staff and by other judges or other public law scholars; therefore, some interviews were obtained through the snowball technique. Given the sensitive nature of judicial decision making, I promised the judges and the central staff anonymity and will not reveal any information about them except that there were seven active judges, one senior status judge, and three central staff members in my sample. In revealing

[54] In 1996, the Immigration and Nationality Act was substantially revised by the Illegal Immigration Reform and Immigrant Responsibility Act (IIRIRA), Pub.L. 104–208, Div. C, 110 Stat. 3009–546. IIRIRA abolished the distinction between exclusion and deportation, rolling the two formerly separate legal actions into a generic action called "removal."

[55] All the interviews with the judges and staff were conducted by the author, and most were in person; only one interview, the interview with Judge H, was conducted over the phone.

only limited information about the judges, I have followed the lead of David Klein and Jonathan Cohen's research, which also utilized interviews with Courts of Appeals judges.[56] Unlike Klein and Cohen, who cited their interviews in a more diffuse manner, I have attributed specific comments to individual judges. These seven active judges constitute 25 percent of the 28 active judges on the Ninth Circuit.

The main goal of conducting interviews with the judges was to clarify and gain insight into the internal processes and experimentation in the Ninth Circuit's adjudicative procedures. Through talking to the interviewees, I was able to piece together a broad account of the internal procedures that the Ninth Circuit as an institution uses to process immigration cases and to understand how the rising immigration caseload affected the individual personnel, not just the institution. These interviews provided first-hand accounts from witnesses who knew the procedures well. The group included at least three judges who had taken part in the court's many experiments in adjudicating immigration appeals. These institutional processes and experiments are not published in the Ninth Circuit's operations manuals and this information is not available from any other source. Therefore, the interviews with key actors represent persons with "the most involvement with the process of interest" and several who had actually participated in many of the experimental attempts of the Ninth Circuit to cope with its immigration caseload.[57] Trying to use random sampling to obtain interviews was not only unnecessary, but it would also have been an inappropriate, and even counterproductive, methodology for my purposes.

The judges who were interviewed all belong to the bench of the Ninth Circuit Court of Appeals. Given the central role the Ninth Circuit has played in immigration appeals, and the fact that, since the 1980s, it has been this circuit more than any other that has been most affected by an increasing caseload of immigration appeals, it was appropriate to limit the judges' and court staff's interviews to the Ninth Circuit. For all intents and purposes, it is the Ninth Circuit that makes operative doctrine for immigration appeals because of the large percentage of appeals

---

[56] David Klein, *Decision Making in the United States Courts of Appeals* (Cambridge: Cambridge University Press, 2000) and Jonathan Cohen, *Inside Appellate Courts: The Impact of Court Organization and Judicial Decision Making in the United States Courts of Appeals.* (Ann Arbor, MI: University of Michigan Press, 2005), 18–19.

[57] Oisin Tansey, "Process Tracing and Elite Interviewing: A Case for Non-Probability Sampling," *PS: Political Science and Politics*, Vol. XL, No. 4 (Oct. 2007): 765.

that circuit adjudicates. In the interviews with the judges and court staff, I pursued two main lines of questioning. (The actual questions can be found in Appendix D.) The first line of questioning was about how the immigration appeals that have disproportionately affected the Ninth Circuit have changed the Ninth Circuit as an institution. The second line of questioning was about how, if at all, the lopsided distribution of immigration appeals in the U.S. Courts of Appeals system has affected the way individual judges adjudicate those cases and other kinds of cases. In both sets of questions, my goal was to assess the effect of the size and nature of the Ninth Circuit's caseload on the circuit and on its judges. The findings from these interviews are concentrated in Chapter 4, which discusses the strategic uses of discretion, and in Chapter 5, which examines the uneven impact of exogenous factors on the U.S. Courts of Appeals system.

ANALYTICAL STRATEGIES

Two assumptions underlie the analytical approach of this book.[58] First, it is an accepted proposition among political scientists conducting law and courts research that judges have policy preferences and that they often strive to realize these preferences in their legal decision making. Second, I adopt Mark Graber and other historical institutionalists' notion that legal decision making, strategic behavior, and attitudinally driven behavior are not discrete; often legal decision making is some combination of all of these approaches. As Graber noted, even as the behavioralists and attitudinalists contend that no judicial decision can be explained "entirely as a legal exercise," likewise, no judicial decision can be reduced to or explained exclusively as "a sincere or sophisticated effort to secure policy preferences."[59] Rather, legal and institutional norms constrain any pursuit of preferences. Therefore, the outcome in cases is often a mixture of legal, strategic, attitudinal, and behavioralist factors and "no element of that compound can be isolated."[60] Graber was writing about several

[58] Elsewhere I have written more extensively about my search for an appropriate methodology for this book. See Anna Law, "In Search of a Methodology and Tales from the Academic Crypt" in *Researching Migration: Stories from the Field*, Louis DeSipio, Manuel Garcia y Griego, and Sherrie Koussoudji, eds. (New York: Social Science Research Council Publications, 2007), 63–80 (available at http://www.ssrc.org/publications/view/42451838–264A-DE11-AFAC-001CC477EC70/).

[59] Mark Graber, "Legal, Strategic or Legal Strategy: Deciding to Decide During the Civil War and Reconstruction" in Ronald Kahn and Ken I. Kersch, eds., *The Supreme Court & American Political Development* (Lawrence, KS: University of Kansas Press, 2006), 35.

[60] Ibid. at 60.

landmark Supreme Court cases from the Civil War and Reconstruction eras, but his contention that legal decisions are often the reflection of multiple sources of preference still holds true when applied to the U.S. Courts of Appeals. The analysis of the patterns in the modes of legal reasoning allowed me to assess how the legal norms interact with institutional structures in construing what actions are allowable or even possible in the U.S. Supreme Court and the U.S. Courts of Appeals.

How is the effect of institutional context empirically ascertainable? My analysis begins by using the concept of "modes of legal reasoning" to assess the effect of institutional context on judicial decision making. The primary variable extracted from the dataset of opinions from the Supreme Court and the Courts of Appeals was the mode of legal reasoning, which is the legal or political idea or rationale that judges and justices use to explain and justify the legal outcomes they reach. Unfortunately, there is no agreed-on set of modes of legal reasoning within legal or political science scholarship. And although Robert Gordon has written about independent "legal forms" and Michael McCann has referred to "modes" of legal argument, no one has tried to operationalize these for empirical purposes.[61] Immigration law scholars have often identified national sovereignty, plenary power, and procedural due process as three distinguishable and recurring themes in immigration cases.[62] There are of course many sorts of themes and ideas that arise in immigration opinions, but as Sheri Berman indicates, "An idea can rise to prominence, influence political life in some way, and then disappear. However, some of the most important ideas – and norms and culture by definition – exert a continuing influence on politics for extended periods of time."[63] Although ideas such as references to race, class, and gender could be included in a complete discussion of the themes that appear in U.S. immigration law, in actuality a much smaller subset of these ideas were cited as the actual justifications for the final disposition of many cases.[64] In addition, many

---

[61] Robert Gordon, "Critical Legal Studies Symposium: Critical Legal Histories," 36 *Stanford Law Review* 57 (1984) and Michael McCann, "How the Supreme Court Matters in American Politics," in Howard Gillman and Cornell Clayton, eds., *The Supreme Court in American Politics – New Institutionalist Interpretations* (Lawrence, KS : University of Kansas Press, 1999), 81.

[62] See, e.g., Legomsky, "Immigration Law and the Principle of Plenary Congressional Power," 6; Motomura, "Immigration Law After a Century of Plenary Power," 545; and Schuck, "The Transformation of Immigration Law," 1.

[63] Sheri Berman, "Ideas, Norms, and Culture in Political Analysis," *Comparative Politics* 33 (2001): 237.

[64] Some readers may be wondering why I have not included race and economics as major themes, especially in the Chinese Exclusion–related cases in 1883–1893. As I read the

of the persistent modes of legal reasoning – such as due process, doctrine, and administrative deference – that appear in immigration cases are also common themes in other areas of public law.

When thinking of modes of legal reasoning, Phillip Bobbit's modalities from his book *Constitutional Fate* come to mind, and some may wonder why I did not just work from his modalities. In *Constitutional Fate*, Bobbit lays out a typology of legal arguments that can be found in legal opinions, briefs, and other legal documents. He argues that legal institutions and actors have mastered and share a distinct "legal grammar."[65] He further notes that some arguments are illegitimate and not compelling in the legal world because they are not a valid part of the legal grammar; he writes, for example, that no lawyer would make, nor judge approve of, an argument based on kinship (nepotism) or religious beliefs.[66] I make a similar argument about my modes of legal reasoning: the institutional context of each level of the courts renders some modes of legal reasoning acceptable and appropriate while causing others to be illegitimate and unconvincing. But ultimately I found Bobbit's typology of legal arguments of limited use for my purposes because his book aims for a different mark. His goal is to define common theories of jurisprudential argument that legitimize judicial review. At the beginning of this project, I considered using Bobbit's modalities but quickly found that they did not match the modes of legal reasoning that were appearing in the immigration cases. Plenary power, as understood in the immigration context, for example, was neither entirely "structural," "historical," "textual," or purely "doctrinal." It is a combination of all of these. The idea started out as an outgrowth of the commerce clause and then seems to have developed a life of its own after that. I found that plenary power, a recurring and influential mode of legal reasoning in immigration law, did not map onto Bobbit's five modalities of legal arguments. Bobbit himself presents an example that is exactly the definition of plenary power. In acknowledging that his modalities are not completely discrete from each other, he wrote, "the constitutional arguments that a particular sort to question is best suited to be decided by one institution of government and ill-suited to another, may in some cases be thought of as equally plausibly as a prudential argument or a structural

opinions, it became evident to me that although race and economics were motivations in the passage of the Chinese Exclusion Act of 1882, these were not sufficient to explain how the Act was enforced in the Supreme Court and Courts of Appeals.

[65] Phillip Bobbit, *Constitutional Fate: Theory of the Constitution* (New York: Oxford University Press, 1982), 6.

[66] Ibid.

one."[67] No doubt the analytical approach in this book owes a great intellectual debt to Bobbit, but my aim was a very different one from his. It was to assess whether the choice of legal reasoning is related to each federal court's distinct institutional setting and location in the judicial hierarchy and the best way to operationalize the concept for empirical purposes was to look for patterns in the modes of legal reasoning across a large number of legal opinions.

If the goal is to better understand the influence of institutional context on judicial decision making, then one must first ascertain the justifications by which judges arrive at their ultimate conclusions. Whereas analysis that focuses on the final disposition of a case does not contribute to one's understanding of the process by which the judicial decision was made, a focus on the rationale for the decision can open a window into the influence of the factors, including institutional settings, that can affect decision making. For example, the data may show that a Court of Appeals judge or Supreme Court justice ruled consistently against the alien and for the government in a series of cases. The disposition or outcome in these cases could be interpreted as meaning that the judge or justice in question is pro-government and anti-alien, when in fact the judge or justice may simply be upholding her fidelity to doctrine or his view of who (the administrative agency or the federal courts) should be the proper fact finder in the case. Fortunately, "what courts say [in legal opinions] often spells what it is they have actually done."[68] Analysis of patterns in the modes of legal reasoning paints a much more nuanced portrait of the formation of judicial preferences among competing ideas and interpretive approaches to decision making than does just looking at legal outcomes. The use of modes of legal reasoning as a conceptual approach takes seriously the content of legal opinions. As Friedman writes:

> In judicial opinions are found the rules that govern the next case, and thus the conduct of institutions and actors in society...At bottom, what law imposes is a requirement of reasoned justification, and reasons are found in the opinion of a court. It is entirely legitimate in law for judges in some circumstances to reach differing answers to the same question; what matters is that judges explain those answers in a plausible and coherent way. They not only must explain why a result is reached in one case; they also must explain how that result squares with the result of other cases.[69]

---

[67] Bobbit, *Constitutional Fate*, 8.
[68] Friedman, "Taking Law Seriously," 266.
[69] Ibid.

Friedman is right that scrutinizing the content of opinions is the only way to understand the doctrinal rules that govern an area of law or the logic behind a particular legal outcome. But these legal opinions and the rationales that judges provide in them tell us much more than the doctrinal rules or legal norms at work in a case; they are a window into judges' perceptions of what their job is and how they are supposed to be doing it.

Within legal opinions, judges advance their arguments and justify outcomes through the use of modes of legal reasoning. Legal reasoning appears in cases as distinctive "modes" by which "adjudicated incidents and relations are decontextualized, treated as prototypical examples of broader categories, and assessed according to abstract principles and highly stylized discursive conventions."[70] So, in effect, the judges are grouping and categorizing certain types of cases together and assessing cases in each group in similar fashion. Therefore it is appropriate to compare the "modes" with each other. The modes of legal reasoning in immigration cases usually take the form of references to judicial principles (equal protection or due process for instance), political or social understandings of power arrangements (such as national sovereignty or plenary power), or simply a legally recognized method of deciding a case (such as statutory interpretation, doctrine, facts/evidence).

Although the modes of legal reasoning that appear in legal opinions are to some extent dictated by the type of case and the fact patterns of the case, nevertheless some of these modes of legal reasoning have functionalist elements where the legal reasoning can be used as an instrument of the judges to fashion their desired policy goals. Meanwhile, other types of legal reasoning and practice, such as plenary power and procedural due process, exemplify political divisions of power between different branches of government and decision making bodies in a hierarchical judicial appeals process.

Some may charge that the modes of legal reasoning approach is inexact or even invalid as a methodology because legal reasoning and justifications cannot be so parsimoniously separated and classified into discrete modes of legal reasoning. The point is well taken that some of the modes of legal reasoning in this study may in fact be overlapping or bleed into each other. Bobbit similarly acknowledged that his typology does not consist of "wholly discrete items" and that the "various arguments illustrated [by his typologies] often work in combination."[71] In the

---

[70] Michael McCann, "How the Supreme Court Matters in American Politics," 81.
[71] Bobbit, *Constitutional Fate*, 8.

immigration context, Hiroshi Motomura has pointed out that procedural due process has become a "surrogate" for substantive due process legal reasoning.[72] Nevertheless, the analysis of modes of legal reasoning has its benefits. Although the modes of legal reasoning may not be completely distinct and detached, I argue that the *motivations* they encapsulate can be more clearly untangled and classified. Furthermore, the modes of legal reasoning analysis, when combined and buttressed by other methodologies, provides quite a bit of leverage on understanding how judges decide cases, especially their thinking about which values (political or legal) are important to them, and how much deference they are willing to accord to other fact finders.

The reliability of this method was further strengthened by its deployment in more than 2,000 observations, thereby allowing the broad assessment of aggregate trends rather than in a few cherry-picked data points. Moreover, the modes of legal reasoning approach, when combined with the multiple methodologies deployed in this study, allows a better assessment and contextualization of the patterns in judges' legal reasoning. On its own, the modes of legal reasoning approach may indeed be limited, but when it is supplemented by other methodologies, one can have more confidence in its results. To discard the modes of legal reasoning approach altogether as inexact or imprecise is to throw the baby out with the bath water and would be, as anthropologist Clifford Geertz once noted, akin to concluding, "as a perfectly aseptic environment is impossible, one might as well conduct surgery in the sewer."[73] Modes of legal reasoning, supplemented with other methodologies, do provide insight into how judges decide cases and not simply what they have decided. Thus, I treat modes of legal reasoning as a heuristic device that is a basic indicator of the nature and contours of the decision making process, but I do not rely on this methodology alone.

To be clear, when I refer to modes of legal reasoning, these are not the same as a body of legal doctrine – although there is some overlap. As recurring modes of legal reasoning (and therefore stable cognitive structures), ideas such as due process and national sovereignty are far more expansive than a line of doctrine. Legal doctrine encompasses only a fairly clearly

---

[72] Hiroshi Motomura, "The Curious Evolution of Immigration Law: Procedural Surrogates for Substantive Constitutional Rights." 92 *Columbia Law Review* 1625–1704 (1992).

[73] Clifford Geertz, *The Interpretation of Cultures* (New York: Basic Books, 1973), 30. Geertz was paraphrasing the economist Robert Solow.

defined set of similarly situated cases; it is but a subset of the broader range of ideas that occur and recur among different types of immigration cases and among the same type of cases with varied fact patterns.

PRELIMINARY FINDINGS

An important initial finding was that both the Supreme Court and the Courts of Appeals draw from the same set of modes of legal reasoning, albeit to varying extents. It was not the case that the Supreme Court used one set of legal reasoning while the Courts of Appeals used another. Indeed, the finding that one set of legal reasoning is common to both courts is an indication that these legal institutions speak in a common grammar. In Chapter 2 one will discover that the two courts utilize these modes of legal reasoning to dissimilar extents. The following list includes the top eight most frequently recurring modes of legal reasoning in both courts and a brief definition for each (Table 2.1). (The complete list of the modes of legal reasoning can be found in Appendix C.)

What is missing from the list is also significant. In immigration cases, ideas about the racial desirability or undesirability of the nationality or race of the alien, or the decision maker's own policy preferences on U.S. immigration policy, may arise. Although judges and justices undoubtedly had these thoughts in mind and may have even referred to them in passing in the opinions, they knew that these ideas were illegitimate grounds on which to base a legal decision and never used those ideas as the actual rationale to justify a legal conclusion.

The definitions of many of these modes of legal reasoning are self explanatory, but a few words of clarification are in order. Any decision that was rendered where the courts referenced specific statutes and provided interpretations and meaning to statutes was classified as "Statutory Interpretation C." (If the interpretation of statutes was guided by another identifiable principle, such as one that the interpretation should be a "sensible construction" or the idea that Congress would have been "explicit" if it had intended a certain action, these were considered "Statutory Interpretation A" and "Statutory Interpretation B" respectively.) A decision was classified as "plenary power" if the opinion mentioned those exact words or if the opinion referenced the idea that the judiciary was not the proper branch to make decisions in this area of policy. Cases construed as "due process" were those in which the court reached a decision by focusing on an error made by the lower court, administrative agency (the BIA), or other administrative decision maker, such as an immigration

TABLE 2.1. *Definitions of Most Frequently Occurring Modes of Legal Reasoning*

• Statutory interpretation C ("StatInterp")	Ascertaining the meaning of a statute or text based on a deductive or textual approach.
• Plenary power ("PlenPow")	Immigration policy is properly the province of Congress and the elected branches; federal courts are not the proper tribunal to make changes to this policy area and therefore the courts will adopt a laissez faire approach.
• Procedural due process ("ProcDueProc")	Any decisions based on an error made by a lower decision making body.
• Doctrine/*Stare decisis* ("Doctrine")	The case was decided in accordance with current case law.
• Administrative deference ("AdminDef")	Deference to the administrative agency (the Board of Immigration Appeals) or to the immigration judge.
• Reasonableness ("Reasonable")	Decision reached by the lower court or administrative agency was "reasonable" or "supported by substantial evidence."
• Fact/evidence ("Evidence")	Decision was made based on review of the facts and evidence, such as evaluations of the credibility and consistency of witnesses and testimony.
• National sovereignty ("NatlSov")	The definition of a sovereign nation is one that can control its borders by defining who may enter and remain in its territory. Therefore, almost any government action toward an alien is permissible.

judge.[74] Cases that were decided based on citation and references to other cases and existing legal doctrine were considered "doctrine/*stare decisis.*"

---

[74] In this category, I have included cases where the courts focused on either an error of process or procedure or the error of applying the wrong legal standard. The inclusion of the latter category is controversial and some may consider these decisions to be based on doctrine rather than an abuse of process. However, in many cases, it was almost impossible to determine how the authors of the opinions themselves were thinking about the case. For example, in cases where the Courts of Appeals opinion reversed the BIA or the immigration judge because of an abuse of discretion, that abuse could have taken the form of failing to apply the correct legal standard or failing to consider or weigh evidence properly. The distinction between correcting a lower court or administrative error based on process versus doctrine was in many instances unclear and difficult to determine. See, e.g., *Young v. Immigration and Naturalization Service,* 459 F.2d 1004 (9th Cir., 1972).

Cases in which the opinion indicated a desire to defer to the judgment of administrative decision makers or the trial judge were classified as "administrative deference." Cases where the courts were deciding based on whether the lower court or administrative agency's decision met a minimal standard of rationality were classified as "reasonable." The legal language often used in these types of cases was to evaluate the decision based on whether the lower court or agency's decision was supported by "substantial evidence." Decisions that turned on the evaluation of the facts or evidence, primarily evaluations of the credibility of evidence and witnesses, were considered "fact/evidence." Finally, cases based on the idea that it is an inherent right of a sovereign nation to define its borders were classified as "national sovereignty." (Further detail about the coding strategy can be found in Appendix B.)

Legal or Judicial Modes of Legal Reasoning

In the following chapters, I unpack the implications of some of these forms of legal reasoning as indicators of institutional change, but here I take a first cut at analyzing the most frequently occurring modes and group them according to whether they are political or legal. Although there is some overlap between the legal and political modes of legal reasoning, some preliminary distinctions can be made. The legal modes of legal reasoning that specify proper norms of operation or recognized methods of deciding cases are specific to legal institutions and distinguish legal institutions from nonlegal ones. The occurrences and recurrences of the legal modes of reasoning also demonstrate the constraining power of law. The political modes of legal reasoning reflect settled understandings of existing power arrangements between institutions and prescribes particular behavior for the courts with regard to these power arrangements. I take up first the legal modes of legal reasoning and then turn to the political modes of legal reasoning.

• **"Statutory interpretation C"** or general statutory interpretation involves judges interpreting statutes and applying them to a set of facts. Statutory interpretation is a large part of the policy making duties of the Supreme Court and increasingly of the Courts of Appeals too. When two parties differ on what a statute really means, the federal courts may break the tie. Judges for a variety of reasons may choose to decide a case on statutory grounds rather than declaring the statute unconstitutional. In Chapter 5, I discuss some of the political and strategic reasons why judges decide cases based on statutory rather than constitutional grounds. Many observers have commented that the ability to interpret law is the ability to make law.[75] In Chapter 5, I also present several examples of the methods and strategies available to judges to make law through interpreting statutes. Although statutory interpretation is a common duty of both the Supreme Court and U.S. Courts of Appeals, this approach presents an opportunity for judges to exercise strategy in pursuing their own policy preference if they wish to do so.

• **Due process** is a mode of legal reasoning that is central to the constitutionally prescribed function and mission of federal courts. It encapsulates the idea of a branch of government that can and should independently evaluate the actions of the elected branches to ensure that proper procedures have been followed, and that before a person's liberty is abridged, a fair and not arbitrary procedure was followed. The employment of this legal reasoning may signify a power struggle between the judicial branch and elected branches of government and their associates, including administrative agencies that fall under the authority of the executive branch's attorney general's office, because the inherent purpose of procedural protections is to check government abuse of power.

• **Doctrine/*stare decisis*** is a mode of legal reasoning that refers to the common law background of the American legal system. The logic behind the fidelity to doctrine is to ensure fairness and consistency of outcome in similarly situated cases. Probably more than any other mode of legal reasoning, the use of doctrine distinguishes judicial institutions from the legislative and executive branches, and it illustrates the hybrid nature of the federal courts. Although these courts, and especially the contemporary Supreme Court, are political institutions, they are still bound by legal doctrine. This mode of legal reasoning allows an assessment of the extent to which settled law matters and how frequently it is a constraining influence.

• **Administrative discretion** is a mode of legal reasoning that signifies deference to another decision making body. The underlying rationale for this mode of legal reasoning is twofold: 1) the administrative agencies have developed expertise in this policy area, and federal appellate judges, who are generalists, should defer to the specialists; and 2) the administrative agencies, such as the Board of Immigration Appeals and the immigration judges, are closer to the facts and the appellate judges should defer

---

[75] See Walter Murphy, *Elements of Judicial Strategy* (Princeton, NJ: Princeton University Press, 1964), 14–15; and R. Shep Melnick, *Between the Lines: Interpreting Welfare Rights* (Washington, DC: The Brookings Institution, 1994), 6.

to their fact-finding conclusions because these bodies were better able to assess the evidence and credibility of witnesses than appellate courts, which were evaluating a cold record.

• **Reasonableness** is also a deferential standard of evaluation of a case. Like its cousin "the rational basis test" in equal protection jurisprudence, if judges adopt "reasonableness" as a standard of review, they are holding the action they are evaluating to a very low threshold of acceptability. This mode of legal reasoning, like procedural due process, can also be a cognitive shortcut of sorts because it requires less analysis to decide whether an act is reasonable or whether it is substantively correct.

• The evaluation of **fact/evidence** is a role usually designated to trial courts rather than to appellate courts. This approach seeks to identify the relevant facts of a case and to evaluate the credibility of testimony and other evidence. As I show in Chapter 4, the evaluation of evidence and fact can take on a strategic cast when judges from the U.S. Courts of Appeals second-guess the factual determinations of an administrative agency official or a lower court and substitute their own assessment of the evidence.

Political Principles

• **Plenary power** is a common theme in immigration exclusion and deportation cases. At its core, the idea is a political (not legal) arrangement among the three branches of government whereby the U.S. Supreme Court, and to a lesser extent the U.S. Courts of Appeals, defer to the judgment of Congress, the executive branch, and executive branch agencies in immigration cases. When a court adopts plenary power as the mode of legal reasoning it is assuming a position of deference (albeit not total abdication) in this area of law. I understand this approach to be a political division of labor between the different branches of government.

• **National sovereignty,** like plenary power, is a common theme and mode of legal reasoning that appears in immigration cases. It is a theme of legal reasoning that recognizes the policy implication aspects of this area of law and particularly the unique national identity functions that immigration law embodies. According to this reasoning, by definition a sovereign nation is one that can control its borders; therefore, any action that the government takes to do so is permissible. Further, its rationale counsels judicial deference.

HOW DO MODES OF LEGAL REASONING
RELATE TO INSTITUTIONAL SETTING?

Modes of legal reasoning offer insight into how justices and judges think about the immigration issue by providing an explanation of why they have decided the way they have. Specifically, some of these modes of legal reasoning reveal judges' and justices' motivations for their decisions. Some modes of legal reasoning reflect judicial understandings of institutional divisions of labor and political power dynamics. Other modes of legal reasoning have built in instrumental elements that provide justices and judges with some agency in reaching their legal conclusions. Rather than just a typology of arguments, modes of legal reasoning reflect the legal and political influences on judicial decision making.

Additionally, as Chapter 6 will show, still other legal forms and reasoning, such as due process and habeas corpus, retain a degree of autonomy from the shifting winds of institutional and social change. This autonomy means that although some legal forms and practices can be temporally contingent, others are more deeply embedded in our legal or political culture and are not merely reflections of or reactions to political, social, or economic forces.[76] Rather, these deeply held legal values and norms constrain judicial behavior and political choices by providing stable and enduring structures that mediate social and political conflict.[77]

Although legal forms and modes of reasoning such as due process maintain some degree of independence from the vagaries of political, social, and economic changes, they are not insulated and hermetically sealed off from larger society. Indeed it would be difficult to understand how modes of legal reasoning employed by lawyers and judges would have any legitimacy or public support if those ideas were divorced from the norms of society. If this were the case, these legal arguments and decisions would have little resonance with the vast majority of Americans. As Gordon notes, it is more likely the case that the modes of legal reasoning, although stable and autonomous to some extent, are a "dialect" of social discourse that takes place in larger society that taps into themes and beliefs that pervade political culture.[78]

---

[76] Gordon, "Critical Legal Studies Symposium: Critical Legal Histories," 102.
[77] Smith "Political Jurisprudence," 98, and Gordon, "Critical Legal Studies Symposium," 88.
[78] Gordon, "Critical Legal Studies Symposium," 90.

Some of these modes of legal reasoning also allow one to assess the way judges perceive their role in relation to other decision makers in other branches of government, or to lower and upper courts. As a starting point, one can begin our analysis by noting whether the judges choose a purely legal principle or whether they choose a mode of legal reasoning that is an idea that derives from society, culture, or political arrangements. To choose the former indicates more of an adherence to the role of judges as legal decision makers and less as policy makers. To choose the latter indicates some sensitivity to the policy dimensions and implications of the subject of immigration. The choice between applying a legal principle or practice or a sociocultural or political one gives us a window into the judges' self-perception of their proper role as policy makers or legal adjudicators.

One can also gain a sense of how judges perceive their roles by assessing how willing they are to challenge or overturn the determinations of other decision makers, including the decisions of administrative agency officials, lower courts, and other branches of government. Themes such as plenary power, administrative deference, and reasonableness are generally indicative of a general deference (or indeed agreement and endorsement in some instances) to another decision making body. When judges use these modes of legal reasoning, it indicates a deferential posture toward Congress or administrative agencies. Conversely, modes of legal reasoning such as procedural due process, statutory interpretation, doctrine, and fact/evidences do not indicate the adoption of a deferential posture – and indeed these modes of legal reasoning can cut either way, working for or against the alien or the government. But as I show in Chapters 5 and 7, these types of legal reasoning have a potential strategic function in common. From examining the patterns of legal reasoning, one may assess whether the judges in these cases are acting in a deferential manner or whether they are acting strategically to reach a desired legal outcome. Along those lines, one may assess whether the Supreme Court is living up to its self-designated role of protecting "discrete and insular" minorities and acting to check executive and congressional overreach or abuse, and whether the U.S. Courts of Appeals are acting as error correctors or as policy makers in their own right. Are the U.S. Courts of Appeals mechanically applying precedent and looking for errors, or are they deviating from precedent and congressional intent?

CONCLUSION

Aliens' legal appeals originate in the immigration bureaucracy at administrative agencies, but many of these appeals end up in the federal courts, particularly the U.S. Courts of Appeals. The treatment of aliens' immigration claims at the two highest federal appellate courts and the relation of that treatment to the institutional evolution of those two courts is the focus of this study. How one frames the question and the methods one chooses to tackle the question are crucial to what the answers will be. In this chapter I have indicated why focusing on legal outcomes or dispositions alone can distort one's understanding of how the Supreme Court and U.S. Courts of Appeals decide immigration cases because legal outcomes miss the rationales for each court's decision making. Concentrating on legal outcomes alone risks classifying cases with dispositions not in the alien's favor as anti-alien when in fact the court may have been deciding based on doctrine or another legal principle, not xenophobia or racial animus. Interpretive content analysis to unearth the modes of legal reasoning in these opinions gets to some of the motivations for these decisions and provides a more complete picture of judicial decision making.

Some important preliminary findings materialize. For one thing, the two highest appellate courts draw from the same set of modes of legal reasoning – but that is just the beginning, not the end of the story. As the following chapter explains, the Supreme Court and U.S. Courts of Appeals utilize the same set of legal reasoning, but to very different extents. Also, some modes of legal reasoning allow discretion and flexibility, while others do not. What does this mean for judges and justices who wish to pursue particular policy preferences? The chapters that follow spell out the causes and implications of the distinctive approaches taken by the Supreme Court and U.S. Courts of Appeals in deciding immigration appeals for the aliens involved in immigration cases and for these legal institutions and actors themselves.

3

The Rise of Two Courts with Differentiated Functions

What is the role of the federal judiciary in the American political system? An examination of the earliest debates about the federal judiciary reveal competing visions of the proper roles, missions, and functions of that institution among the founders. It becomes apparent, when tracing the evolution of the judiciary, that the design, establishment, and modification of the judiciary were the result of political accommodation of an array of sometimes conflicting interests. Instead of being the outcome of a carefully designed master plan, the institutional development of the U.S. Supreme Court and U.S. Courts of Appeals illustrates what historical institutionalists refer to as the "cumulative consequences of partial reforms."[1] And without a plan that had as its priority the long-term efficacy of the judiciary, the trajectory of these two courts has a spawned a series of unintended consequences, including a rise in the prestige of the Supreme Court and a sharpening division of labor between the Supreme Court and the Courts of Appeals. The judicial system has evolved in a different way than the founders expected. Yet the contemporary federal judiciary has succeeded in fulfilling the aspirations of the founders for the normative role and mission of the institution – albeit with different structural forms to protect such values.

The chapter opens with analysis of the Federalists' and Anti-Federalists' conceptions of the role, mission, and functions of the federal judiciary. These debates are illuminating because they represent the baseline for assessments of the proper role of the federal judiciary in the American

---

[1] Karen Orren and Stephen Skowronek, *The Search for American Political Development* (New York: Cambridge University Press, 2004), 80.

political system. The second section of the chapter focuses on three factors that have contributed to the widening in functions and missions of the Supreme Court and the Courts of Appeals: key pieces of legislation,[2] the "judicialization" of immigration policy, and the choice of enforcement strategies in U.S. immigration policy. The chapter closes with an empirical assessment of the consequences of the division of labor in the federal court system for alien litigants.

THE FEDERALISTS AND ANTI-FEDERALISTS ON THE JUDICIARY

The Federalist and Anti-Federalist deliberations about the functions, shape, and form of the federal judiciary took place at a time when the institution was not yet in existence. Therefore the debates at this point were based on the idea, rather than the reality, of a judicial institution. The pre-ratification debates represent the very beginning of the institutional development process. Many of the initial critiques and defenses of the federal judiciary failed to anticipate the structural changes that would enhance the standing and influence of the Supreme Court.

The central concern animating the disputes between the Federalists and the Anti-Federalists on the Constitution was the distribution of power between the national and state government units that would be codified in the founding document. The discussions between the Federalists and Anti-Federalists over the proper form, function, and structure of the federal judiciary was colored by federalism concerns. The Anti-Federalists were generally suspicious of a concentration of power at the national level and preferred to keep authority close to the people by retaining power in local

---

[2] Rather than recount every legislative act modifying the judiciary, a task that others have ably performed, I focus my discussion here on key transformative legislation that altered the mission or role of the federal courts. For accounts of legislative acts creating the federal judiciary, see Felix Frankfurter and James Landis, *The Business of the Supreme Court: A Study in the Federal Judicial System* (New York: Macmillan, 1927; reprinted 2007); Stanley Kutler, *Judicial Power and Reconstruction Politics* (Chicago: University of Chicago Press, 1968); Maeva Marcus, ed., *Origins of the Federal Judiciary: Essays on the Judiciary Act of 1789* (New York: Oxford University Press, 1992); William M. Wiecek, "The Reconstruction of Federal Judicial Power, 1863–1875" in 13 *American Journal of Legal History* 1969:233–59; Charles Gardener Geyh, *When Courts & Congress Collide – The Struggle for Control of America's Judicial System* (Ann Arbor: University of Michigan Press, 2007), especially chapters 1 and 2; "History of the Federal Judiciary" at http://www.fjc.gov/hostiry/home.nsf; and Russell R. Wheeler and Cynthia Harrison, "Creating the Federal Judicial System," 3rd ed. (Washington, D.C.: Federal Judicial Center, 2005) (available at www.fjc.gov/public/pdf.nsf/lookup/Creat3rd.pdf/$File/Creat3rd.pdf).

government units. To the Anti-Federalists, a distant national government was unlikely to be cognizant of or sympathetic to local concerns, and such a situation invited the kind of tyranny the colonies had only recently left behind in breaking with England. To the Federalists, only a strong national government could stifle bickering between the states and localities and quell insurrections, such as Shays's Rebellion, that threatened the young nation's stability. While the Anti-Federalists embraced popular democracy as highly desirable, the Federalists viewed the broad extension of democracy as opening the door to mob rule, and thus a threat to order and stability. The Federalists desired a strong national government that would reign in the popular passions and parochial prejudices that they believed was inherent in local government that lacked impartiality.

These fundamental differences in worldview carried over into the debates about the judicial branch. Given their wariness of federal power, the Anti-Federalists favored a limited federal judiciary, which they felt would check federal tyranny and preserve the power of state courts.[3] They attacked both the structure and functions of the prospective federal judicial institution. Through "Brutus," in 1787, they launched an opening salvo against the judicial branch, charging that an extensive network of federal courts would, "in the common course of things, ... eclipse the dignity, and take away from the respectability, of the state courts... and in the course of human events it is to be expected, that they will swallow up all the powers of the courts in the respective states."[4] The Anti-Federalists were only half right in this prediction; the state courts today do retain jurisdiction in many areas of law and it would be incorrect to say that they have been wholly "swallowed up." However, Brutus correctly foresaw the federal courts' rise in profile and prestige and their eventual eclipse of state courts.

The Anti-Federalists also worried about the structural arrangement of the proposed government system and what this would mean for federal court power over individuals and states. Early on, the Anti-Federalists perceived the political dimensions of this separation of powers arrangement and they objected especially to the independent power of the Supreme Court. The Anti-Federalist Brutus observed that, "[the authors of the constitution] have made the judges independent, in the fullest sense

[3] Wheeler and Harrison, "Establishing the Federal Judicial System," 2.
[4] Melancton Smith, "Anti-Federalist 1" in Herbert J. Storing, ed., *The Anti-Federalist: Writings by the Opponents of the Constitution* (Chicago, IL: University of Chicago Press, 1985), 113. The identity of "Brutus" is uncertain, but historians think it is the pseudonym used by Melancton Smith.

of the word. There is no power above them, to control any of their decisions. There is no authority that can remove them, and they cannot be
controlled by the laws of the legislature. In short, they are independent
of the people, of the legislature, and of every power under heaven. Men
placed in this situation will generally soon feel themselves independent of
heaven itself."[5] In the Anti-Federalists' view, the issue here was a lack of
accountability. What would happen if the Supreme Court made an error
or abused its power? Where could an aggrieved litigant turn for redress
after the ruling of the Supreme Court? This fear of the finality of the
Supreme Court was then and still is a concern, but the Anti-Federalists
would have been surprised to learn that today, the U.S. Courts of Appeals,
not the U.S. Supreme Court, are, for the vast majority of appellants, the
courts of last resort. Brutus failed to anticipate a series of developments
that would produce a bottleneck in the flow of cases to the Supreme
Court and Courts of Appeals.

In response to the Anti-Federalists' fears about the finality of Supreme
Court decisions, the Federalists pointed to their rationale for an independent judiciary that would result from providing life tenure to federal
judges. In the *Federalist 78*, Publius wrote:

This independence of the judges is equally requisite to guard the Constitution
and the rights of individuals from the effects of those ill humors which the arts of
designing men, or the influence of particular conjunctures, sometimes disseminate
among the people themselves, and which, though they speedily give place to better information and more deliberate reflection, have a tendency in the meantime,
to occasion dangerous innovations in the government and serious oppressions of
the minor party in the community.[6]

Publius and the other Federalists noted that it is precisely the intention
that the judges should *not* be politically accountable to the other branches
and to public opinion that would allow the judiciary to fulfill its function as an independent check on the other branches. The Federalists saw
judicial independence as desirable; the Anti-Federalists thought just the
opposite.

Another major point of disagreement between the Federalists and
Anti-Federalists was rooted in the functions that the judiciary would
serve in the American political system, and, especially, whether those
responsibilities would enhance the power of the national entity at the

---

[5] Melancton Smith, "Anti-Federalist 20" in Herbert J. Storing, ed., *The Anti-Federalist* (Chicago: University of Chicago Press, 1985), 183.
[6] Alexander Hamilton, "Federalist 78" in Clinton Rossiter, ed., *The Federalist Papers* (New York: Penguin, 1961), 469.

local government units' expense. Both sides were working from projections of how a judiciary, if it should exist, would function. Either to play down the influence of the judiciary or because this assessment took place at a time when the power of judicial review was not clearly understood, the Federalists believed that the judiciary would not be a powerful branch at all relative to the power of the legislative and executive branches. In a famous passage from *Federalist 78*, Publius wrote:

> The judiciary from the nature of its functions, will always be the least dangerous to the political rights of the Constitution; because it will be least in a capacity to annoy or injure them. The executive not only dispenses the honors, but holds the sword of the community. The legislature not only commands the purse but prescribes the rules by which the duties and rights of every citizen are to be regulated. The judiciary, on the contrary, has no influence over either the sword or the purse; no direction either of the strength or of the wealth of the society, and can take no active resolution whatever. I may truly said to have neither FORCE nor WILL but merely judgment; and must ultimately depend upon the aid of the executive arm even for the efficacy of its judgment.[7]

Publius concluded that the judiciary would be the "weakest of the three departments of power; that it can never attack with success either of the other two; and that all possible care is requisite to enable it to defend itself against their attacks."[8] Publius and the Federalists viewed the functions of the judiciary as severely limited, and these limits were a source of overall weakness of the institution when compared with the elected branches. In these assessments, it is unclear whether the Federalists were purposely downplaying the issue to win Anti-Federalist support or whether they were just plain wrong because of their inability to predict the rise of judicial power.

Debates also erupted over the duties and powers of the federal judiciary. The Federalists pointed to the ability of the judiciary to render judgment as a limitation on the power of the institution; the Anti-Federalists pointed to that same function as a cause for concern and a potential source of an abuse of power. It was not just the structure of the judiciary that concerned the Anti-Federalists. Brutus was remarkably prescient in recognizing the power of statutory and constitutional interpretation. First, he anticipated that given the separation of powers arrangement, there would be no other institution to check the Supreme Court's interpretation of the Constitution; he wrote, "the supreme court then will

---

[7] Alexander Hamilton, "Federalist 78" in Clinton Rossiter, ed., *The Federalist Papers* (New York: Penguin, 1961), 465 (capitalization in original).
[8] Ibid. at 465–66.

have a right, independent of the legislature, to give construction to the constitution and every part of it, and there is no power provided in this system to correct their construction or do it away."[9] Secondly, Brutus predicted that the Supreme Court would use its interpretative opportunities to enhance the power of the national government. Regarding situations where the Supreme Court had exclusive jurisdiction over certain areas of law or jurisdiction concurrent with the states, he predicted:

In such cases, therefore the laws of the state legislature must be repealed, restricted, or so construed, as to give full effect to the laws of the union on the same subject. From these remarks it is easy to see, that in proportion as the general government acquires power and jurisdiction, but the liberal construction which the judges may give the constitution, those of the states will lose their rights, until they become so trifling and unimportant, as not to be worth having.[10]

Here Brutus overestimated the power of the federal judiciary to render the state courts completely meaningless, but he did appreciate the control inherent in the construing and construction of constitutional and statutory language long before the Supreme Court was even to exist and actually flex its interpretative muscles.

Although they are here today, the existence of the lower federal courts was by no means inevitable. In the pre-ratification debates one finds evidence that the creation of the lower federal courts was a move to appease the Anti-Federalists, who were concerned about the accessibility of federal justice. The overall goal of the Anti-Federalists was to minimize the influence of the federal courts while preserving the power of state courts. They grudgingly conceded that there was a need for the inferior courts so that all the litigation would not be routed to the Supreme Court, but they suggested that the state courts could assume these functions instead of creating inferior federal courts. The Anti-Federalists had reason for their concern about the accessibility of the federal courts given the difficult travel conditions in colonial America. They argued that if the federal courts were not easy to get to for local litigants, then these courts would be open to only the rich who could afford to travel there. Brutus wrote, "it appears, that the administration of justice under the powers of the judicial will be dilatory; that it will be attended with such a heavy expense as to amount to little short of denial of justice to the poor and

---

[9] Melancton Smith, "Anti-Federalist 15" in Herbert J. Storing, ed., *The Anti-Federalist* (Chicago: University of Chicago Press, 1985), 185.

[10] Melancton Smith, "Anti-Federalist 12" in Herbert J. Storing, ed., *The Anti-Federalist* (Chicago: University of Chicago Press, 1985), 172.

middling class of people who in every government stand most in the need of the protection of the law."[11] The Federalists responded that having the state courts take on some of the appellate functions would be unwise because the state courts could not be impartial in many of the legal questions, given that state judges lacked the protection of life tenure. Publius wrote:

> The most discerning cannot forsee how far the local tribunals of the jurisdiction of the national causes; whilst every man may discover that courts constituted like those of some of the States would be improper channels of the judicial authority of the Union. State judges, holding their offices during pleasure, or from year to year, will be too little independent to be relied upon for an inflexible execution of the national laws.[12]

Publius indicated that the state tribunals should not take on some of the intended functions of federal appellate courts because state judges are not insulated from political pressure as federal judges are. He also believed that the state could not be impartial in applying federal law.

So why were the federal courts created and for what purposes? From the pre-ratification debates, we learn that the Federalists wanted an independent judiciary that would be able to check the executive and legislative branches without fear of political or electoral retaliation. The Anti-Federalists were not opposed to the existence of a federal judiciary per se, but they were concerned that some of the functions of the federal judiciary would usurp the influence of state courts and local juries and that the federal courts would only be accessible to those who could afford to travel to them. Also, the Anti-Federalists were concerned that there would be no recourse for litigants who disagreed with the Supreme Court's decisions.

Because the deliberations between the Federalists and the Anti-Federalists over the judiciary took place at a time when the judiciary was not actually in existence yet, some of their criticisms missed the mark. That some of these fears strike us as quaint today speaks to the great evolutionary strides the judiciary has taken over the years. But to appreciate the range of the institution's development fully, one must first begin with the original intent for the institution, which is what these pre-ratification debates represent. Moreover, the dissimilar visions about the judiciary

---

[11] Melancton Smith, "Anti-Federalist 14" in Herbert J. Storing, ed., *The Anti-Federalist* (Chicago: University of Chicago Press, 1985), 180.

[12] Alexander Hamilton, "Federalist 81" in Clinton Rossiter, ed., *The Federalist Papers* (New York: Penguin, 1961), 486.

and the broader national government would continue to circumscribe the growth and expansion of the federal judiciary for another hundred years. Indeed, these disputes would recur in the politics surrounding the various congressional acts that created the federal judiciary piece by piece. Neither the Federalists' nor the Anti-Federalists' ideas would completely triumph over the other. The legislation creating the federal courts shows that, "in every case controversies were adjusted by compromise rather than by exclusive acceptance of competing conceptions regarding American federalism."[13] The Federalists' and Anti-Federalists' views about the structure, functions, and operations of the federal judiciary, which was to take shape in the legislative acts that brought the federal judiciary into existence, renewed the tensions between these two contending viewpoints that would have to be managed.

LEGISLATION SHAPING AND TRANSFORMING THE ROLE OF THE COURTS

In the development of the federal judiciary, congressional legislation has been the means by which the structure, operations and, therefore, the institutional contexts of the courts have been created and altered. Again and again these legislative changes were driven by practical necessities and political considerations that were historically contingent. The cumulative result of these alterations to the courts' institutional settings has been a progressive narrowing of the jurisdiction of the Supreme Court, resulting in a divergence of mission and function between the Supreme Court and the Courts of Appeals. J. Woodford Howard, Jr. has characterized the contemporary Supreme Court and Courts of Appeals as institutions that have "fully differentiated functions."[14] This situation resulted in part because the congressional acts creating the judiciary lacked guiding principles of institutional design.

Although the debates between the Federalists and the Anti-Federalists articulated different roles for the judicial branch to play, the legislative branch was actually charged with the creation of the institution through successive congressional acts. Richard Stevens writes that the brevity of the constitution on judicial design meant the need for legislation "to bring into being the structures, the bare lineaments of which are set out

[13] Frankfurter and Landis, *Business of the Supreme Court*, 3.
[14] J. Woodford Howard, Jr., *Courts of Appeals in the Federal Judicial System: A Study of the Second, Fifth, and District of Columbia Circuits* (Princeton, NJ: Princeton Univeristy Press, 1981), 5.

by the Constitution."[15] The federal judicial system was of course not created overnight; the structures of the institution itself as well as its influence grew slowly over time. As Robert McCloskey once wrote, "The Court, like an individual, grew up slowly."[16] Each act that fashioned the judiciary created or changed the workings of the judiciary through determinations of how many federal courts there would be, how many and which judges would staff these courts, and what jurisdiction each court would have. Evidence indicates that the early Congress conceived of the Supreme Court as an appellate court at the top of the judicial hierarchy, but not necessarily as one appellate court that would function all that differently from the lower federal appellate courts.[17] The writers of the early congressional acts did not intend that the Court would be transformed into the powerful policy maker and political actor that it has become today. Neither could the members of Congress have predicted that the Supreme Court would become the august body that it is today in the public consciousness, while the lower federal courts command far less public recognition.

One striking thing about the ratification debates was that no aspect of the federal court structure was inevitable – not even the creation of the inferior courts. All aspects of the institution were open to debate and negotiation. Although Article III of the Constitution had provided that, "The judicial power of the United States, shall be vested in one Supreme Court, and in such inferior courts as the Congress may from time to

---

[15] Forward by Richard Stevens to Frankfurter and Landis, *The Business of the Supreme Court*, xxi.

[16] McCloskey, *The American Supreme Court*, 25.

[17] One indication of the lack of respect for the Supreme Court by the founders in the country's early years was a failure to provide or plan for physical space for the Court. According to Frankfurter and Landis, while the White House and the Capitol were slated to house the executive and legislative branches, the early Court held sessions in a hotel lobby, a tavern, and the basement of the Capitol building (13). The marble "temple" that houses the Court today was not built until 1937. Moreover, Akhil Amar argues that social convention has artificially enhanced the stature and reputation of the Supreme Court through our rhetorical references to the various personnel in the federal courts. He indicates that the constitutional text itself does not require different titles for the various judges in the federal courts except the special designation of one member as "Chief Justice." He concludes, "Thus, the modern practice of referring to Supreme Court officers as 'justices' and lower federal court officials as 'judges' derives not from the words of the Constitution but ... from those of the first Judiciary Act." In fact, Amar notes that the framers viewed the status and duties of the lower court judges and the Supreme Court judges to be "equal to one another" (Akhil Amar, "Jurisdiction Stripping and the Judiciary Act of 1789" in Maeva Marcus, ed., *The Origins of the Federal Judiciary*, 45).

time ordain and establish" there was much debate during the ratification conventions on what that text meant with respect to the establishment of inferior courts.[18] Some representatives thought the constitutional language required the creation of inferior courts while others thought that the inferior courts were optional and that their establishment was at the discretion of Congress. Representative James Jackson, for example, read the constitutional language with the latter interpretation. He wrote, "the word 'may' is not positive, and it remains with Congress to determine what inferior jurisdiction may be necessary and what they will ordain and establish."[19] In repairing to the text of the constitution, supporters as well as opponents of the creation of inferior courts both were able to find textual evidence and support for their position.

The very fact that the founders placed Congress in charge of deciding whether and how to fashion the lower federal courts illustrates the political expediency of the creation of the lower federal courts. It is generally understood that the lower federal courts were created because of the Federalists' mistrust of transferring federal jurisdiction to the state courts and because of their wish to create, at least in theory, a federal judicial branch of government that was distinct from state courts.[20] This explanation gets to one of the motivations for the lower federal courts, but it does not address why the creation of these courts was not specified in the Constitution itself. The reason is that the Federalists were trying to finesse the issue. The Anti-Federalists were most unhappy at the prospect of the existence of the federal courts in general and feared in particular that a proliferation of a system of lower federal courts would make obsolete the power of state courts. In committing the creation of the lower federal courts to Congress, the Federalists chose political vagueness over certainty.[21] In so doing, they muted Anti-Federalist opposition to these courts and delayed the political battle for another day. That these debates took place in a time where the federal court system was merely an abstract idea, rather than an already operating institution with a track record, enabled this political move to succeed. Indeed it is quite possible that neither the Anti-Federalists nor the Federalists had a good idea of

[18] Marcus and Wexler, "The Judiciary Act of 1789," 17.
[19] Cited in Marcus and Wexler, "The Judiciary Act of 1789," 18.
[20] Gerald Casper, "The Judiciary Act of 1789 and Judicial Independence," in Maeva Marcus, ed., *Origins of the Federal Judiciary*, 286; Charles Gardener Geyh, *When Courts & Congress Collide: The Struggle for Control of America's Judicial System* (Ann Arbor, MI: University of Michigan Press, 2007), 46.
[21] Geyh, *When Courts & Congress Collide*, 32.

what the Supreme Court, much less the lower federal courts, would look like and how it would function. As Charles Geyh writes:

The delegates were committed to an independent judicial branch, but theirs was a commitment in concept only. Unhappy experiences with judicial dependence on the crown prior to the Revolution had given way to equally unhappy experiences with judicial dependence on the legislatures afterward, leaving the delegates desirous of decision-making and structural judicial independence as a theoretical matter, but with precious little practical experience to guide them.[22]

In institutional development, ignorance of the founders/creators is often bliss. The ability to foresee the powerful institutions in their own right that the U.S. Courts of Appeals would grow into would have thrown these courts' very creation in doubt.

The federal judiciary was created as the third branch of government for a number of reasons. The founders, influenced by reading Montesquieu and other political theorists, were committed to the idea of creating a government with a separation of powers. Furthermore, the Federalists viewed the federal judiciary as a means of furthering their goal of consolidating national power over state power. The growth of commerce and trade also required a politically stable environment and the framers envisioned the federal courts as the enforcers of national laws that would settle state disputes. The fear of "parochial prejudice, dealing unjustly with litigants from other states and foreign countries, undermined the sense of security necessary for commercial intercourse."[23] Therefore, another major impetus for the creation of the federal courts was an attempt by the national government to quell and mediate disputes between states, litigants from different states, and aliens to pave the way for a strong national economy.

Toward these ends, the First Judiciary Act of 1789 created the basic structure of the judicial hierarchy. The Act also divided the country into three districts that corresponded to state lines and set the jurisdiction of the courts. The 1789 Act then created a six-member U.S. Supreme Court at the top of the judicial hierarchy. Below the Supreme Court were the circuit courts, which would convene twice each year and would sit in the districts.[24] The circuit courts would be composed of two Supreme Court justices and one district judge from each circuit. These circuit courts were the predecessors of the contemporary U.S.

---

[22] Geyh, *When Courts & Congress Collide*, 35.
[23] Frankfurter and Landis, *The Business of the Supreme Court*, 9.
[24] Wheeler and Harrison, "Creating the Federal Judicial System," 4.

Courts of Appeals and these circuit courts existed concurrently with the Courts of Appeals from 1891 until 1911, when they were abolished. Below the circuit courts were the district courts, which were staffed by the one judge of the district. The district courts were trial courts, with a primary mission of finding facts and evaluating evidence. The circuit courts and the Supreme Court were appellate courts intended to serve the function of error correction.

Even though many elements of the Federal Judiciary Act of 1789 were of Federalist design, the Act also included political compromises with Anti-Federalist forces. The Act answered Anti-Federalists' concerns about a far away tyranny by tying the federal courts closely to the "legal and political cultures of the states."[25] Additionally, it limited federal trial court jurisdiction to admiralty and diversity cases, cases where the U.S. was a plaintiff, and federal criminal cases, and in so doing was more restrictive than even the Constitution stipulated. The concession to the Anti-Federalists was to allow federal courts to take over in cases involving federal questions only if a diversity element[26] was present. To tie the federal courts closely to the political culture of the states, the First Judiciary Act ensured that the federal district court lines would correspond to state lines and that the district judges must reside in those districts. Further, the Act established a circuit-riding requirement for Supreme Court justices so that the justices would be acquainted with local laws and customs. These requirements were designed so that the federal courts would not be completely insulated from local customs, cultures, and concerns, thereby allaying the Anti-Federalists' fears of distant and tyrannous federal officials.[27]

The First Judiciary Act of 1789, which brought the federal judiciary into existence, was very much shaped by the immediate political and fiscal concerns of the time. The actual text of the Constitution's Article III provided little guidance for the creation of the structure of the judiciary. The First Judiciary Act of 1789 represents what was politically possible in 1789 and "not so much the powers granted by the Framers in 1787."[28] The evidentiary trail shows an act that was meant to be responsive to the political concerns of the day.[29] These concerns included building public

[25] Wheeler and Harrison, "Creating the Federal Judicial System," 6.
[26] "Diversity" refers to litigation that involves residents of different states as opposed to residents of the same state.
[27] Wheeler and Harrison, "Creating the Federal Judicial System," 6–8.
[28] Marcus and Wexler, "The Judiciary Act of 1789," 30.
[29] Marcus and Wexler, "The Judiciary Act of 1789," 27.

support for a nascent federal government, creating economic and political stability to enable the flourishing of commerce, and settling disputes between states, rather than being the product of any science or vision of institutional creation and design.

The First Judiciary Act of 1789 and the Evarts Act of 1891 serve as the legislative bookends to the structure of the contemporary federal judiciary; the First Judiciary Act created the basic hierarchical structure of the judiciary and the Evarts Act developed that structure by creating the U.S. Courts of Appeals. The mission and status of the Supreme Court was dramatically altered with the passage of the Evarts Act in 1891. The 1891 Act, also known as the "Circuit Courts of Appeals Act," marks a critical juncture in institutional development where the development paths of the U.S. Supreme Court and U.S. Courts of Appeals took different forks in the road. Just as Franklin Delano Roosevelt's presidency marks the divide between the historic and modern presidency, the Evarts Act separates the historical and modern judicial regimes where the Supreme Court and U.S. Courts of Appeals diverged in their roles and functions in very significant ways. Prior to the 1891 Act, the Supreme Court was still functioning as a court of review, although with an increasingly narrowing jurisdiction; and the circuit courts were functioning as appellate courts that dealt with matters not routed to the Supreme Court. After the Evarts Act, the Supreme Court truly became a political and policy court, and the Courts of Appeals, although they continued in their primary appellate function, also developed a policy making power that was independent of the Supreme Court's policy power.

The Evarts Act was a response to two problems that were impeding the functioning and efficacy of the federal courts: the increasingly cumbersome and unworkable circuit riding system and the burgeoning backlog of cases at the Supreme Court. Understaffed circuit courts and huge inconveniences to the justices caused by the obligation to ride circuit persisted after the Evarts Act was passed on March 13, 1891. In the Evarts Act, Congress took the major step of creating the circuit courts of appeals (later renamed the "U.S. Courts of Appeals"), which would be staffed by designated circuit court judges instead of a combination of circuit-riding Supreme Court justices and district judges. The Act was written also to address the backlog of Supreme Court cases. For the first time, Congress gave the Supreme Court discretionary review over its docket. Under this Act, the courts of appeals were given final jurisdiction over admiralty and diversity cases, patent and revenue cases, and criminal prosecutions. All these types of cases could still be appealed to the Supreme Court, but the Act stipulated that, rather than a mandatory review, the Court would grant review through a writ of *certiorari*.[30]

The Evarts Act shifted a large portion of the appellate caseload from the U.S. Supreme Court over to the new U.S. Courts of Appeals, thereby setting up the U.S. Courts of Appeals as the primary appellate courts and the federal district courts as the primary trial courts.[31] The Act also alleviated the circuit-riding problems and workload pressures by bifurcating the appeals stream. The "intrinsically more important issues" were routed to the Supreme Court while the "more numerous but less difficult issues" were sent to the new appellate courts. Except for the abandoned Act of 1801, the Evarts Act of 1891 was the first act to provide major structural reform to the judiciary.[32]

The significant structural modifications to the judicial institution created by the Evarts Act had lasting consequences for the functioning of the federal judiciary. The Evarts Act significantly shaped the duties and mission of the Supreme Court and the Courts of Appeals by setting the two courts along diverging paths of development. The creation of the circuit courts of appeals and the subsequent routing of more mundane issues to these courts, combined with the granting of discretionary control over the docket of the Supreme Court, greatly enhanced the standing and influence of the Supreme Court in the federal system. The fact that only the Supreme Court was given the power to issue writs of *certiorari* paved the way for further enhancement of the Supreme Court's profile and influence at the expense of the lower federal courts. The Court's prestige and perceived importance were raised in the public consciousness because it became, at least in theory, the court of last resort, the final stop in the litigation chain. Henceforth, all eyes would turn to the Supreme Court for a final pronouncement on legal and policy issues. At the same time, this Act laid the groundwork for the increasing insulation of the Courts of Appeals from Supreme Court supervision.

The remainder of the history of the federal judiciary consists of a progressive narrowing of the jurisdiction of the U.S. Supreme Court, increase in prestige of the U.S. Courts of Appeals, and expansion of the bureaucracy supporting the federal courts.[33] The Judiciary Act of 1916, for

---

[30] O'Brien, *Storm Center*, 153.
[31] Wheeler and Harrison, *Creating the Federal Judicial System*, 18.
[32] Frankfurter and Landis, *The Business of the Supreme Court*, 99–100, 103.
[33] Please refer to Frankfurter and Landis, *The Business of the Supreme Court*, Chapter VI, on the creation of the Conference of Senior Circuit Judges, a body that was created to address administrative and operational issues of the U.S. Courts of Appeals as well as to provide input in congressional legislation affecting the courts.

example, was passed to help the Supreme Court keep up with its docket by "shutting off cases of minor importance"; this was accomplished by giving the Courts of Appeals and state courts final review over certain types of cases. The intent was to leave the Supreme Court free to review cases that were important to "whatever the national interest might be."[34] At the same time, the Courts of Appeals enjoyed an increase in their prestige, at least among members of the bar and the rest of the legal community.

Whereas the initial creation of the circuit courts as intermediate courts met with both public skepticism and open opposition because of the strongly held belief among litigants and lawyers that they had the right to take their appeal to the highest court in the land, the U.S. Courts of Appeals, by the early twentieth century, had established a measure of respect among members of the bar and the public and "[t]hese courts were now taken for granted as courts of great authority."[35] Even as the U.S. Courts of Appeals enjoyed their heightened prestige and respect, their standing in public perception never rivaled or even approached the stature of the Supreme Court.

The structure of the federal judiciary and the flow of litigation wrought by the Evarts Act remain intact today. The effects of this structure were further exaggerated by exponentially growing caseloads. This growth in caseloads, combined with the progressively narrowing Supreme Court jurisdiction and the Court's increasing discretion over its docket, created a bottleneck of cases at the U.S. Courts of Appeals. These courts did not have the prominence that the Supreme Court enjoyed in the public consciousness, but their influence was no less because of the numbers and types of cases in which these courts had final review. Increasingly, and especially in the large and growing body of subconstitutional issues, the U.S. Courts of Appeals became the creators of operative doctrine in many areas of law, including immigration law.

THE JUDICIALIZATION OF IMMIGRATION POLICY

The First Judiciary Act, the Evarts Act, and many other pieces of legislation set the structure of the judicial hierarchy, determined each court's jurisdiction over certain issues, and set whether each court could control its own docket. However, institutional growth is not just dictated

---

[34] Frankfurter and Landis, *The Business of the Supreme Court*, 255.
[35] Frankfurter and Landis, *The Business of the Supreme Court*, 258.

by the rules and structures of the institutions. Factors outside the federal judiciary interacting with the institutional structures of the courts also contributed to the widening divergence in function of the Supreme Court and U.S. Courts of Appeals. The chief engine driving innovation and development in the federal court system has been an exponentially growing caseload. Chapter 5 explores the nature of the relationship between caseload pressures and institutional growth. This section examines two main factors that have created the rise in the federal courts' immigration caseload: the judicialization of immigration policy, as aliens discovered early that they would meet with a comparatively favorable response from the appointed, rather than the elected, branches of government; and the nature of the national strategies to enforce immigration laws, which emphasizes the number of apprehended violators of those laws.

One reason that the federal courts' immigration appeals caseload has steadily increased over time is that aliens and their supporters have, from the very beginning, realized the efficacy of going to the federal courts for relief from harshly discriminatory and severely restrictionist legislation such as the Chinese Exclusion Act. Aliens, especially the Chinese, came to an early and crucial realization that, although Congress created all legislation regulating immigration, it was often the federal courts, the lower federal courts in particular, that were responsible for interpreting and ultimately applying these acts. Moreover, aliens went to the federal courts for relief from discrimination, deportation, and exclusion because, lacking the legal right to vote, they had few other avenues of recourse in the political system. They could not prevail upon the elected branches of government to help them.

Charles McClain was among the first to point out that Chinese immigrants, especially, exhibited political savvy and initiative in fighting discriminatory laws directed at their community. He convincingly refutes the charges that the Chinese were politically backward and not cognizant of American political institutions and practices. McClain writes, "The nineteenth-century Chinese-American community may, because of language, have been more isolated from mainstream society than other immigrant groups in certain respects, but lack of political consciousness was not one of its distinguishing characteristics...Far from being passive or docile in the face of official mistreatment, they reacted with indignation to it and more often than not sought redress in the courts."[36] Their responses

---

[36] Charles J. McClain, *In Search of Equality: The Chinese Struggle against Discrimination in Nineteenth-Century America* (Berkeley, CA: University of California Press, 1994), 2–3.

to government-sanctioned discrimination were organized and swift. In her study of lower federal court cases, mostly district court cases, Lucy Salyer similarly found that the Chinese were politically astute enough to go "forum shopping" when they realized that they were more likely to get a favorable outcome in federal district and circuit courts rather than before the executive administrative agencies in charge of immigration.[37]

In the years leading up to the eventual passage of the Chinese Exclusion Act, the Chinese had come into economic competition with white ethnic immigrant groups and native-born Americans. Motivated by racism and further fueled by economic competition, California had passed a series of laws designed to oppress and harass the Chinese in the hopes that the Chinese would leave the area.[38]

Based on their analysis of primarily U.S. District Court cases, McClain and Salyer demonstrated that, far from being politically unaware, diffident, or hesitant, the Chinese community fought back with an array of strategies that revealed their mastery and understanding of how to put pressure on the political system and government officials. Prominent members of the community wrote letters of protest to public officials, recognized the need to hire a lobbyist who would press their cause, and engaged in campaigns of civil disobedience. Through the Chinese Six Companies (the de facto nongovernmental representative and advocate of the Chinese)[39] and Chinese diplomats in Washington, D.C., the community regularly protested the treatment of the Chinese to all levels of the U.S. government. However, the centerpiece of their resistance effort was to go to the federal courts to contest official discrimination. Not only did the Chinese take their grievances to court, they did so with the best legal talent they could hire.[40] Appeals from Chinese immigrants flowed into state and later the federal district courts in large numbers to fight discriminatory state laws that impinged on their ability to earn, work,

---

[37] Salyer, *Laws as Harsh as Tigers*, xvi.
[38] These ordinances were passed in San Francisco in particular; among the most infamous were the cubic air ordinance and the queue ordinance. The former was a law to prevent large numbers of Chinese from living in close quarters. In police raids, violators of the cubic airspace ordinance were jailed unless they paid a fine, but instead of paying the fine, many of the Chinese decided to remain in jail for a few days. When the authorities realized this, they passed the queue ordinance. In those years, Qing dynasty law mandated that men wear their hair in long queues. The queue ordinance mandated that Chinese men who were sent to jail would have their scalps shaved, in large part to humiliate them. (See McClain, *In Search of Equality*, 65–9, which details the Chinese legal challenge to these two ordinances.)
[39] Salyer, *Laws as Harsh as Tigers*, 40.
[40] Salyer, *Laws as Harsh as Tigers*, 70, and McClain, *In Search of Equality*, 205.

and live – to seek equal protection of the laws.[41] These efforts were one of the first examples of organized and sustained political litigation with the goal of changing public policy toward the Chinese.

Beginning in 1882, the Chinese also went to all levels of the federal courts to challenge immigration exclusion and deportation laws. Salyer reports that in their foray into the federal district courts especially, the Chinese met with remarkable success. At this point in immigration history, the decision of whether to admit aliens at U.S. ports of entry had been left to the local collector of the Treasury Department. When would-be Chinese immigrants received unfavorable determinations by the collector, they would appeal to the federal district courts for a writ of *habeas corpus*. In the federal district courts, the Chinese obtained high rates of success in overturning the Treasury Collector's negative immigration decisions; the district courts were far more liberal in their interpretation of statutes and acceptance of supporting evidence than was the Collector. One reason was that institutional context mattered greatly; the administrative agency officials felt much more public pressure to enforce Chinese exclusion policies, while federal judges were insulated because of their life tenure from political and electoral pressure. The Treasury Department's own statistical estimates showed that by 1885 the courts, mainly the federal district courts, were responsible for landing 2,695 Chinese, or 20 percent of the total number that were landed since the passage of the Exclusion Act. And by 1888, Treasury Department estimates showed that 4,091 Chinese had gone to the federal courts to challenge the Collector's decisions and 85% had obtained favorable outcomes there.[42]

The inevitable question that arises is, "Why were the Chinese faring so well in the federal district and circuit courts?" Salyer's answer is: "The success of the Chinese in the federal courts is surprising given traditional accounts emphasizing judicial deference in immigration cases. The intervention of the federal trial courts in San Francisco suggests that judges played a more active role, at least initially – a fact missed by legal scholars – perhaps because they have focused on the Supreme Court and East Coast European immigrants."[43] Salyer and McClain's works are

---

[41] See generally McClain, *In Search of Equality.*

[42] Salyer, *Laws as Harsh as Tigers,* 72, 20. Salyer notes that Judge Morrow, who sat on the district court from 1891 to 1897 and the circuit court from 1897 to 1924, had strongly and publicly supported Chinese exclusion as a member of Congress in the 1880s. Joseph McKenna, who was a circuit court judge from 1892 to 1897, was Morrow's colleague in the House, and he also pushed for Chinese exclusion.

[43] Salyer, *Laws as Harsh as Tigers,* xv.

important in raising the distinction between the institutional contexts of government institutions, namely the dissimilar incentives of those institutions in which the officials are elected and federal judicial institutions in which the judges and justices are appointed for life. But Salyer had also raised a more subtle point: the institutional settings within different levels of the *same* institution may also be diverse. It is precisely because of the influence of the dissimilar institutional settings of the U.S. Supreme Court and the U.S. Courts of Appeals on decision making that led the Chinese to fare better in the lower federal courts than in the Supreme Court.

It is worth systematically examining why the Chinese did so well in these courts. The institutional context and incentives operating in the lower federal courts increased the aliens' chances of success in a number of ways. Given that many federal district judges had openly supported Chinese exclusion policies, it was by no means a foregone conclusion that they would put those personal and political feelings aside when adjudicating Chinese immigrants' cases. Salyer attributed the Chinese legal success in the district courts to the institutional norms of the district courts, which involved respect for the doctrine of *habeas corpus,* and the application of "judicial evidentiary standards" that contributed to Chinese victories. She noted in particular the important institutionally based norms of "treating cases individually and applying general principles to decision making" that the judges felt should be extended to all litigants in a court of law, not just Chinese ones.[44] Given the particular intuitional context of the federal district courts, the judges were bound by evidentiary rules, doctrinal rules, and an expectation derived from their institutional role, and felt obligated to set aside their personal feelings about the Chinese in favor of the judge's obligation to evaluate each case according to the rule of law.

Proximity to the litigants as well as frequent exposure to the large numbers of them also worked to influence district court judges' decisions. In his biography of district court Judge Ogden Hoffman, Christian Fritz surmises that the federal district courts in California often ruled in favor of aliens because they were physically confronted with literally thousands of petitioners daily in their courtrooms and were forced to put a human face on the cases.[45] The factfinding function of these courts, combined with the sheer crush of humanity that invaded the courtrooms,

[44] Salyer, *Laws as Harsh as Tigers,* 69.
[45] Christian G. Fritz, *Federal Justice: The California Court of Ogden Hoffman – 1851–1891* (Lincoln, NE: Nebraska University Press, 1991).

hammered home the plight of the Chinese as individual litigants, not an abstract or amorphous class of people. About Judge Hoffman's approach to the Chinese cases, Fritz wrote:

> Unlike most critics of Chinese immigration, Hoffman was forced to deal with the Chinese on a personal, day-to-day basis. Despite his generalized bias toward the Chinese, in his court he did not face "the Chinese" but rather individualized Chinese petitioners. The thousands of separate hearings individualized the Chinese, forcing Hoffman to see and hear from them as human beings with distinct explanations and histories that had to be appraised...Hoffman, for instance, expressed his delight at being able to avoid separating Chinese children from their parents. Likewise, both he and Sawyer [another district court judge] admired and respected qualities of the Chinese individuals even as they decried the limitations of the race.[46]

Contrast this approach of the district courts to that of the Supreme Court, which only heard a small number of immigration cases, and one of the effects of institutional context on judicial decision making becomes very clear. Whereas trial courts, such as the district courts, were physically confronted by a deluge of Chinese claimants (to the point that Ogden Hoffman's court was referred to as a "habeas corpus mill"[47]), the Supreme Court saw far fewer immigration cases and its rulings were driven by concerns about creating precedents. Comparing the approach of district judges Hoffman and Sawyer to adjudicating Chinese immigration cases with the approach of Stephen Field, who was a Supreme Court justice, Fritz noted, "Unlike Field, who heard only test cases in which the Chinese petitioner at hand was largely incidental and symbolic of many others similarly situated, Hoffman and Sawyer could not maintain Field's detachment."[48] Although the district courts took an individualized approach to the litigants, the Supreme Court approached each case as a vehicle with which to make a broad statement about a whole similarly situated class of cases. Indeed, the individualized versus aggregate approach to cases is one of the main institutional features that differentiates the trial courts from the appellate courts.

Although the Chinese may have been the first ethnic group to discover that the federal district and circuit courts were a more receptive forum than were administrative agencies, they were not the only nationality to

---

[46] Fritz, *Federal Justice*, 247–48.

[47] Christian G. Fritz, "A Nineteenth Century 'Habeas Corpus Mill': The Chinese Before the Federal Courts in California," *American Journal of Legal History*, Vol. 32, No. 4 (Oct., 1988), 347–72.

[48] Fritz, *Federal Justice*, 248.

avail themselves of the protections and procedures of the federal courts. In the years 1891 to 1924, when the Chinese were beating a well-worn path to federal courtrooms, aliens of 12 other nationalities also took their cases as far as the U.S. Courts of Appeals. However, it is not surprising that the Chinese were the nationality most frequently represented in federal immigration cases because they were going to court in droves to challenge the Chinese exclusion law, the first federal immigration law to single out an ethnic group for discriminatory treatment. It is quite possible that other immigrant groups took note of the success of the Chinese litigation campaign and turned to the federal courts to replicate this legal strategy.[49] Indeed, in subsequent years one sees a growth not only in the raw number of immigration cases being appealed to the U.S. Courts of Appeals, but also an expansion in the number and array of nationalities of aliens going to the federal courts for relief from the federal government's enforcement of immigration policies. By 1970, 48 different nationalities of aliens went to court in immigration proceedings. By 1990, it was 85 different nationalities, and in the years 2001 and 2002, there were 116 different nationalities represented in the immigration cases at the three U.S. Courts of Appeals. From the growth over time in the number of distinct nationalities represented in the U.S. Court of Appeals system, one can see that many other nationalities besides the Chinese went to the federal courts for relief in immigration proceedings.

Their weak political position encouraged aliens to head to the federal courts rather than rely on members of the elected branches of government for relief. This was supported by the fact that the immigration laws had built in a perhaps unintended incentive for aliens to take their appeals as far up in the federal court system as possible. The further up the federal

---

[49] The numbers are relatively small between the years 1891 and 1888 because of a law passed in 1891 that sought to make the determinations of the inspectors and officers of the Treasury Department (which then had control over the admission of immigrants) final. There was to be no recourse to the federal courts. Curiously, the law explicitly omitted the Chinese from this requirement; it applied only to aliens who were not Chinese laborers, leaving the Chinese free to continue to appeal to the federal courts. Historians are not completely clear on the impetus for this little-known provision of the 1891 Act, but Salyer speculates, "Congress did know, however, of Chinese immigrants' use of the federal courts to contest admission cases, and it seems likely that it wished to avoid such litigation with non-Chinese immigrants." Why the Chinese were not barred by this "finality clause" is unknown, but a similar provision was inserted into the Chinese Exclusion Act of 1888. A snafu in ratification of the law threw the legality of the provision into doubt, however, and the Circuit Court of Appeals for the Ninth Circuit (and later the Supreme Court) regarded the finality clause as never having actually become law (Salyer, *Laws as Harsh as Tigers*, 27–8).

judicial hierarchy an alien can take her case, the longer she can drag out her stay in the United States. The longer immigrants' stay is extended, the more chance they have to develop and gain deportation-mitigating "equities" (factors that work in the alien's favor in his or her argument against deportation), such as the parentage of a U.S. citizen's child, or marriage to a U.S. citizen or lawful permanent resident.[50] Further, the hope among aliens is that the longer they are able to remain in the country, the longer time there is in which Congress will perhaps pass new legislation that would grant them relief from their deportation.

BORDER ENFORCEMENT STRATEGIES

Early on, aliens had figured out they would meet with more favorable treatment at the hand of the judicial branch rather than at the hands of administrative bureaucracies or elected officials. Their movement to the federal courts was further encouraged by the manner in which the U.S. government has chosen to carry out its immigration policy. The volume and nature of the immigration appeals flowing to the federal courts has much to do with the federal government's immigration enforcement strategies. From decade to decade, the United States, like any other country, has claimed sovereign control over its borders, but the focus of what constitutes a national threat has shifted over time.[51] The 1880s through the 1890s was a period of nation building in which the United States and its political institutions, including the U.S. Supreme Court, went out of their way to assert the country's national sovereignty. These strident assertions of nationhood are on display in the bombastic language found in foundational immigration cases such as *Chae Chan Ping v. United States* (1889)[52] and *Fong Yue Ting v. United States,* (1893).[53] In *Chae Chan Ping*, for example, the Court stated, "The power of exclusion of foreigners being an incident of sovereignty belonging to the government of the United States as a part of those sovereign powers delegated by the constitution, the right to its exercise at any time when, in the judgment of the government, the interests of the country require it, cannot

---

[50] See, e.g., *United States ex rel. Marcello v. District Director of Immigration and Naturalization Service,* 634 F.2d 964 (5th Cir. 1981) for an example of a typical abuse of the judicial process by an alien to lengthen his stay and avoid deportation.

[51] Peter Andreas, *Border Games: Policing the United States – Mexico Divide* (Ithaca, NY: Cornell University Press, 2001), 3.

[52] 130 U.S. 581.

[53] 149 U.S. 698.

be granted away or restrained on behalf of any one."[54] Similarly, in *Fong Yue Ting,* the Court majority opined, "The right to exclude or to expel all aliens, or any class of aliens, absolutely or upon certain conditions, in war or in peace, being an inherent and inalienable right of every sovereign and independent nation, essential to its safety, its independence and its welfare..."[55]

The 1920s through the early 1950s were dominated by the theories of Social Darwinism and white supremacy, and then by the Red Scare. As Daniel Tichenor has argued, in the 1950s the federal government struck a Faustian deal to restrict eastern and southern European immigration while tolerating illegal Mexican migration.[56] Kitty Calavita goes even further in arguing that there is evidence that the federal government actually encouraged illegal immigration; the INS and Border Patrol both had policies of lax enforcement against Mexican migration during harvest season.[57] More important, Calavita argues that the Bracero Program (1942 to 1964), which allowed Mexican migrants to take temporary agricultural work in the United States, fulfilled two political functions by simultaneously appeasing growers' demands for cheap and accessible workers and giving the INS a temporary reprieve from public pressures to control illegal Mexican migration.[58] The 1960s brought the Civil Rights revolution and its political atmosphere of racial tolerance spilled over to the Immigration Act of 1965, which was by all accounts inclusive and expansionist in its elimination of the national origins discrimination.[59] The watershed 1965 Act replaced a racist national origins selection system with a racially neutral preference system that selects immigrants based on their family relations to those in this country or because of their employment skills. The decade of the 1980s was characterized by a shift in immigration policy to a focus on combating illegal immigration that

---

[54] 130 U.S. 581, 609.

[55] 149 U.S. 698.

[56] Testimony of Daniel J. Tichenor, Research Professor, Eagleton Institute of Politics and Department of Political Science, Rutgers University, New Brunswick, New Jersey, before the U.S. House of Representatives Committee on the Judiciary, Subcommittee on Immigration, Citizenship, Refugees, Border Security, and International Law, March 30, 2007, 7–9 (available at www.judiciary.house.gov/hearings/March2007/Tichenor070330.pdf).

[57] Calavita, *Inside the State: The Bracero Program, Immigration, and the INS* (New York: Routledge Press, 1992), 33.

[58] Calavita, *Inside the State*, 111, 140.

[59] See David Riemers, *Still the Golden Door: The Third World Comes to America* (New York: Columbia University Press, 1992). See especially chapter 3 for an excellent account of the political factors that contributed to the passage of the 1965 Act.

culminated in the Immigration Reform and Control Act of 1986 (IRCA), which for the first time criminalized the hiring of illegal aliens. Today, however, the employer sanctions provisions of IRCA have been deemed a failure; IRCA's ignoble legacy is the creation of a cottage industry for the manufacture and distribution of fraudulent documents. The mid-1980s is also when Peter Andreas noted a "sharp escalation of border policy," when the policing of our nation's borders moved from "low politics to high politics."[60]

The 1990s were marked at first by a period of immigration inclusion with the passage of the Immigration Act of 1990 (IMMACT) that expanded visa numbers for legal immigration categories. By 1996, the pendulum had swung back to the restrictionist side with the passage of the Antiterrorism and Effective Death Penalty Act (AEDPA), which was passed soon after the Oklahoma City bombing.[61] The AEDPA sharply curtailed the availability of *habeas corpus* review for certain classes of criminal aliens. In that same year, Congress passed the Illegal Immigration Reform and Immigrant Responsibility Act (IIRIRA), which expanded the criminal grounds for the removal of aliens and significantly changed the deportation and exclusion procedures.[62] These two acts were viewed by immigration advocates as an assault on and rollback of aliens' rights. The 1996 reforms were followed up by the REAL ID Act of 2003, which made further changes to the availability of judicial review for aliens in removal proceedings.[63] Among its many provisions, the REAL ID Act barred the district courts from *habeas* review of aliens' removal claims, instead routing these appeals to the U.S. Courts of Appeals where aliens can file a "petition for review." The REAL ID Act also barred judicial review of many discretionary decisions related to immigration. Immigration proponents viewed these pieces of legislation as draconian responses to criminal aliens who were allegedly abusing the legal system to prolong their stay in the United States. Advocates of these changes perceived them as closing a loophole that had been abused.

The enforcement strategies of the federal government in the past two decades have also had consequences for the number and nature of cases flowing to the federal courts. As Andreas described in his book *Border Games – Policing the United States–Mexico Divide*, the escalation of border enforcement in the mid-1980s was fueled by media images and the

---

[60] Andreas, *Border Games*, x, 3.
[61] Public Law 101–649 and Public Law 104–132, respectively.
[62] Public Law 104–208, Div. C, 110 Stat. 3009–546.
[63] Public Law 109–13.

public image that the border was "out of control."[64] Andreas persuasively argued that the escalation of border enforcement was an exercise in the federal government's use of "images, symbols, and language to define the problem" and to demonstrate to the public what was being done about it. Far from being a practical policy solution that actually brought the southern border under control, the enforcement methods were "suboptimal in the means–ends calculus."[65] Why would the federal government engage in this elaborate exercise of building fences and increasing border patrol staff if these measures did not have any discernable effect on deterring illegal immigration and the transportation of drugs into the United States? Enforcement methods that are not actually effective can still be *politically* effective; the federal government's projection of the image that it is taking steps to crack down on the border problem wins political points because it mimics progress being made. "Stupid policies can be smart politics," he wrote.[66] The border enforcement strategy that began in the 1980s and continues to concentrate resources on the southern border is a part of political theatre and an example of symbolic politics in action.

One INS official that Andreas interviewed flatly stated, "The border is easy money politically. But the interior is a political minefield."[67] Interior enforcement efforts have drawn fire not only from immigrant communities and their advocates, but from business owners and leaders who charged that the INS was hurting their business. The escalated border enforcement approach taken by the federal government beginning in the mid-1980s has "limited the range of acceptable policy solutions."[68] Some might argue that this enforcement strategy from a political standpoint obviates the need to vigorously pursue other kinds of enforcement strategies.

Even with strong evidence that jobs draw illegal aliens rather than public benefits, free education for their children, or driver's licenses, recent and ongoing border enforcement strategies filter few resources to interior enforcement, especially worksite enforcement that could concentrate on busting and penalizing U.S. employers who are also breaking U.S. immigration laws to employ illegal aliens. By 2002 there were 18,043 border patrol agents and approximately 3,092 interior inspectors.[69]

[64] Andreas, *Border Games*, 8–9.
[65] Ibid.
[66] Andreas, *Border Games*, 9, 148.
[67] Andreas, *Border Games*, 147.
[68] Ibid. at 32.
[69] Migration Policy Institute, "Immigration Enforcement Spending Since IRCA," November 2005, No. 10, pg. 8 (available at http: www.migrationpolicy.org/ITFIAF/ FactSheet_Spending.pdf).

Moreover, the technological resources, funding, and numbers of interior enforcement agents at the agency formerly known as INS, now known as Immigration Customs and Enforcement (ICE), lags far behind comparable resources and funding allocated to the U.S. Customs and Border Protection (CBP). Border control received 58 percent of the enforcement resources in 2002; interior investigations received a mere 9 percent of the resources.[70] Disproportionate budget and personnel increases continue to flow toward CBP and border enforcement efforts and not to the augmentation and expansion of ICE and interior enforcement.

At issue is not just the disproportionate focus on and funding of border enforcement and interior enforcement, but also the way existing resources are deployed in interior enforcement. In 2003, as part of a new U.S. Immigration and Custom Enforcement program, DHS personnel were earmarked for "abscondee removal teams." This group, called the National Fugitive Operations Program (NFOP), has enjoyed rapid expansion in recent years in both size and funding. As a Migration Policy Institute (MPI) report described it, NFOP is "a massive operation with a very narrow congressional mandate: locating dangerous individuals with existing removal orders."[71] However, according to MPI, the practice of NFOP has not been consistent with the program's mandate and originally intended purpose. DHS has had enforcement procedures in place for a while in which Fugitive Operation Teams (FOT) charged with apprehending criminal aliens typically set forth "the number of fugitive alien targets" that the team was expected to apprehend in a specific time frame.[72] It is not clear from DHS policy whether these "targets" were hard quotas, or merely aspirational guidelines, but these targets seem to have put pressure on FOTs to meet numerical quotas by apprehending ordinary status violators who did not have criminal backgrounds beyond the breaking of immigration law.[73] The MPI report authors speculated

---

[70] Ibid.

[71] Margot Mendelson, Shayna Strom, and Michael Wishnie, "Collateral Damage: An Examination of ICE's Fugitive Operations Program," 3. This is a report prepared under the guidance of Muzaffar Christi and Doris Meisner for the Migration Policy Institute, February 2009 (available at www.migrationpolicy.org/pubs/NFOP_Feb09.pdf).

[72] Mendelson et al., "Collateral Damage," 7.

[73] Two news reports seem to treat the numerical guidelines as firm targets. See for example Spencer S. Hsu, "Immigration Priorities Questioned; Report Says Focus on Deporting Criminal Apparently Shifted," *Washington Post*, February 5, 2009, A2. In the article Hsu refers to "arrest quotas." Nina Bernstein, "Despite Vow, Target of Immigrant Raids Shifts," *New York Times*, February 4, 2009, A1. Bernstein writes of the internal directives to raise "arrest quotas" for FOTs in 2006.

"The 1,000-arrest-per-team guidance established in January 2006 places significant pressure on FOTs to make hundreds of arrests."[74] Specifically, the report noted:

[T]he quota system, and its crediting of nonfugitive arrests, does not encourage FOTs to direct scarce resources to higher-priority apprehensions; in fact, assuming it is more resource intensive to capture one person who threatens national security than ten arbitrary unauthorized immigrants, a team determined to reach 1,000 arrests would be wise to ignore hard-to-locate national security threats and concentrate on the least dangerous immigrants, including nonfugitives.[75]

The authors documented the NFOP's recent activities, including a breakdown of the number and kinds of apprehensions. NFOP was discovered to be mainly apprehending "low-hanging fruit," or aliens who were noncriminal offenders who had happened to be in the wrong place at the wrong time during a raid, and were simply easier to catch than more serious criminal offenders and the most dangerous fugitives who were actively evading arrest.

The particular strategies of immigration enforcement, which focuses on apprehension and eschews worksite enforcement and criminal prosecutions against U.S. employers, and goes after garden-variety immigration status violators instead of criminal aliens, has had profound effects on the immigration caseloads in the federal courts, especially the federal district courts and U.S. Courts of Appeals. These courts cannot control their dockets as the Supreme Court can. Because the government has chosen to focus on border enforcement that involves the building of physical structures such as walls and fences and amassing border patrol guards along the southern border to intercept and block would-be illegal crossers, statistics become very important to prove the efficacy of these strategies (as are catchy team names, such as National Fugitive Operations Program). The apprehension numbers, exacerbated by arrest quotas, demonstrate to the public that the border enforcement strategies are working because the apprehension numbers represent illegal aliens that would have infiltrated our border defenses had the border patrol and INS not apprehended them.[76] Andreas compares the focus on apprehension statistics

---

[74] Mendelson et al., "Collateral Damage," 19.

[75] Mendelson et al., "Collateral Damage," 19.

[76] But apprehension numbers are deceptive because, as Wayne Cornelius has shown, when we double- and triple-fortify part of the border between the United States and Mexico, as with the high-profile INS programs "Operation Hold the Line" and "Operation Gatekeeper," apprehensions in those sectors will decrease, but this does not preclude the circumvention of those crossing areas and a subsequent increase of crossings in

to the Vietnam War-style "body count" strategy.[77] But because the border enforcement and apprehension statistics approach focuses on aliens, who are politically easier targets than the U.S. employers who hire them, this approach has increased the number of immigration cases in the federal courts, rather than create a parallel stream of criminal cases targeting the offending U.S. employers, who also violate immigration laws. The arrest quotas of the NFOP also seem to ignore quality in favor of quantity; instead of removing violent criminals, the NFOP has apprehended mostly noncriminal aliens for the sake of meeting numerical quotas.

After the 9/11 terrorist attacks in 2001, the Bush administration seemed to have adopted a new policy of immigration enforcement that turned toward interior enforcement. The policy continues to emphasize apprehension numbers and stepping up the pace and frequency of deportations, but it does so through high profile and large-scale raids on businesses. The *New York Times* reported that during the Bush administration, "Immigration and Customs Enforcement officials, facing intense political pressure to toughen enforcement, removed 221,664 illegal immigrants from the country over the last year, an increase of more than 37,000 – about 20 percent – over the year before, according to the agency's tally."[78] More recently, although President Obama's administration seems to have scaled back on high-profile raids in which aliens are rounded up, but efforts begun by President Bush to identify and deport illegal aliens who are in local jails have been expanded.[79]

In addition to media reports and government reports, other research entities, such as the Transactional Records Access Clearinghouse (TRAC), also confirm the increase in immigration prosecutions in the last few years.[80] TRAC noted a "heightened level of DHS immigration referrals"

---

border areas that are more remote and dangerous. See Wayne Cornelius, "Impacts of Border Enforcement on Unauthorized Mexican Migration to the United States," Sept. 26, 2006 (available at http://borderbattles.ssrc.org/Cornelius/).

[77] Andreas, *Border Games*, 99.

[78] Julia Preston, "As Pace of Deportation Rises, Illegal Families Are Digging In," *New York Times*, May 1, 2007, A1.

[79] Julie Preston, "U.S. Shifts Strategy on Illicit Work by Illegal Immigrants," *New York Times*, July 2, 2009, A1; and Spencer S. Hsu, "U.S. to Expand Immigration Checks to All Local Jails: Obama Administration's Enforcement Push Could Lead to Sharp Increase in Deportation," *Washington Post*, May 19, 2009, A1.

[80] TRAC is an independent, nonpartisan research center that describes itself as "a data gathering, data research and data distribution organization associated with Syracuse University." TRAC gathers information and statistics primarily through the use of the Freedom of Information Act (FOIA) (available at http://trac.syr.edu/aboutTRACgeneral.html).

beginning in 2004 and continued into the first six months of FY2005. In an August 2005 report, TRAC added, however, that "When changes in the overall immigration enforcement effort are examined, it would appear that the Bush Administration has in fact adopted an across-the-board get-tough policy: more referrals, more prosecutions and more convictions."[81] Whether the apprehensions and prosecutions derive from border apprehensions or interior apprehensions, the increase in prosecution has led to more persons being caught, many who then headed to the federal courts to avoid deportation and removal.

The across-the-board ratcheting up of enforcement has meant that more immigration cases have poured into the federal court system, although not all apprehensions and prosecutions end up there. Most aliens who are apprehended, unless they have a criminal background, are first offered the option of voluntary departure where they may choose to depart the United States of their own volition and at their own expense. If an alien chooses to challenge a deportation, he or she is placed in deportation or removal proceedings. The advantage of challenging one's removal in first the administrative agency system and then the federal courts is, first, that it prolongs one's stay in the United States, and then because, especially for aliens convicted of aggravated felonies, the legal consequences of deportation are very severe. The disadvantage is that if an alien is finally found to be deportable, he or she is banned from returning to the United States for ten years and barred for life if convicted of an aggravated felony.[82]

The effect on the federal courts of the government's recent border enforcement strategies has been a rise in the number of deportation cases streaming into the federal courts.[83] Had the government's strategy instead concentrated on vigorous worksite enforcement of employer sanctions against U.S. employers, for example, there would have been a

---

[81] "Criminal Enforcement of U.S. Immigration Law" (available at http://trac.syr.edu/tracins/latest/131/).

[82] 8 U.S.C. § 1229a, subsection 7, stipulates, "(7) Limitation on discretionary relief for failure to appear. Any alien against whom a final order of removal is entered in absentia under this subsection and who, at the time of the notice described in paragraph (1) or (2) of section 239(a) [8 USCS § 1229(a)], was provided oral notice, either in the alien's native language or in another language the alien understands, of the time and place of the proceedings and of the consequences under this paragraph of failing, other than because of exceptional circumstances (as defined in subsection (e)(1)) to attend a proceeding under this section, shall not be eligible for relief under section 240A, 240B, 245, 248, or 249 [8 USCS §§ 1229b, 1229c, 1255, 1258, or 1259] for a period of 10 years after the date of the entry of the final order of removal."

[83] Solomon Moore and Ann M. Simmons, "Immigrant Pleas Crushing Federal Appellate Courts," *Los Angeles Times*, May 2, 2005 ("Tougher enforcement of immigration laws has also funneled more cases into the system"), 2.

very different stream of cases headed into the federal courts. This strategy would have yielded more criminal prosecution cases of U.S. employers of U.S. citizens or lawful permanent residents, not civil charges such as those in deportation and exclusion proceedings. A TRAC report, "Recent Trends in INS Enforcement," indicated that "The sharp jump in INS criminal enforcement actions has had an important impact on the federal criminal justice system. The surge in INS activities, for example, was the major contributor to the increase in the overall number of federal prosecutions – which went to 90,832 in FY 2001 from 76,818 in 1992."[84] These enforcement strategies not only affected the criminal justice system, they also affected the federal courts by sending a large number of certain types of cases to those courts.

TWO COURTS WITH DIFFERENTIATED FUNCTIONS: CONSEQUENCES FOR ALIEN LITIGANTS

The confluence of congressional legislation first creating the structures and rules of the federal judicial system, the decision of immigrants of an array of nationalities to go to the federal courts to defend challenges to their immigration status, and the rise of immigration enforcement beginning in 1986, had the combined effect of further distancing and distinguishing the U.S. Supreme Court and the U.S Courts of Appeals in their functions. By the turn of the twentieth century, a consensus had been reached in the political system about the division of labor of the Supreme Court and lower federal courts. The Supreme Court was to be reserved for important legal and policy questions; the U.S. Courts of Appeals would maintain much of their error correction function.

In his landmark book, *Courts of Appeals in the Federal Judicial System: A Study of the Second, Fifth, and District of Columbia Circuits*, J. Howard Woodford discerned the functions of the federal appellate courts. Among his overall findings were that the Supreme Court and the Courts of Appeals have a dissimilar mix of cases, different sources and sets of litigants, and unlike natures and outcomes of decisions.[85] These are crucial distinctions, to be sure. This book augments Howard's findings by

---

[84] Available at http://trac.syr.edu/tracins/findings/aboutINS/insTrends.html. The report refers to the Immigration and Naturalization Service because the Department of Homeland Security was not created until 2002.

[85] J. Woodford Howard, Jr., *Courts of Appeals in the Federal Judicial System: A Study of the Second, Fifth, and District of Columbia Circuits* (Princeton, NJ: Princeton University Press, 1981).

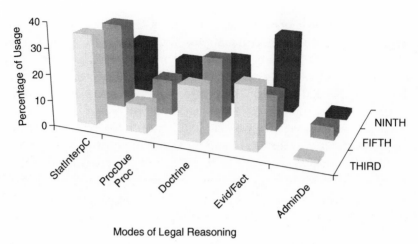

FIGURE 3.1. Frequency of Modes of Legal Reasoning in the Third, Fifth, and Ninth Circuits, 1881–2002

showing that the two courts differ in an additional dimension, which is their divergent approaches in deciding cases. This divergence in turn has implications for the success of alien litigants in immigration cases before these courts.

As a first cut at the data, the frequency (in percentages) of the modes of legal reasoning selected by the Third, Fifth, and Ninth Circuits were compared with each other.

What Figure 3.1 shows is that the three Courts of Appeals adjudicate immigration cases in relatively similar ways, as indicated by their use of the modes of legal reasoning to similar degrees. The wider variance in the use of facts and evidence among the circuits can be attributed to the much larger number of asylum cases that are received by the Ninth Circuit, cases that are largely fact-driven. Similarly, the higher-frequency use of statutory interpretation in the Third and Fifth Circuits can be attributed to those two circuits' receiving more deportation cases than does the Ninth Circuit. These deportation cases most often involve disputes over statutory meanings. Meanwhile, the Ninth Circuit has a much larger percentage of asylum cases than the other two circuits, and these cases are overwhelmingly decided based on evaluations of facts and evidence. Although there are some regional variations, because of the mix of immigration cases in each circuit, Figure 3.1 shows that the Third, Fifth, and Ninth Circuits generally use the same modes of legal reasoning to comparable extents, indicating that these courts take similar approaches in deciding their cases.

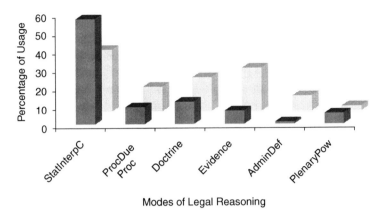

FIGURE 3.2. Modes of Legal Reasoning by Court, 1881–2002

A more striking empirical picture develops when one compares the modes of legal reasoning most often used by these three Courts of Appeals with the modes of reasoning in the Supreme Court.

Figure 3.2 shows that although the U.S. Supreme Court and the three U.S. Courts of Appeals use the same set of legal reasoning, they do so to dissimilar extents. The Supreme Court uses statutory interpretation far more frequently than do the Courts of Appeals in deciding cases. In fact, among all the modes of legal reasoning, the Supreme Court uses statutory interpretation as a mode of legal reasoning most often, in a full 57 percent of the immigration cases. Statutory interpretation at the Supreme Court was far and away the most frequently used legal reasoning, with doctrine trailing as a distant second in 12 percent of the cases. Meanwhile, the U.S. Courts of Appeals' legal reasoning is more evenly distributed among a number of different approaches: fact/evidence (27 percent), statutory interpretation (26 percent), doctrine (21 percent), and procedural due process (15 percent). The fact that the U.S. Courts of Appeals' modes of legal reasoning are more evenly distributed among several approaches than the Supreme Court's shows that the Courts of Appeals are performing a number of institutionally designated functions.

Regarding the functions of the Supreme Court and the Courts of Appeals, Howard had specifically remarked about two separate functions performed by the federal appellate courts. One task is for these courts to carry out "'error correction,' in which appellate courts hold trial courts and agencies accountable under law." The other job is to carry out "'institutional review,' in which appellate courts umpire conflicts among different branches of government and declare general principles of legal policy."[86] The patterns of the modes of legal reasoning illustrated by Figures 3.1 and 3.2 empirically confirm Howard's findings.[87] In spending the majority of its time weighing in on statutory interpretation, the Supreme Court is conducting "institutional review" by serving as tie-breaker in intercircuit conflicts and having the last word in statutory interpretation conflicts. As well, the Supreme Court is actively creating public policy by infusing vague statutes with the justices' preferred meaning. Meanwhile, the contemporary Courts of Appeals substantially retain their originally intended error correction function, as illustrated by their continued usage of procedural due process, doctrine, and fact/evidence as modes of legal reasoning. What the data also indicates, however, specifically in the 26 percent of the cases in which the Courts of Appeals have used statutory interpretation, is that even as the Courts of Appeals continue to perform their error correction function, they are also growing into policy makers in their own right. These courts' policy making ability derives from their frequent and increasing opportunities to interpret statutes and the correspondingly waning likelihood that, if a decision is appealed, the Supreme Court will grant *certiorari* and review the U.S. Courts of Appeals' work.

The Supreme Court now concentrates on important policy and political issues. The Courts of Appeals continue with their error correction. But what exactly does this mean for alien litigants in immigration cases? The consequence for alien litigants has been that they have fared less well in winning their appeals in the Supreme Court than the Courts of Appeals and this situation has much to do with the distinctive manners in which the Supreme Court and the Courts of Appeals approach deciding cases. The reasons are multifold and very much tied to institutional context. First, given the hierarchical structure of the federal judicial system, the Supreme Court, by virtue of its position at the top of the system, has often acted as the tie-breaker and final arbiter of policy questions, especially when lower courts disagree. Although an alien may have won an appeal at the Courts of Appeals level, that decision may be overturned if

---

[86] Ibid. at 7.
[87] Howard's data range covered the years 1965–1967 and a diversity of appeals; my data cover the years 1881–2002 but include only immigration cases. Nevertheless, in analyzing the modes of legal reasoning, one can see that the differentiated functions of the two courts can also be shown through analysis of the manners in which they have decided cases.

the Supreme Court takes the case, often for a political or policy reason that is of little concern to the individual litigant in the case. Second, an alien is likely to receive a more favorable outcome depending on whether the court treats the case individually or as a representative of a larger class of similarly situated cases, and the Courts of Appeals are much more likely than the Supreme Court to take the former approach. Third, if the alien is asserting that there has been an error of law or fact made by the administrative agency, the Courts of Appeals, not the Supreme Court, are likely to be the courts that will address their issues. As the following examples will show, all of these phenomena result from the particularized functions of each court.

The Supreme Court as Tie-Breaker and Policy Maker

There is evidence of the Supreme Court behaving as a policy court as early as the Chinese exclusion period. Congressional passage of the Chinese Exclusion Act in 1882 and subsequent amendments did not settle the issue of what that policy meant. It was left to the federal courts to interpret and carry out the provisions of the Acts. The circuit courts in the 1880s and early 1890s were confused about whether the Chinese Exclusion Act should be enforced by race or by nationality. The confusion was understandable given that this was a time when even academic understandings of race, ethnicity, nationality, and biology were unclear and often conflated all these categories as if they were overlapping and interchangeable. Different circuits had contrasting strategies in dealing with the enforcement of the Chinese Exclusion Act. In *United States v. Douglas* (1883),[88] Justice Nelson of the Massachusetts circuit ruled that an ethnic Chinese alien born in Hong Kong was admissible and exempt from the Chinese Exclusion Act based on his nationality. He was not a Chinese citizen, but a British subject residing in Hong Kong. In this case, the Massachusetts circuit read the intent of the Chinese Exclusion Act to be *nationality* based.

Within one month of the *Douglas* decision, *In re Ah Lung* (1883)[89] was decided in the California Circuit. Judge Field, then sitting as a California circuit judge, ruled that another Chinese laborer from Hong Kong was excludable based on his *race*. The California circuit interpreted the intent of the Chinese Exclusion Act to exclude "all laborers of the Chinese race."[90] One circuit had decided that enforcement of the Chinese

[88] 17 F. 634.
[89] 18 F. 28.
[90] 18 F. 28, 32.

Exclusion Act turned on nationality, and another circuit on the opposite coast had determined that enforcement of the Act should be triggered by race. The situation of the conflicting circuit decisions was ripe for Supreme Court review.

The circuit courts could not agree on whether nationality or race should be controlling, and the Supreme Court never really settled the issue definitively because all the challenges to the Chinese Exclusion Acts that reached the Supreme Court involved Chinese nationals – not ethnic Chinese from countries other than China. Yet one can extrapolate from a series of decisions that the Court itself had settled on a racialist application of the Act. This approach is evidenced in *Yamataya v. Fisher*, "That Congress may exclude aliens of a particular race from the United States; prescribe the terms and conditions upon which certain classes of aliens may come to this country; establish regulations for sending out of the country such aliens as come here in violation of law; and commit the enforcement of such provisions, conditions and regulations exclusively to executive officers, without judicial intervention, are principles firmly established by the decisions of this court."[91] The passage is an example of the plenary power doctrine, but in it the Court also opines that race, rather than ethnicity, is an acceptable ground for exclusion of aliens.

The historical example of the Supreme Court in the Chinese exclusion era shows the Court's potentially powerful role as policy maker and tie-breaker. In opining that the Chinese Exclusion Act should be defined in racial rather than national origin terms, the Supreme Court made a very significant policy pronouncement, not just a legal one. The power exists only in potential form because the Supreme Court must affirmatively choose to rule on the issue by granting a case *certiorari*. Thus, this example also shows that the Supreme Court's main power derives from its ability to make one ruling that will have ramifications for many other similarly situated cases. The U.S. Courts of Appeals, in contrast, derive their main power in the sheer number of cases they adjudicate and the fact that if the Supreme Court does not grant an appeal *certiorari*, the Court of Appeals becomes the court of last resort.

Individual vs. Group Adjudication

Another effect of the division of labor and differentiation in function between the U.S. Supreme Court and the U.S. Courts of Appeals is

---

[91] *United States v. Wong You*, 223 U.S. 67.

illustrated in the way in which the two courts approach immigration appeals. As mentioned, the Supreme Court, by virtue of the small number of cases it accepts and its contemporary role as a policy court, typically takes one case to make a policy or political pronouncement about a large class of similarly situated cases. Meanwhile, the U.S. Courts of Appeals continue to adjudicate cases on an individual basis and have the expectation that administrative agency officials will do the same.

The deportation case of *Reynoso v. Immigration and Naturalization Service* (9th Cir. 1981)[92] lays out several different approaches the U.S. Courts of Appeals could take in adjudicating cases. The Reynosos, a Mexican couple who had entered the United States illegally, were applying for suspension of deportation; this would have set aside their deportation order and permitted them to remain in the United States. The majority on the panel concluded that the Board of Immigration Appeals (BIA) had not abused its discretion in concluding that, although the couple had met other statutory requirements to qualify them for suspension of deportation, they had not shown that their repatriation would result in "extreme hardship." The majority wrote:

[T]here is nothing to distinguish the hardship of these petitioners from that of any of the thousands of other Mexican nationals who annually enter the United States illegally and who then accumulate seven years of good time in this country....If this court were to grant relief in this case we would be holding that the hardship involved in returning to a former, lower material standard of living automatically requires a remand in every deportation case that fits the residential and charter requirements of § 1254.[93]

In a long dissent, Judge Pregerson wrote that he believed the case law of the circuit should be read so that the "hardship requirement should not be set too high."[94] But Pregerson's main objection was to the manner in which the majority had conflated the Reynosos' case with the situation of countless other Mexican nationals. Pregerson wrote:

The majority ignores the totality of facts that related to the Reynosos and, instead invokes a floodgates argument in characterizing their situation as similar to that of "any of the thousands of other Mexican nationals who annually enter the United States illegally and who then accumulate seven years of good time in this country." The evil in this approach is its stereotypical treatment of all Mexican aliens who seek to remain in this country. Moreover, this approach flouts the long-established rule that each hardship case must be decided on its own facts. In

[92] 627 F.2d 958.
[93] 627 F.2d 958, 959.
[94] 627 F.2d 958, 961.

reviewing the Board's decision denying an application for suspension of deportation, our role is to examine each case on its own merits, rather than to speculate about "thousands" of other matters not before us.[95]

The majority's merging of the Reynosos' case with so many others is more commonly the approach taken by the Supreme Court when it decides cases because the Court decides cases with an eye toward setting precedent for a large class of similar cases.

Such an approach places the litigants in the individual cases at a disadvantage. Although a case-by-case approach by no means guarantees an individual litigant a victory, it can skew the decision in favor of the individual. As Pregerson in his dissent reminded the majority, "Not every alien who seeks to remain in this country has elderly permanent resident parents who are at least partially dependent upon their petitioner children for support. Nor does every alien suffer, as will the Reynosos if deported, the pain of separation from a large extended family of permanent resident parents, sibling, nieces, and nephews."[96] As the Ninth Circuit itself had stated in *Banks v. Immigration and Naturalization Service* (9th Cir. 1979), "This type of discretionary determination [of whether an alien had demonstrated "extreme hardship"] is not bound by hard and fast rules; each case must be decided on its own facts."[97] The *Reynoso* court was confronted with choosing between adjudicating the case by taking into consideration the very specific circumstances of that couple's situation (as Judge Pregerson's dissent urged), or taking the approach the majority eventually took in collapsing any individual distinctiveness of that family's situation, and generalizing the Reynoso's situation to that of "thousands of other Mexican nationals." Yet, given the institutionally based incentives and imperatives, the Supreme Court is more likely to adopt the generalizing approach taken by the *Reynoso* majority, while the Courts of Appeals have more incentive to adopt the approach urged by Judge Pregerson's dissent. Are the Supreme Court and Courts of Appeals precluded from either approach? No, of course not, but the institutional structures, especially the judges' and justices' perceptions of their roles and missions, are very much tied to their institutional setting and those settings predispose the Supreme Court toward one approach and the Courts of Appeals toward another.

[95] 627 F. 2d 958, 963 (some internal citations omitted).
[96] 627 F.2d 958, 963.
[97] 594 F.2d 760, 762.

This individualized approach to adjudicating cases is not limited to the Ninth Circuit; a panel of the Fifth Circuit also adopted this adjudicative strategy. In *Barthold v. Immigration and Naturalization Service* (5th Cir. 1975)[98], Barthold, a Haitian alien, arrived in Miami without inspection and claimed asylum a day later. The hearing and subsequent Fifth Circuit appeal was based on his asserted right to counsel in deportation hearings. In reviewing that claim, the unanimous opinion stated, "It is clear that any right an alien may have in this regard is grounded in the fifth amendment guarantee of due process rather than the sixth amendment right to counsel...Therefore, we analyze the proceedings in terms of their fundamental fairness on a case-by-case basis."[99] In evaluating the case as a Fifth Amendment due process case, the Fifth Circuit panel sidestepped the issue of a deportation proceeding's civil nature (which does not entitle a claimant to legal counsel at public expense) and focused on the due process aspect of access to counsel instead. Such analysis required a case-by-case adjudication and individualized analysis in order to make a determination of whether due process was met in that case.

In addition to their own tendencies toward adopting individualized approaches to deciding cases, and especially when using a due process lens to do so, the U.S. Courts of Appeals have generally held administrative agencies to the same standard of individualized review and have been highly critical of "boilerplate" decisions. The Armenian Christian asylum case of *Hartooni v. Immigration and Naturalization Service* (9th Cir. 1994)[100] is a good example of the Courts of Appeals holding the Board of Immigration Appeals to this standard. The majority wrote:

We are not permitted to credit such an inaccurate, conclusory, and boilerplate decision...The Board's decision was premised on a nonexistent credibility finding. It provided only one questionable reason for the denial. And it failed to explain why it discounted the compelling evidence corroborating Hartooni's story...In view of these failures and the compelling evidence in favor of Ms. Hartooni's claims, we hold that the Board's action was arbitrary and capricious.

The *Hartooni* case and many other Ninth Circuit cases cited *Castillo v. Immigration and Naturalization Service* (9th Cir. 1991)[101], a Nicaraguan asylum case in which the Ninth Circuit laid out the standards for evaluating whether the BIA's decision was supported by substantial evidence.

[98] 517 F.2d 689.
[99] 517 F.2d 689, 690–691.
[100] 21 F.3d 336.
[101] 951 F.2d 1117.

Indeed, *Castillo* was the precedent-setting case in this regard. The *Castillo* panel wrote:

[I]n order for this court to conduct a proper substantial evidence review of the BIA's decision, the Board's opinion must state with sufficient particularity and clarity the reasons for denial of asylum. Boilerplate opinions, which set out general legal standards yet are devoid of statements that evidence an individualized review of the petitioner's contentions and circumstances, neither afford the petitioner the BIA review to which he or she is entitled, nor do they provide an adequate basis for this court to conduct its review. Those Board opinions that lack an adequate statement of the BIA's reasons for denying the petitioner relief must be remanded to the Board for clarification of the bases for its opinion. There are no steadfast rules regarding what constitutes an adequate Board decision.[102]

In writing that "there are no steadfast rules regarding what constitutes an adequate decision," the Ninth Circuit underscored the importance of individualized review. The Fifth Circuit shares this view, as illustrated in the deportation case of *Ramos et al. v. Immigration and Naturalization Service* (5th Cir. 1983):

We recognize that the immigration authorities are burdened by a heavy case load. It is not our intention to require of them lengthy exegeses on immigration law or extended discussion of evidentiary minutiae. All we insist upon is a sufficient indication that they have a fair understanding of what the alien's various relevant contentions of hardship, supported by the evidence, actually are; that they have meaningfully considered and evaluated each of these contentions; and that they provide a statement of the reasons why, in their opinion, these contentions do not, individually and in the aggregate, establish "extreme hardship."[103]

This statement is quite remarkable. In it, the Fifth Circuit acknowledges that they are mindful of the crushing caseloads of the administrative agencies, but the *Ramos* court clearly laid out their minimal expectations of what constitutes a proper adjudication to these administrative agencies, a review that must include individual assessments of an alien's specific situation.[104]

---

[102] 951 F.2d 117, 1121 (internal citations omitted).

[103] 695 F.2d 181, 188.

[104] See also *Mikhael v. Immigration and Naturalization Service*, 115 F.3d 299 (Fifth Circuit 1997) ("Nonetheless, we are charged with ensuring that the BIA has exercised its expertise in hearing a case.") See *Abdel-Masieh*, 73 F.3d at 585 (reversing BIA's decision and holding that its [the BIA's] decision must reflect meaningful consideration of the relevant substantial evidence supporting the alien's claim); and *Ullah v. Immigration and Naturalization Service*, 1995 U.S. App. LEXIS 38397 (9th Cir. 1995) ("[I]n determining that Ullah did not qualify for asylum or withholding of deportation, the BIA set out only general legal standards which failed to provide any evidence of an individualized review of Ullah's contentions and circumstances.").

The diversity in functions of the U.S. Supreme Court and the U.S. Courts of Appeals means that the two courts take dissimilar approaches in adjudicating cases; the Supreme Court takes a group-determination approach, while the Courts of Appeals are far more likely to take an individualized approach. I neither argue that the Supreme Court exclusively takes a group adjudication approach, nor do I argue that the Courts of Appeals exclusively adopt a case-by-case approach. What these cases show, however, is that the Courts of Appeals view individualized, case-by-case adjudication as very much a necessary and appropriate part of their mission and function. A residual benefit of this phenomenon is that an alien is more likely to win her case when a court takes an individualized approach, rather than when the alien's specific facts and claims are subsumed into a larger class of cases. An alien fairs better when her case is adjudicated on the basis of the unique facts than when her case is used as a vehicle to make a policy point about thousands of other similar cases. To reiterate, the individualized approach does not guarantee an alien victory, but it does increase the likelihood of it.

Checking Bureaucratic Errors

Although the founders conceived of a generic "judicial branch" that would counterbalance the power of the elected branches and their agents, it has largely fallen upon the federal district courts and Courts of Appeals to check the behavior of and correct the errors and abuses of the bureaucracy. The error correction, and sometimes ombudsman, role of the U.S. Courts of Appeals is yet another piece of evidence that the U.S. Supreme Court and the lower federal courts have evolved into very different institutional animals. Fifty-two percent of all U.S. Courts of Appeals cases in the dataset were appeals from the Board of Immigration Appeals. When one looks only at the unpublished decisions, the percentage of cases in the U.S. Courts of Appeals originating from the Board of Immigration Appeals is 78 percent. Between the published and unpublished decisions, a significant percentage of immigration cases are being appealed from the Board of Immigration Appeals (Table 3.1).

Given the large percentage of immigration appeals that originate in the administrative agencies, the U.S. Courts of Appeals' error correction and watchdog roles become all the more important. There has also recently been much concern about the professionalism, fairness, and evenhandedness accorded to immigrants by the immigration bureaucracy, particularly

TABLE 3.1. *Percentage of Immigration Appeals in the Courts of Appeals by Origin*

All cases in database	805 (52%) BIA	839 (48%*) federal district courts
Unpublished cases	356 (78%) BIA	8 (.02%*) federal district courts

*The percentages do not add up to 100 because a small percentage of appeals originate in the highest state courts.

the administrative officials such as immigration judges and the BIA.[105] Concerns about the efficiency and quality of administrative review and the effect on the judges of the Courts of Appeals is discussed in more detail in Chapter 5.

The immigration judges and the BIA, both of which are part of the Executive Office of Immigration Review, are two decision making bodies that are administrative (as opposed to judicial) in nature and one of the functions of the federal courts is to oversee administrative agency decisions and check any abuses of power or discretion. If there is a lack of confidence in administrative agency decisions and a belief that there are widespread abuses, as has been illustrated by recent high-profile reports criticizing immigration judges and the BIA, then there is added pressure on the federal court system. Given the small number of cases the Supreme Court accepts (205 cases between the years 1881–2002 compared with the 1,994 cases in the Third, Fifth, and Ninth Circuits for the same period), the burden falls squarely upon the Courts of Appeals to detect and rectify any administrative agency abuses and errors. In reality, it is the U.S. Courts of Appeals, rather than the U.S. Supreme Court, that have become the last lines of defense against bureaucratic errors and abuses.

There are laws and rules governing which types of administrative decisions are subject to judicial review. As Jerry Mashaw has noted, "Administrative law became in substantial part law describing the barriers to judicial review of administrative action."[106] The Administrative

---

[105] A comprehensive report dated July 31, 2006, by the Transactional Records Access Clearinghouse, a nonpartisan research division of Syracuse University, showed wide and troubling disparities in the asylum approval rates among the nation's 208 immigration judges. Also see "Immigration Appeals Swamp Federal Courts" by Claire Cooper and Emily Bazar in the *Sacramento Bee*, September 5, 2004, A1, criticizing the "boilerplate" decision text and sometimes sloppy decision making of the Board of Immigration Appeals.

[106] Jerry L. Marsaw, *Due Process in the Administrative State* (New Haven, CT: Yale University Press, 1985), 25–6.

Procedure Act (APA) defined judicial review as essentially a review of procedure and process. Some decisions that involve an "exercise of discretion" by the Attorney General of the United States and designated administrative agencies, such as the BIA, are not subject to judicial review, but other types of administrative decision are. The Supreme Court initially spelled out what immigration agency actions are covered by the federal APA in *Marcello v. Bonds* (1955).[107] However, many of the Courts of Appeals panels have adopted the position that it is for them to determine whether judicial review is warranted in each case. For example, in *Ravancho v. Immigration and Naturalization Service* (3d Cir. 1981), a suspension of deportation case, the majority voted to remand the case to the BIA because the Board had made several factual errors:

> We read the Supreme Court's *Wang* decision as reiterating the basic precept, which our prior opinion had also referred to, that Congress entrusted to the Attorney General, and not to the courts, discretion to determine whether a petitioner has shown extreme hardship to warrant suspension of deportation. We do not read that decision as foreclosing all judicial review regarding such matters, since such review is expressly provided in the statute. While the scope of such review may be narrow, it extends at least to a determination as to whether the procedure followed by the Board in a particular case constitutes an improper exercise of that discretion.[108]

In his dissent, Judge Aldisert argued that the majority had treated the precedent set by the Supreme Court case, *Immigration and Naturalization Service v. Wang* (1981), in a "cavalier" manner and that case was relevant to this one because it dealt with "the appropriate scope of judicial review of INS discretion."[109] The bureaucracy's claim of administrative discretion in some cases goes directly against the error-correction function of the federal courts and it is evident in many cases that the U.S. Courts of Appeals are walking a tightrope between administrative discretion and exercising their institutionally prescribed error-correction function.

I do not suggest that the Supreme Court willfully ignores bureaucratic abuses and errors. All the federal courts are still courts of law, not purely political institutions. As a result, the federal courts, including the U.S. Supreme Court, are still bound by legal norms of procedural fairness. Indeed Chapter 6 presents numerous examples of the Supreme

---

[107] 349 U.S. 302 (1955).
[108] 658 F.2d 169, 176 (some internal citations omitted).
[109] *Immigration and Naturalization Service v. Wang*, 450 U.S. 139, and *Ravancho v. Immigration and Naturalization Service*, 658 F.2d 169, 171.

Court's insistence on procedural protections for aliens even in the face of the dominance of the plenary power doctrine. Moreover, political battles erupted between Congress and the federal courts collectively when Congress tried to limit judicial review over discretionary decisions in the mid-1990s. In indicating that discretion has its limits, Justice Scalia's opinion, in which he concurred in part and dissented in part, in *Immigration and Naturalization Service v. Doherty* noted that while he agreed that both suspension of deportation and adjustment of status are discretionary grants of relief, "even discretion, however, has its legal limits."[110] Nevertheless, this particular viewpoint, to insist on holding administrative discretion to legal limits despite congressional directives to be deferential, is much more frequently expressed by the Courts of Appeals. The situation is due to two factors: the large number and volume of cases the Courts of Appeals adjudicated compared with the Supreme Court and the primary error correction function of the Courts of Appeals. It was also clear from cases that when the U.S. Courts of Appeals scrutinized exercises of administrative discretion, these courts' insistence on holding administrative discretion to compliance with legal standards of due process and basic fairness derived from the judges' belief that such judicial review was in line with the mission and duty of their court.

The U.S. Courts of Appeals' perceptions that they are playing their proper role in providing judicial review (and ultimately judicial oversight) over administrative agency actions is tied to the judges' role perception and transcends the ideological reputation of the circuit as well as the individual ideologies of the judges. An *en banc* panel of the Ninth Circuit, for example, has held that the BIA's broad discretion to deny motions to reopen is not beyond judicial review." *Watkins v. Immigration and Naturalization Service* (9th Cir. 1995).[111] The panel in *Watkins* bluntly concluded:

In this case, the BIA's actions were simply irrational...The BIA's denial of the motion to reopen in this case for the sole reason that petitioner appealed her deportation order was an abuse of discretion. It was arbitrary, irrational, and capricious because every motion to reopen could be denied on these grounds. This standard leaves the BIA free to decide cases based on whim or prejudice. This is especially true where, as in this case, the BIA does not consider all relevant factors and fails to articulate a reasoned basis for its decision.[112]

---

[110] *Immigration and Naturalization Service v. Doherty*, 502 U.S. 314, 329 (Scalia, J., Stevens, J., Souter, J., dissenting).
[111] 63 F.3d 844, 855 (some internal citations omitted).
[112] 63 F.3d 844, 850–851.

Similarly, in *Sida et al. v. Immigration and Naturalization Service* (9th Cir. 1981), the panel, in fairly strong language, chided the BIA:

Just as an alien is entitled to consideration of all relevant factors that may establish extreme hardship, an alien should be entitled to consideration of new evidence presented in support of a motion to reopen. Otherwise we open the door to potentially arbitrary administrative decisions as to what new evidence will be considered and what new evidence will be cast aside. The better approach requires the BIA to consider an alien's newly available evidence and to rule on the merits; it does not allow the BIA to refuse to consider new evidence whenever it feels that the alien, for whatever reason, does not merit any consideration.[113]

Likewise, the Fifth Circuit, in *Hernandez Cordero v. Immigration and Naturalization Service* (5th Cir. 1987), which was decided *en banc*, adopted a similar approach. Four other judges, including Judge Edith Jones, who was considered for elevation to the Supreme Court by President George W. Bush, joined the dissent, authored by Judge Rubin:

The majority opinion professes to adhere to the statutory mandate that federal courts review decisions made by subordinate government officials, but in fact the opinion adopts a standard of review that renders administrative decision making unreviewable. The court thus abandons these "honest, dependable, hardworking members of society" to the indifference of the bureaucracy...This interpretation strips the phrase "extreme hardship" of virtually all content and abdicates our responsibility under the Administrative Procedure Act to assure against arbitrary and capricious administrative action.[114]

The dissent also added that they had taken into consideration the position of the decision maker:

In determining what Congress intended to be the breadth of administrative discretion and the scope of judicial review over its exercise, we should also consider the rank of the official whose decision is reviewed. Congress may rightly decide that cabinet officers deserve more latitude in making decisions than is accorded lower-ranking civil servants in making routine pronouncements. As the majority opinion recognizes, however, it was not the Attorney General who made or reviewed this administrative decision. He has delegated his authority to 65 special inquiry officers, as the statute labels them, who have by regulation been elevated in title to judges. Their decisions are in turn subject to review only by an internal group, the Board of Immigration Appeals. Neither the Attorney General, his Deputy Attorney General, nor any of his Assistant Attorneys General has ever considered whether deportation of the Hernandez family would occasion them extreme hardship. This decision was made in the depths of the bureaucracy...The leitmotiv of the majority opinion is, "Let the bureaucracy do as it will." The

[113] 665 F.2d 851, 854.
[114] 819 F.2d 558, 564.

Administrative Procedure Act, however, commands us to review the decisions of such administrative officers to determine whether they have made a clear error of judgment. If they have, the decision is an abuse of discretion.[115]

This statement indicates the panel's skepticism at granting blanket deference to administrative agency personnel, especially to a faceless bureaucrat "in the depths of the bureaucracy." This quote also illustrates the politics of deference that is discussed in more detail in Chapter Five. Much of the disagreement between the Courts of Appeals and among the judges themselves is about the proper level of deference to give to administrative decision makers. The tension in the circuits and among judges is rooted in the clash of the Courts of Appeals' (and to a lesser extent the Supreme Court's) institutional function as error correctors and statutory directives to defer.

The contemporary U.S. Courts of Appeals continue to take their error-correction role and their task of policing the bureaucracy seriously. Indeed, in a number of cases, the Courts of Appeals chastised the INS in very blunt language for not following its own rules, and put the agency on notice that the courts would be closely scrutinizing them. In an asylum case of a man from El Salvador, *Rios-Berrios v. Immigration and Naturalization Service* (9th Cir. 1985)[116] the INS had argued that Rios-Berrios, who spoke no English and who had been transported to an INS detention center far away from where he was apprehended, had knowingly waived his right to counsel in the deportation hearing. The majority noted that under such circumstances, the adjudication "demanded more than lip service to the right of counsel declared in statute and agency regulations."[117] The panel further noted, "We are not in favor of an agency treating the statutes and regulations by which it is governed as casually as it viewed them here. We will continue to take a close look at a claim such as that raised by petitioner, especially where so fundamental a question as right to counsel of one's choice is concerned."[118]

The Fifth Circuit also adopted the same approach in the deportation case of *Jung Ben Suh v. Immigration and Naturalization Service* (5th Cir. 1979).[119] Suh had arrived on a nonimmigrant visa, overstayed, and now found himself in deportation proceedings. In vacating and remanding the case, the Fifth Circuit panel wrote that the INS was in error in having

[115] 819 F.2d 558, 567.
[116] 776 F.2d 859.
[117] 776 F.2d 859, 863.
[118] 776 F.2d 859, 863–864.
[119] 592 F.2d 230.

accepted and adjudicated Suh's application for an employment visa in the first place when the agency knew that there were no visa numbers available. They wrote, "We do not look with favor upon the INS violation of its own regulations...He would have secured adjustment of status and avoided deportation."[120] These were but a few examples of the actions of the Courts of Appeals in continuing their role of scrutinizing administrative agency actions.

Whereas Kitty Calavita and others have noted that Congress dodged contradictions in immigration policy by delegating tremendous authority and discretion to the "less visible and politically vulnerable administrative enclaves" such as the INS, federal judges operate by an entirely different calculus.[121] Federal judges, as unelected officials, do not need to respond to public pressure about the efficacy of immigration enforcement. Indeed the whole point of their life tenure is to allow them to check executive, legislative, and administrative agency abuses without fear of political or electoral reprisal. And this is precisely the role the U.S. Courts of Appeals continue to perform, far more so in fact than the Supreme Court, which is preoccupied by policy and political concerns.

CONCLUSION

The Supreme Court that was originally designed as an appellate court that just happened to sit at the top of the judicial hierarchy has now largely ceased to be a true "court of review."[122] The vast majority of the Court's appellate functions have been taken over by the U.S. Courts of Appeals; today, these are effectively the courts of last resort for nearly all federal litigants. Whereas those courts were originally created to help alleviate the Supreme Court's caseload, the Courts of Appeals have developed into courts that "initiate and conclude many policy questions of federal litigation."[123] In fact, neither the U.S. Supreme Court nor any of the U.S. Courts of Appeals is quite performing the same functions today for which each was originally designed.

The increase in federal caseloads in general, not just the immigration caseload, has further reinforced the parallel but distinctive development paths of the Supreme Court and Courts of Appeals. The contemporary

---

[120] 592 F.2d 230, 232 (some internal citations omitted).

[121] Kitty Calavita, *Inside the State: The Bracero Program*, 9.

[122] Richard J. Richardson and Kenneth N. Vines, *The Politics of Federal Courts* (Boston, MA: Little, Brown and Company, 1970), 149.

[123] Richardson and Vines, *The Politics of Federal Courts*, 128–29.

Supreme Court and Courts of Appeals now perform unique functions and, at times, seem to have goals and missions that are contrary to each other. The Supreme Court today is primarily a policy and political court as it routinely serves as tiebreaker among lower courts. The Courts of Appeals retain much of their originally designed error correction function. But because the U.S. Supreme Court grants *certiorari* to so few cases, it is effectively the U.S. Courts of Appeals that are charged with oversight over the vast and extensive administrative bureaucracy in immigration and other areas of law. This is not to say that the Supreme Court has forsaken all its institutional roles as a legal institution; it remains a legal institution, but the Supreme Court and Courts of Appeals today have distinct roles in the federal judicial hierarchy.

This division of labor has profound consequences for litigants. For better or for worse, the Courts of Appeals are set up to do more individualized review of the cases while the Supreme Court, by virtue of its evolved position at the top of judicial hierarchy, is geared toward aggregate review. As the examples in this chapter demonstrate, although it is no guarantee of a victory, one has a better chance of winning if one's case is adjudicated with an individualized approach, rather than having one's case chosen by the Supreme Court to use as a means of setting precedent for a broad set of similarly situated cases.

The federal judiciary as a whole embodies sometimes-conflicting missions and functions. The Supreme Court especially has had to balance its policy making and political role with its still ongoing mission as a court of law. Both sets of institutionally derived contexts prescribe certain kinds of behavior for the Court, whose imperatives sometimes are at odds. What one learns from this case of intercurrence within the federal judiciary is that such a phenomenon may serve a practical function: the ostensible mission conflict within the *same* institution can be accommodated, and to some extent mitigated, by a differentiation in function and in the various segments of the judiciary. Such a division of labor does not preclude all mission conflict within the federal courts, but it does reduce the frequency of such conflict.

Orren and Skowronek have noted that institutions may not be synchronized in function or design because different institutions have dissimilar reasons for their creation, a phenomenon that they term "intercurrence." In the development of the federal judiciary, one can see a segment of the hierarchy that has risen in stature and prestige far outstripping that of the lower federal courts. Along with the increased prestige of the Supreme Court came revised roles and altered missions and expectations of that

Court and of the Courts of Appeals. Often these new roles and missions bore little resemblance to the early conceptualizations of the institution. As one will see in the next chapter, sometimes the roles and missions of the U.S. Supreme Court and of the U.S. Courts of Appeals work at cross-purposes. American political development scholars have noted that this kind of internal conflict and contradiction is a hallmark of institutional design process where new policies are overlaid over existing policy choices and the institutions are in fact created "at different times" and often for "quite contrary purposes."[124] The institutional development of the federal judiciary illustrates that different components within the *same* institution may also be characterized as intercurrent.

[124] Karen Orren and Stephen Skowronek, "Beyond the Iconography of Order: Notes a 'New Intuitionalism,'" in Lawrence C. Dodd and Calvin Jilson, eds., *The Dynamics of American Politics: Approaches and Interpretations* (New York: Westview Press, 1993), 311–30; and Karen Orren and Stephen Skowronek, *The Search for American Political Development* (New York: Cambridge University Press, 2004), 112.

4

Interstitial Policy Making in the U.S. Courts of Appeals

The federal courts are distinct from the immigration bureaucracy, Congress, and the presidency because, as courts of law, they embody institutional rules and norms that are indigenous and specific to legal institutions, such as doctrinal constraints and the hierarchical nature of the appellate process. Unlike the legislative and the executive branches, where overt and aggressive political maneuvering to obtain one's objective is allowable and expected, in the judicial branch this same behavior in the appointed branch of government is construed as inappropriate, if not illegal. As a result, while some modes of legal reasoning, such as textualism, structuralism, doctrine, and others are acceptable in deciding cases, other modes of legal reasoning, such as one's personal views (in this instance, on immigration policy or toward particular nationalities) or personal whims, are illegitimate in the context of legal decision making.[1]

Nevertheless, there are still opportunities for judges and justices to engage in behavior with an intent to reach one legal result over another. While much of the tactical maneuvering that goes on at the Supreme Court takes place in the form of interactions and reactions of the justices to each other, similar behavior at contemporary U.S. Courts of Appeals is subtler. As Judge A characterized it, the nature of the U.S. Courts of Appeals is that those courts are "interstitial policy makers."[2] In the

[1] Ronald Khan and Ken Kersch, "Introduction," in Ronald Khan and Ken Kersch, eds., *The Supreme Court & American Political Development* (Lawrence, KS: University of Kansas Press, 2006), 17–18.
[2] Interview with Judge A, 6/18/07. All pronouns used to refer to the judges are feminine and may not match the actual sex of the judge.

U.S. Courts of Appeals, purposive action manifests less in the interaction between judges and much more in the judges' personal judgments in exercises of discretion and creative statutory interpretation. Still, these exercises of discretion are subject to institutional limits and supports.

The nature of judicial decision making, with its reliance on positive law and the concomitant indeterminacy of text, leaves openings for judges to pursue their policy choices if they wish to. The hierarchical structure of the appellate process, the fact that each person has a different threshold of belief in judging evidence, and the very adjudicative procedures of the U.S. Courts of Appeals themselves, all also provide openings for exercises of discretion. The discretionary exercises found in the set of immigration cases in this study included determining the level of scrutiny brought to bear on the facts of the case, raising or lowering one's threshold of belief while evaluating the credibility of witnesses and evidence, and determining whether to defer to the preceding decision making body or to second-guess it. In addition, these exercises of discretion are made with regard for the relations between the decision making bodies above and below the U.S. Courts of Appeals, namely the U. S. Supreme Court and the administrative agency units given the sequencing of the litigation chain.

Judges at any level of the judiciary have always had opportunities to interpret law. And it is now an accepted maxim among public law scholars that the power to interpret law is to make law. However, the contemporary Courts of Appeals, by virtue of their increasing independence from the Supreme Court, and as compared with the historical circuit courts and U.S. Courts of Appeals, have more opportunities given the much larger number of cases they adjudicate, and arguably more institutionally created incentives to engage in creative interpretation and exercises of discretion. None of the behavior described in this chapter is illegal or remotely approaches the level of civil disobedience. Indeed, the behavior detailed in this chapter demonstrates that one need not go outside the bounds of legality or professionalism to effectively realize one's policy preferences. The goal of this chapter is neither to test a model of judicial decision making, nor to make the argument that U.S. Courts of Appeals judges always or even frequently engage in these types of behavior. Instead the aim is to delineate a range of options and opportunities that policy-oriented judges have and to show how these are enabled and limited by institutional norms and structures. In so doing, I explicate the processes and mechanisms that characterize purposive behavior and its relations to the institutional structures that motivate and create opportunities for their behavior at the U.S. Courts of Appeals. My approach overlaps to some extent with some game theory studies that also take into account the influence of institutional structures.[3] The difference is that the historical institutionalist approach of this book attempts to study the influence of institutional norms and structures across time.

In *Federalist 78*, Hamilton worried that the federal judiciary would be the weakest and "least dangerous branch" of government because of its inability to control the armed forces, as the president did, or to control the mechanisms of taxation and revenue, as the Congress did. Mostly, Hamilton worried that the judicial branch would not have any real power because, he noted in the well-known quote, "The judiciary...may truly be said to have neither FORCE nor WILL, but merely judgment."[4] When they wrote those words, the framers could not have known that the judicial branch, and the Supreme Court in particular, would evolve into the powerful institution that it is today. The contemporary Supreme Court is now a coequal branch of government with the Congress and the presidency, thereby negating any early concern that the judicial branch would be overrun by the other two branches of government. Moreover, Hamilton and the framers of the constitution greatly underestimated the creativity of the judges of the federal judiciary to exercise their judgment in savvy ways, not just to register their opinion, but also to actually create law and policy. It turns out that "mere judgment" can be a powerful tool in the hands of those members of the U.S. Supreme Court and the U.S. Courts of Appeals who wish to reach a particular legal outcome.

HOW IS POLICY MADE IN THE U.S. COURTS OF APPEALS?

Given the focus on the Supreme Court in most political science research on the court system, there are many fine studies that explore what constitutes strategic behavior at the Court. In the context of rational choice scholarship and its variants, "strategic behavior" in the courts has a very precise meaning. As defined by Lee Epstein and Jack Knight, "strategic decision making is about *interdependent* choice: an individual's action is, in part, a function of her expectations about the actions of others."[5] Epstein and Knight's work was inspired by Walter Murphy who, in his

---

[3] See, e.g., McNollgast, "Politics and the Courts: A Positive Theory of Judicial Doctrine and the Rule of Law," 68 *Southern California Law Review* 1631 (1995).

[4] Alexander Hamilton, *Federalist 78*, "The Judiciary Department," *Independent Journal*, Saturday, June 14, 1788. (Original capitalization.)

[5] Lee Epstein and Jack Knight, *The Choices Justices Make* (Washington, DC: Congressional Quarterly Press, 1998), 12. (Emphasis in original.)

classic work *Elements of Judicial Strategy*, detailed some of the internal interactions and horse-trading that may go on at the Supreme Court in various stages of the decision making process and especially at the stage where draft opinions are circulated.[6] In that vein, Epstein and Knight further documented and expounded on the strategic behavior that takes place at the Supreme Court. Key to Epstein and Knight's definition of "strategic behavior" is the interdependent nature of the judges' decision making. As they explain it, "To say that a justice acts strategically is to say that she realizes that her success or failure depends on the preferences of other actors and the actions she expects them to take, not just on her own preferences and actions."[7] Yet there are many different varieties of behavior that can be construed as strategic, including but not limited to the Supreme Court justices' decision to grant certiorari or not, judges' decisions about when to write a separate opinion, and the factors that make a U.S. Courts of Appeals case more or less likely to be granted *en banc* review.[8] Common to all of the studies on these types of behavior is a focus on the actions and reactions to actors on the court and in the court above or below it in the litigation sequence of the appeal.

As a collegial court with nine members, the Supreme Court is certainly fertile ground for the study of strategic and what I term "purposive" behavior. Murphy, Epstein and Knight, and many others have also indicated that much of this behavior at the Supreme Court is in response to institutional norms, conventions, and structures (such as the "Rule of Four" to grant *certiorari*). However, their research does not zero in on the particular effects of institutional setting, and much of their discussions of strategic and purposive behavior on the Supreme Court focuses on the interaction of the justices with each other. Instead, this book shifts the emphasis to spotlight the constraining effects of institutional setting on judicial decision making.

I use the word "purposive" to distinguish the analytic approach taken in this book from the judicial politics literature on "strategic" behavior, which has a very specific meaning that refers to the judges or justices

[6] Murphy, *Elements of Judicial Strategy*. See chapter 2, "Marshalling the Court."

[7] Epstein and Knight, *The Choices Justices Make*, 12.

[8] See, e.g., Gregory A. Caldeira, John R. Wright, and Christopher J.W. Zorn, "Sophisticated Voting and Gate-Keeping in the Supreme Court," *Journal of Law, Economics and Organization* 15(3):549–72; Tracey George, "The Dynamics and Determinations of the Decision to Grant En Banc Review," 74 *Washington Law Review* 213–74 (1999); H.W. Perry, Jr., *Deciding to Decide: Agenda Setting in the United States Supreme Court* (Cambridge: Harvard University Press, 1991); and Murphy, *Elements of Judicial Strategy*.

anticipating and reacting to the actions of other judges and justices and other political actors. By contrast, the analytical approach in this book posits that legal decisions are informed by the interplay of legal, strategic, and attitudinal elements. The purposive approach rejects the notion that legal outcomes are the direct output of a judge's or justice's policy preferences. Put differently, the motivations influencing a judge or justice to reach one legal outcome are more than a reflection of their preferred policy outcomes; there is the intervening and constraining effect of institutional norms and structures of the U.S. Supreme Court and U.S. Courts of Appeals. Although there is no tolerance for naked politics in the federal courts and the rules and norms of the courts are "not infinitely malleable,"[9] judges can still behave in a purposive manner even within these limits. In fact, the rules, norms, and structures can simultaneously constrain and allow legal decision making by, on the one hand, permitting and perhaps even encouraging the exercise of certain types of discretion, while on the other hand circumscribing other types of purposive action.

Many other studies have examined the nature of strategic or purposive behavior at the Supreme Court; however, fewer have assessed the same phenomenon at the U.S. Courts of Appeals.[10] In the existing strategic studies on the Courts of Appeals, many focus on the strategic elements of *en banc* review or how dissents at the Courts of Appeals may raise a red flag and induce the Supreme Court to grant review, should the case be appealed further.[11] What is the parallel behavior in the U.S. Courts of Appeals when decisions are made by a panel of three judges? The membership on these panels is neither set nor predictable. In the Ninth Circuit Court of Appeals, for example, a computer program randomly

[9] Walter Murphy, *Elements of Judicial Strategy* (Princeton, NJ: Princeton University Press, 1973), 31.

[10] A study by McNollgast, "Politics and the Courts: A Positive Theory of Judicial Doctrine and the Rule of Law," examines strategic behavior of the Supreme Court and how and when it might police lower courts that are not in doctrinal compliance. However, the focus is not on the purposive actions that lower courts judges might take to pursue their policy preferences.

[11] Barry Friedman notes in "Taking Law Seriously," *Perspectives in Political Science* 4, No.2 (2006), 265, that "[w]hile everyone seems to have some sense of what it means for a Supreme Court justice to act strategically, this is less clear for the lower courts." Some exceptions are Virginia A. Hettinger, Stefanie A. Lindquist, and Wendy L. Martinek, "Comparing Attitudinal and Strategic Accounts of Dissenting Behavior on the U.S. Courts of Appeals," *American Journal of Political Science* 48: 123–37 (2004); David Klein's *Decision Making in the U.S. Courts of Appeals* (New York: Cambridge University Press, 2000); Frank Cross and Emerson Tiller, "Judicial Partisanship and Obedience to Legal Doctrine: Whistleblowing on the Federal Courts of Appeals," 107 *Yale Law Journal* 2155–76 (1999).

selects and forms panels of three judges to hear cases. Similarly, aside from the rule that the Chief Judge must sit on every *en banc* panel, a computer also randomly draws the *en banc* panels of fifteen judges at the Ninth Circuit. To be sure, many of the kinds of considerations documented on the Supreme Court, such as the necessity of obtaining the required threshold number of votes to assure one's majority position, also occur at the U.S. Courts of Appeals, which are collegial courts. However, there are significant differences in the types of behavior available to the judges of the U.S. Courts of Appeals and the justices of the U.S. Supreme Court.

H.W. Perry and others have examined the phenomenon of "defensive denials" and "aggressive grants"[12] in regard to the Supreme Court justices' strategy in deciding whether or not to grant a case *certiorari*; such behavior has no direct parallel at the Courts of Appeals. While the Supreme Court can pick and choose its cases, the Courts of Appeals cannot and therefore must adjudicate all cases properly appealed to it. In short, purposive behavior in the U.S. Courts of Appeals is necessarily different from such behavior at the U.S. Supreme Court for the simple reason that strategies available to Supreme Court judges may not be available to Courts of Appeals judges given that the rules, operational procedures, and norms governing the different levels of the courts are not the same.

Conversely, some kinds of actions are available at the Courts of Appeals and not at the Supreme Court. For example, Burton Atkins writes about strategies that flow "as a consequence of the decision making rules operative in the appellate circuits courts" such as for a judge to wait for "the luck of the draw" in the construction of the three-judge panels to place her on a panel with like-minded judges who share her policy point of view.[13] He also refers to some of the strategic considerations that U.S. Court of Appeals judges might take into account, such as in deciding which cases to send for an *en banc* hearing.[14] Atkins is right that "the options available to a policy-oriented judge depend to some extent upon formal decision–making rules which operate within the court."[15] Although both the U.S. Supreme Court and the U.S. Courts of Appeals gain opportunities to pursue their policy preferences through vague text, other kinds of purposive behavior in the Courts of Appeals

[12] Perry, *Deciding to Decide*, 198–212.
[13] Burton M. Atkins, "Decision Making Rules and Judicial Strategy on the United States Courts of Appeals," *The Western Political Quarterly* 25, 4 (1972): 626–42, 626–7.
[14] Ibid. at 630–1.
[15] Ibid. at 627.

are attributable to the specific rules and norms of operation of those courts that are not available at the Supreme Court.

SOURCES OF POLICY MAKING OPPORTUNITIES

As illustrated in the Ninth Circuit, policy making in immigration appeals derive in part from two main decision making rules that function on top of the usual policy making opportunities inherent in statutory interpretation. The first is the composition of the panel and the second is the internal procedure of the Ninth Circuit's screening panels that allows any one judge to "kick" a case back to the oral argument track which, as explained in Chapter 5, provides more detailed judges' review of the case than the screening track cases. Indeed Judge G said in her interview, "Of *course* it matters to the aliens which mix of judges they [the aliens] get on their panel!" She further explained that in many cases, it comes down to a judge's basic attitudes toward people's rights, and that this is true in all kinds of cases and not just immigration cases.[16] Judge D stated, "You can predict the outcome of [immigration] cases based on the panel composition. Some people will always vote against aliens; some people will always vote for them. No one will tell you this."[17] These judges' comments beg the question of exactly how panel composition matters at the U.S. Courts of Appeals. How does a judge purposively realize her policy preferences in immigration cases?

One may also wonder about the role of ideology in judicial decision making. The relationship of the ideology of the judges to the way they decide immigration cases is a tricky one; in other contexts, such as in congressional studies and voting behavior, the immigration issue does not manifest as a classically ideological issue. To further complicate the matter, in the judicial arena, there are also confounding influences on a judge's ideology created by the constraints of institutional structures and norms. Elsewhere a coauthor and I have assessed the question of ideology and asylum cases in the Courts of Appeals.[18] The point is that institutional settings, which shape the role perception of judges and justices, are

[16] Interview with Judge G, 7/27/07.
[17] Interview with Judge D, 6/13/07.
[18] Anna O. Law and Margaret S. Williams, "Understanding Judicial Decision Making in Immigration Cases at the Courts of Appeals." Paper prepared for presentation at the 2009 Midwest Political Science Association Convention in Chicago, IL, April 2–5, 2009 (available at http://www.allacademic.com/meta/p_mla_apa_research_citation/3/6/3/8/1/p363814_index.html).

interactive variables mediating any influence of ideology on legal decision making. In that sense, ideology is not really the relevant unit of analysis and is almost superfluous. The reason is that one who is acting based on their ideological proclivities must still operate within the institutional constraints of a court of law. Instead, the question that this book strives to answer is, "Regardless of their ideology, what options do pro-alien or pro-government judges have in deciding a case to reach a desired outcome?" and "How do institutional contexts constrain or encourage the pursuit of a preferred legal outcome?"

As is the case for the Supreme Court, one source of purposive behavior at the Courts of Appeals derives from the limits of positive law and the corresponding flexibility created by statutory interpretation. However, additional opportunities for the pursuit of one's policy preferences also arise when a case is fact driven and fact intensive, as are many immigration cases, especially asylum cases. These policy making opportunities are enhanced by the hierarchical setup of the appeals process and the docket control mechanisms of the Courts of Appeals and the Supreme Court. A judge or justice may also exercise her discretion in a number of ways that can influence the final disposition of a case. These exercises of discretion, for example, can determine the level of scrutiny a judge or justice brings to a case, which has implications for the outcome of the case. The hierarchical structure of the appeals process and the fact that the Supreme Court accepts so few cases for review may create additional incentives for Courts of Appeals judges to exercise their discretion with a goal toward realizing their policy preferences.

The Limits of Positive Law

Many opportunities to make law by interpreting law are gained from the confines of positive law, law that is created in civil society. This is the case because text cannot be written to cover every conceivable permutation of human experience and behavior, nor can text be guaranteed to elicit the same interpretation and understanding from multiple readers. Furthermore, as R. Shep Melnick and others have noted, although statutory interpretation is not commonly regarded as a form of strategic or purposive behavior, the fact is that for federal judges, there are "no generally accepted, authoritative methods" of how to interpret statutes.[19]

---

[19] R. Shep Melnick, *Between the Lines: Interpreting Welfare Rights* (Washington, DC: The Brookings Institution, 1994), 6.

As Justice Antonin Scalia lamented, "We American judges have no intelligible theory of what we do most."[20] Inherent in the nature of positive law are blanks and areas of fuzziness that allow and sometimes even require a judgment call on the part of the judges. In *The Elements of Judicial Strategy*, Murphy pointed to the federal judiciary's ability to interpret statutes and executive orders as a source of the judiciary's power. The power of statutory interpretation flows from the limitations of positive law itself, in particular the "broad language of the constitution," conflicting pieces of legislation, and the "limitations inherent in the use of words."[21] When confronted with conflicting statutes, judges are free to choose the version that comes closest to their preferred legal outcome, or, as Melnick described, to read between the lines "in order to give specific meaning to vague legislative language."[22] Opaque language and competing statutory language virtually invite judges to read their own interpretations and policy preferences into the text. Even when the text is not vague, the "limitations inherent in the use of words" means that words and text lack the precision of conveying one precise meaning to the exclusion of others.[23] Also, if one word or phrase can hold multiple meanings, then judges can adopt a meaning different from that adopted by the previous decision makers. Murphy termed judges' reading or interpreting their own preferences into text as "judicial legislation under the guise of statutory interpretation."[24] Melnick noted that statutory interpretation is a tool that can be used by judges who are "wary of experimentation but eager to do good."[25] The opinions in this study were replete with examples supporting Murphy and Melnick's contentions that statutory interpretation is a source of judicial power and enables the pursuit of policy preferences.

The Rise of Statutory Interpretation

Statutory interpretation as a mode of legal reasoning has become a powerful tool for policy-minded judges to pursue their preferences. Figure 4.1 shows that although the U.S. Supreme Court utilizes statutory interpretation in immigration cases more frequently than do the U.S. Courts of

[20] Antonin Scalia, *A Matter of Interpretation: Federal Courts and the Law* (Princeton, NJ: Princeton University Press, 1997), 14.
[21] Murphy, *Elements of Judicial Strategy*, 14–15.
[22] Melnick, *Between the Lines*, 6.
[23] Murphy, *Elements of Judicial Strategy*, citing John Marshall, 15.
[24] Murphy, *Elements of Judicial Strategy*, 14.
[25] Melnick, *Between the Lines*, 40.

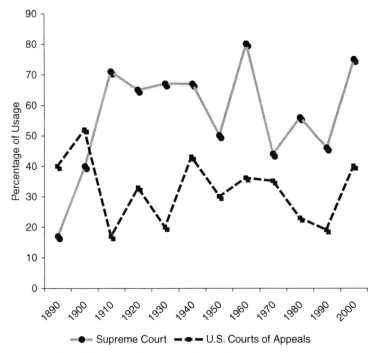

FIGURE 4.1. Use of Statutory Interpretation, 1881–2002

Appeals, the two courts have consistently used this mode of legal reasoning over time. Figure 4.1 also shows that although the Supreme Court uses statutory interpretation in a higher percentage of cases than the Courts of Appeals, in recent decades the Courts of Appeals are also more likely to use statutory interpretation. The increase in the use of statutory interpretation by the U.S. Courts of Appeals, combined with the miniscule number of cases to which the Supreme Court *certiorari* means that over time, the Courts of Appeals have become policy makers in their own right in a growing number of cases.

The proliferation of statutory interpretation at both levels of the courts can be attributed to a number of factors. There has been a trend toward the profusion of statutes that are simultaneously more vague and more complex than prior pieces of legislation on the subject. Additionally, there is a drift toward the legislative process becoming increasingly complicated, with the onset of an era of divided government that has produced sometimes vague and incoherent statutes.[26] Some of these trends were

[26] Melnick, *Between the Lines*, 28–31.

certainly true of immigration policy, where there has been an increase in the number of statutes over time. Adding to these developments are the factors discussed in the previous chapter that boosted the immigration caseload, such as the judicialization of immigration and the selective enforcement strategies of the federal government beginning in the mid-1980s. All of these processes worked together to greatly increase the overall number of immigration appeals headed to the federal courts and to multiply the opportunities for purposive behavior through statutory interpretation.

In addition to determining whether laws and government actions are consistent with the Constitution of the United States, a large portion of the cases that come before the U.S. Supreme Court and U.S. Courts of Appeals require the justices or judges to be tie-breakers in a dispute about what a particular law or statute actually means. Supreme Court judges are routinely asked to interpret statutes; increasingly, the Courts of Appeals judges also must spend a significant amount of time at this task. The rise of statutory interpretation has opened the door for policy making by the Courts of Appeals. The close reading of the cases in this study revealed that there are a number of informal and sometimes unstated processes whereby judges can engage in creative textual or statutory interpretation to reach a desired result. One way to do so is by second-guessing the decision making body that came before.

Given that statutory interpretation and the evaluation of facts and evidence are two of the most frequently used modes of legal reasoning in the U.S. Courts of Appeals, one gains a general sense of the number of opportunities presented by these approaches to deciding cases. Unlike the flexibility created by vague text, the purposive opportunities created by the exercises of discretion involve judges' bringing different levels of scrutiny to bear on the facts of a case. There is also evidence suggesting that the level of scrutiny judges bring to a case may well affect the outcome when the cases are fact/evidence driven, like many of the thousands of political asylum cases in immigration. The remainder of this chapter investigates the processes by which these two modes of legal reasoning can be deployed purposively by U.S. Courts of Appeals judges and how the two approaches are constrained and encouraged by institutional structures of the federal judiciary and the immigration bureaucracy.

Unclear or Vague Language

Statutory interpretation is a powerful tool at both the U.S. Supreme Court and the U.S. Courts of Appeals in engaging in purposive decision making, but does this process involve the interpretation of facts or the interpretation of law? In his article "Taking Law Seriously," Barry Friedman criticizes political science research on law and courts for conflating distinctions between questions of law and questions of fact, a distinction that is a crucial one in the legal world because as Friedman explains, "it often defines who the relevant decision maker is…Whether trial is by judge or jury, appellate courts tend to defer to factual determinations of lower courts."[27] According to Friedman, the fact versus law distinction not only signifies who the decision maker should be, but it also prescribes the level of discretion an appellate court should accord the determination/interpretation of the text or legal term given by the fact finder. He offers the example of the term "probable cause" where the interpretation of that term is one of law instead of fact because such interpretation "depends on resolution of deeper policy questions." In addition, the determination of probable cause is to be "reviewed de novo (afresh) on appeal."[28] It is true that in many of the cases in this study, where the U.S. Courts of Appeals were asked to undertake statutory interpretation, the judges were required to define terms such as "extreme hardship" and "good moral character," which law professors such as Friedman would clearly classify as determinations of law. However, in many other immigration opinions, the judges were required to determine the meaning of seemingly straightforward words such as "adultery" and "custody." Are these determinations of law or determinations of fact? For many terms like "probable cause" or "due process" it seems clear that a legal determination is required. But the law versus fact distinction is not a clean binary and there is no clear dividing line between the determination of law and the determination of fact. As illustrated by some of the examples to follow, when there is no clear distinction between the interpretation of law and the interpretation of fact, the hierarchical structure of the appellate process becomes significant. In effect, regardless of whether they are engaging in interpreting law or facts, U.S. Courts of Appeals judges are overriding the determinations of the adjudicators below them in the appellate chain.

Realizing the policy making potential and flexibility inherent in statutory interpretation, the Supreme Court has attempted to limit the range of interpretation by advising the lower courts to defer to administrative policy makers if these policy makers have put forth a "reasonable" interpretation of the statutes. In *Chevron v. National Resources Defense*

---

[27] Friedman, "Taking Law Seriously," 268.
[28] Friedman, "Taking Law Seriously," 268.

Council (1984), the Supreme Court advised that in interpreting statutes, if the intent of Congress is clear, then "that is the end of the matter" because the court and the administrative agency must give way to the intent of Congress.[29] However, if the court determines that Congress "has not directly addressed the issue," or that the statute "is silent or ambiguous on the issue," then the court may *not* "simply impose its own construction on the statute."[30] Instead, the court should decide whether the administrative agency has put forth a "permissible" construction of the statute.[31] In the *Chevron* case the Court made clear that the federal court "may not substitute its own construction of a statutory provision for a *reasonable* interpretation made by the administrator of an agency."[32] Although this doctrine attempts to limit when an appeals court may exercise its statutory interpretation powers, it has not prevented purposive behavior because the *Chevron* formula begs the question of what is a "reasonable" interpretation. In the view of less deferential appellate judges, *Chevron* applies only in cases where the statute and congressional intent are clear; if it is not clear, then all bets are off and the judges may render their own interpretation in lieu of an interpretation they now deem unreasonable. However, more deferential judges might take the opposite view and accept the administrative agency's interpretation as long as it is reasonable. The structure of the appellate process again becomes determinative; the Supreme Court simply cannot or will not police all the Courts of Appeals panels that have not, in the Court's view, shown sufficient *Chevron* deference to the administrative decision makers.

The fact that the contemporary U.S. Courts of Appeals enjoy a substantial degree of insulation from Supreme Court supervision has augmented the opportunities and incentives for judges to take liberties in statutory interpretation. Simply put, the U.S. Courts of Appeals adjudicate tens of thousands more cases than the Supreme Court does. The Supreme Court in recent years has granted oral argument to about 80–100 cases (not just immigration cases) from the more than 7,000 petitions on all kinds of cases that it receives each year.[33] With regard to immigration cases in particular, between the years 1881 and 2002, the Supreme Court decided 200 immigration cases; the eleven U.S. Courts of Appeals decided a

[29] 467 U.S. 837, 843–44.
[30] 467 U.S. 837, 843.
[31] Ibid.
[32] Ibid. at 844. (Emphasis added.)
[33] Lawrence Baum, *The Supreme Court* (9th ed.), (Washington, DC: Congressional Quarterly Press, 2007), 100–101.

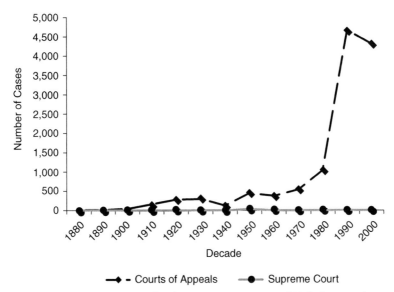

FIGURE 4.2. Immigration Caseload at Supreme Court and U.S. Courts of Appeals, 1881–2002

combined total of 12,371 immigration cases in the same period. That the U.S. Courts of Appeals are more likely than not to be the last decision making body to handle the appeal means that it is these judges' preferred interpretations of statute and uses of discretion that will stand. As Figure 4.2 shows, the reality of the modern judicial hierarchy is that all eleven U.S. Courts of Appeals collectively are now realistically the court of final appeal for almost all federal litigants, including alien litigants.[34]

Moreover, because the Supreme Court is now a policy court, it is more likely to grant *certiorari* to cases with constitutional issues at stake. As a result, many cases that engage in mere statutory interpretation are likely to fly under the radar altogether.[35] Certainly the opportunity to read one's own policy preferences into vague or imprecise language exists whether the possibility of reversal by the Supreme Court is 2 percent or 90 percent, but the incentive to do so is increased with a low possibility of reversal. I could not ask about incentives for purposive or strategic behavior, or the frequency of such behavior, in my interviews with the judges without

[34] John P. McIver, "Scaling Judicial Decision: The Panel Decisionmaking Process of the U.S. Courts of Appeals," *American Journal of Political Science* 20, No. 4 (1976): 749–61, 749.
[35] Melnick, *Between the Lines*, 24–5.

offending them, so I did not ask.[36] However, many of their comments revealed they were cognizant of an array of purposive techniques to reach a particular legal outcome.

In the immigration context, an invitation to interpret comes up in several specific and recurring instances. In general deportation cases, an alien is fighting to retain the right to stay in the country and not be expelled. Under U.S. immigration law, an alien (including those illegally residing in this country) may contest her deportation by presenting evidence why she should remain in the United States. Before the 1996 legislative reforms created generic grounds for "cancellation of removal," there was a class of categories called grounds for "suspension of deportation" that allowed an alien who met certain criteria to avoid deportation and to remain in the United States as a lawful permanent resident. Aliens who meet the following criteria can avoid deportation under the suspension of deportation standard: a) they have been in the country continuously for ten years; b) they have been "of good moral character"; c) they have not been convicted of certain crimes; and d) their deportation will result in "exceptional and extremely unusual hardship" for parents, a spouse, or children who are citizens or lawful permanent residents. In these legislatively mandated categories there is room for interpretation because the statute goes no further in defining "good moral behavior" and "exceptional and extremely unusual hardship." Requirements of "good moral behavior" (or its historical variant, "good moral character") are also legally defined criteria that must be met in other types of immigration procedures, including naturalization applications and applications for voluntary departure, an alternative to deportation. Moreover, it is not just vague legal terms such as "exceptional and extremely unusual hardship" that invite creative interpretation. Even mundane words with seemingly plain meanings, such as "departed" and "adultery," can also elicit judicial creativity.

WHAT IS "EXTREME HARDSHIP"?

A vague legal term such as "extreme hardship" has invited much creative interpretation. What exactly constitutes extreme hardship? Any alien who has spent any amount of time in the United States can point to some hardship that he or she will endure if deported. Yet the range of the factors that constitute hardship is quite large and one may construe

---

[36] Please refer to Appendix C for the list of questions that were asked of the judges.

hardship broadly or narrowly. Hardship can be economic, psychological, or social in nature. Aliens who have fought their deportation have argued that their wages would not be as high in their home country as in the United States, that they would lose revenue because of the forced liquidation of their land holdings, or that their children will face worse educational opportunities in their home country, and that they and their children will be psychologically traumatized by being uprooted from familiar family and friends and dropped into an unfamiliar environment. Other aliens have taken another tack by arguing the extreme hardship that their deportation would visit on their relatives who are U.S. citizens or lawful permanent resident relatives. With regard to the above-mentioned and fairly common arguments against an alien's deportation, there is existing case law governing those situations.[37] However, in cases where aliens provide a reason for claiming hardship that does not fall under existing doctrine, the judges have to decide whether the argument raised constitutes extreme hardship. Additionally, judges have some room to decide how to weigh different types of hardship. Should they consider each claim of hardship discretely, or should they toll the cumulative effects of the claimed hardship? The judges' decisions in these instances can lead to a person's deportation or a suspension of deportation or cancellation of removal.

An example of the effect of multiple interpretive options is found in the case *Immigration and Naturalization Service v. Wang* (9th Cir. 1981),[38] which eventually reached the Supreme Court. The Wang case involved two Korean aliens, husband and wife, who overstayed their temporary visas after initially entering as treaty traders. The couple subsequently had two children, both born in the United States, and bought real estate, including a business. They applied to the U.S. Courts of Appeals for a suspension of deportation and eventually to the U.S. Supreme Court on a motion to reopen their appeal, based on the extreme hardship that would fall on their U.S.- born children. Even though the range of legal issues that can

---

[37] *Fong Choy Yu v. Immigration and Naturalization Service*, 439 F.2d 719 (9th Cir. 1971) (a claim of economic disadvantage in alien's country of origin does not meet the standard of extreme hardship), *Mendez v. Major*, 340 F.2d 128 (8th Cir. 1965) (the possibility of inconvenience to the citizen child is not a hardship of the degree required of "extreme hardship"), *Choe v. Immigration and Naturalization Service* 597 F.2d 170 (9th Cir. 1979) (an alien cannot gain favored status merely because he has a child who is a United States citizen), *Hassan v. INS*, 927 F.2d 465, 468 (9th Cir. 1991) ("Common results of deportation, without more, are insufficient to prove extreme hardship.").

[38] 450 U.S. 139.

be reviewed are more limited under a motion to reopen than under a petition for review, both the Ninth Circuit and the Supreme Court's rulings struggled to define extreme hardship. In overturning the Ninth Circuit's grant of a motion to reopen, the Supreme Court acknowledged, "The crucial question in this case is what constitutes 'extreme hardship.' These words are not self-explanatory, and reasonable men could easily differ as to their construction." The Court added that the Ninth Circuit had erred in construing the term "liberally" in order to "effectuate its ameliorative purpose."[39] In an *en banc* hearing of the case, the Ninth Circuit had chosen to interpret the term "extreme hardship" broadly and in a way that combined the effects of harm to the Wangs' two minor U.S.–born children, and the Wangs' economic interests in order to weight the "total potential effect" of deportation of the Wang family.[40]

The disagreement between the Supreme Court and Ninth Circuit in this case turned not only on the semantic meaning of the words "extreme hardship" but also on whose interpretation should carry more weight. The Supreme Court admonished the Ninth Circuit for not giving enough deference to the Board of Immigration Appeals's interpretation of what constituted "extreme hardship." The Supreme Court wrote, "the Court of Appeals improvidently encroached on the authority which the Act confers on the Attorney General and his delegates...the Act commits their definition in the first instance to the Attorney General and his delegates, and their construction and application of this standard should not be overturned by a reviewing court simply because it may prefer another interpretation of the statute."[41] When statutory terms are not clear, the meaning of the term as well as whose interpretation should prevail are at issue.

The *Wang* case illustrates two openings in the decision making process for U.S. Courts of Appeals judges to pursue their policy preferences via statutory interpretation. When given multiple possible interpretations of vague terms, one may choose the interpretation that best conforms with one's policy preferences. But another opportunity for pursuing one's desired outcome arises even after a party has already asserted one possible interpretation of a vague term such as "extreme hardship." The appeals process is set up in hierarchical fashion. Therefore, the last decision making body to hear the case is the body whose interpretation will prevail. In the *Wang* case, the Wangs began in an administrative hearing before

[39] 450 U.S. 139, 144.
[40] 450 U.S. 139, 149.
[41] 450 U.S. 139, 144.

an immigration judge. When the Wangs lost, they appealed to the Ninth Circuit, which assigned it to a panel of three judges. The appeal then went to an *en banc* hearing with eleven judges. Eventually the appeal reached the Supreme Court. At each stage of the appeal, the decision making body could either agree with the decision maker below and affirm the decision or could reverse the decision and substitute its own interpretation. Keep in mind, however, that the *Wang* case is rare because it is one of the few cases to run the entire length of the appeals process. Given the small number of cases from the U.S. Courts of Appeals that the U.S. Supreme Court agrees to adjudicate, it is the U.S. Courts of Appeals that are almost always the courts of last resort. The hierarchical structure of the judiciary becomes a significant determinant of whose interpretation reigns supreme.

DISPUTES OVER EVERYDAY WORDS

Whereas *Wang* dealt with "extreme hardship" in the context of a deportation case, *Umanzor v. Lambert* (5th Cir. 1986),[42] was an asylum case where the Fifth Circuit was charged with divining the meaning of two seemingly quotidian terms, such as "in custody." Umanzor, an alien from El Salvador, had entered illegally and now found himself in deportation proceedings. He applied for asylum to avoid deportation. First the district court had to determine whether Umanzor was eligible to apply for judicial review of his detention. The relevant statute, 8 U.S.C. § 1105a(a)(9), provides that "any alien held in custody pursuant to an order of deportation may obtain judicial review thereof by *habeas corpus* proceedings." While his lawyer was filing the *habeas* motion in court, Umanzor was taken into custody by the Immigration and Naturalization Service and placed on an airplane to be deported. The district court had argued that Umanzor was not entitled to contest his detention in court because he was not "in custody" of the U.S. government because he was aboard a commercial airliner when his attorney filed his *habeas corpus* appeal in court. The Fifth Circuit disagreed with this interpretation, writing:

We have little difficulty in concluding that Umanzor was under actual physical restraint by the government's agent – the airline – at the moment the habeas petition was filed. Umanzor was imprisoned inside of the aircraft, against his will, until the aircraft completed the flight and he was released. Since the district

[42] 782 F.2d 1299.

court had jurisdiction over the INS director against whom the writ issued, *habeas* jurisdiction attached.[43]

Umanzor's ability to challenge his detention turned on the Fifth Circuit's understanding of the term "in custody." Because the Fifth Circuit ruled that he was indeed in custody, he was entitled to file a *habeas corpus* claim.

As the *Umanzor* and *Wang* cases illustrate, courts are sometimes called upon to give meaning to both unclear legal terms and everyday words, often in the very same case. The deportation case of *Brea-Garcia v. Immigration and Naturalization Service* (3rd Cir. 1976)[44] is a good example. The immigration code at 8 U.S.C. § 1254(e) (1971) allows the Attorney General to permit an alien in deportation to depart the United States voluntarily if the alien has demonstrated, among other requirements, "good moral character." Yet, the legal term "good moral character" is not defined in the Immigration and Nationality Act, except in the negative sense in section 1101(f), which lists classes of persons who shall not be regarded as having good moral character. In *Brea-Garcia*, a Dominican man was seeking voluntary departure after being found deportable. Voluntary departure is desirable and preferable to deportation because the alien can avoid the criminal stigma of deportation and can more easily reenter the United States. A grant of voluntary departure is discretionary by immigration officials and requires a person to be of "good moral character" for the five years prior to application for voluntary departure. Under the categories of persons and actions that lacked good moral character was the designation of anyone who has "committed adultery" as designated by section 101(f)(2). The problem for the Third Circuit was that "adultery" was not defined anywhere in the federal immigration statute.

What was the confusion about this everyday term? In this case, it lay in the question of whether the determination of what is "adultery" is a legal determination, a factual determination, or a determination contingent on one's own moral view of what constitutes adulterous behavior. The *Brea-Garcia* case illustrates the difficulty of classifying such discretionary determinations. Brea-Garcia argued that his behavior did not constitute "adultery." He had entered the United States on a nonimmigrant student visa with his wife and had overstayed the visa. While still married to his Dominican wife, he had sexual relations with another

[43] 782 F.2d 1299, 1302.
[44] 531 F.2d 693.

woman and fathered a child with her. His wife eventually moved back to the Dominican Republic, where she obtained a divorce from Brea-Garcia. Although he was free at this point to marry his mistress, he failed to do so and fathered a second child out of wedlock with her. Around this time, Brea-Garcia was picked up by immigration authorities and ordered deported because of his visa overstay. He applied for voluntary departure before an immigration judge, who denied his request based on his adultery, which prevented him from demonstrating good moral character. Brea-Garcia appealed to the Board of Immigration Appeals and married the mother of his two children. The Board of Immigration Appeals remanded the case back to the immigration judge in light of the new developments. The immigration judge declined to grant voluntary departure on the second appeal despite the marriage, and reinstituted the deportation order, stating that Brea-Garcia's adultery had occurred in the previous five years. He further observed, "that marriage to the present wife was delayed apparently so she could first obtain a visa as the unmarried child of a legal resident parent even though the delay resulted in a second birth out of wedlock. The subsequent marriage should not operate as a remission of the adultery which had evidently destroyed Brea-Garcia's first marriage."[45] In reinstating the deportation order, the immigration judge resorted to a New Jersey state definition of adultery, because there was no clear federal definition of adultery. Had the judge determined that Brea-Garcia's behavior did not constitute adultery, Brea-Garcia would have qualified for suspension of deportation; instead, he was eventually deported.

SEPARATION OF POWERS AND THE POLITICS OF INTERPRETATION

In addition to the disputed meaning of "adultery," the *Brea-Garcia* case is also instructive because it traces the history of how Congress tried to limit the extent of interpretations of "adultery" by the U.S. Courts of Appeals and how these courts have responded. One can see from the different approaches taken by the circuits the corresponding array of possible legal outcomes for aliens in immigration cases based on the judiciary's interpretation of the word "adultery." When the immigration judge used a state definition of adultery to deport him, Brea-Garcia protested and argued that it was unfair to subject aliens with immigration violations to

[45] 531 F.2d 693, 695.

the whims of state civil laws that had nothing to do with immigration. The Third Circuit countered that, before passage of the Immigration and Nationality Act of 1952, "determination of good moral character was even more of a patchwork than Brea-Garcia contends has been produced by reference to state law. Section 101(f) did not exist, so good moral character was entirely undefined."[46] In what was viewed by the U.S. Courts of Appeals as an attempt to limit the discretion inherent in interpreting an imprecise term such as adultery, Congress added Section 101(f) to the U.S. Code to ensure that "good moral character" would exclude anyone who had committed adultery as defined by any state law.[47]

The Third Circuit reported that, in response to the congressional attempt to limit interpretative license of the federal courts, these courts became "uncomfortable with the diversity of state definitions of adultery and disliked having the condition of an alien's moral character conclusively dictated by his chance decision as to which would be his state of residence."[48] The Ninth Circuit, D.C. Circuit, and several district courts adopted more liberal definitions of the statute, interpretations that would not automatically construe any state law that defined adultery to trump good moral character automatically. Generally, these courts declined to deem adultery a lack of good moral character unless the adultery was "behavior which is unquestionably inconsistent with good moral character."[49] The Third Circuit declined to follow this path, asserting that to do so would provide too much variability and also that such a move would be in contravention of congressional intent. The Third Circuit further noted:

The collateral issues which the *Moon Ho Kim* test [from a Ninth Circuit case] would inject into the already complex and time-consuming immigration procedures are endless. The immigration judge would be compelled to sit as an arbiter of the viability of marriages, a task which few mortals are qualified to undertake. He would also be required to determine what quantum of adulterous conduct constitutes a threat to the vague and amorphous concept of "public morality." The matter would not end with his decisions. Appeals unquestionably would be taken on these issues, which are at most tangential to the real question before the judge. We believe these avenues of inquiry unnecessarily would burden and further complicate immigration hearing procedures.[50]

In this statement, the Third Circuit warned of the perils of judicial interpretation, which has the possibility of creating an endless cycle of

[46] 531 F.2d 693, 696.
[47] 531 F.2d 693, 696.
[48] 531 F.2d 693, 696.
[49] 531 F.2d 693, 697.
[50] 531 F.2d 693, 697.

interpretations based on an array of possible definitions of one statutory term such as "good moral character."

That Congress responded to the courts' behavior at all is unusual. The structural complexity of the American political system, with its intentionally built-in multiple veto points that are designed to force compromise and slow down the legislative process, make congressional response to judicial actions rare and slow. As Melnick wrote, the same aspects of the American political system that "conspire to multiply the number of statutory issues that come before the judges, to encourage judges to look beyond the letter of the law" are the same structural attributes of the system "that reduce (but not eliminate) the possibility that judicial decisions will be overturned by subsequent legislation."[51] Therefore, any congressional response to judicial action, regardless of its efficacy, is rare.

The *Brea-Garcia* case displays some of the politics surrounding congressional and judicial disagreements over terms given the policy ramifications. In an effort to circumscribe and limit the interpretations of "adultery" and "good moral character," Congress legislated measures to standardize the treatment of adultery under federal law. In fact, the attempt may have made matters worse by having the effect of making aliens involved in immigration proceedings liable for deportation based on arbitrarily and varying state definitions of adultery. In turn, several of the U.S. Courts of Appeals and district courts resisted what they viewed as overly punitive applications on aliens and these courts generated more liberal readings of the federal law in order to reach a pro-alien result in certain cases. The semantic confusion created by words such as "good moral character" and "adultery" are not only openings for judges to read their own policy preferences into legal decisions, but may also precipitate judicial disputes with other branches of government over the range of allowable interpretation. And the reality is that unless the Supreme Court drastically increases the number of cases it accepts on appeal from the U.S. Courts of Appeals, or the legislative process becomes more streamlined than it now is, the U.S. Courts of Appeals will have relatively free rein to make their own judgments about the proper meaning of words, text, and statutory language in general.

The problems and opportunities presented by unclear text are not unique to the U.S. Courts of Appeals; certainly the U.S. Supreme Court also confronts these same difficulties and opportunities. I maintain, however, that the incentive to interpret a statue in a manner that leads to one's

---

[51] Melnick, *Between the Lines*, 8.

desired legal outcome increases for the U.S. Courts of Appeals judges
when the possibility of reversal by the Supreme Court is understood to be
remote. In addition, there really are no other forms of sanctions that can
be applied to Courts of Appeals judges who do not follow congressional
directives or Supreme Court doctrine about discretion. As Frank Cross
points out, "The Supreme Court cannot 'expel' the circuit court from its
jurisdiction or financially punish the court, the sort of tools that might
encourage compliance."[52] Similarly, in J. Woodford Howard's landmark
study of the Courts of Appeals, his survey noted that these judges were
not particularly concerned about Supreme Court reversal.[53]

I am not suggesting that the U.S. Courts of Appeals judges interpret statues to bend unclear and vague language to their whim in every
instance that they engage in statutory interpretation. The low rates of
pro-alien decisions, an average of 32 percent among the three U.S. Courts
of Appeals in this study, are proof that the judges are not being improperly activist and running amok in granting alien claims.[54] The three circuits show comparable rates of pro-alien grants in immigration cases
(Figure 4.3). The allegedly liberal Ninth Circuit is not granting alien petitions left and right, nor is the allegedly conservative Fifth Circuit denying
all alien claims. The slightly higher pro-alien rate of the Third Circuit is
attributable to the much lower number of asylum claims in that circuit
than in the Ninth. (The data show that unpublished opinions that are
mainly in the Ninth Circuit sample of cases, particularly unpublished
political asylum opinions, have the lowest pro-alien rates.) So although
there are minor variations in the pro-alien grant rates among the three
circuits, Judge A is right; the empirical evidence bears out her claim that
"as a rule of thumb, the alien loses."[55] Also, these data suggest that the
three circuits are carrying out their duties in remarkably like manner.

---

[52] Frank B. Cross, *Decision Making in the U.S. Courts of Appeals* (Palo Alto: Stanford University Press, 2007), 101.

[53] J. Woodford Howard, Jr., *Courts of Appeals in the Federal Judicial System* (Princeton, NJ: Princeton University Press, 1981), 163–65.

[54] See Kanstroom, "The Better Part of Valor," in which his quantitative findings reveal that among the vast majority of cases from 1996 to the present that involve discretion-ary grounds, more than 90 percent are denials. He writes, "Those who suggest that the federal courts are too highly interventionist in discretionary immigration cases should consider these data" (193).

[55] Interview with Judge A, 6/12/07. See also Law and Williams, "Understanding Judicial Decision Making in Immigration Cases at the U.S. Courts of Appeals," 21, noting that "All judges appear to be disinclined to vote pro-alien across circuits, throughout our study period, even in the Ninth Circuit."

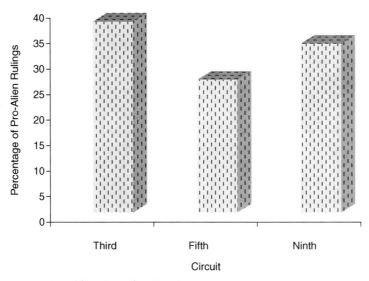

FIGURE 4.3. Pro-Alien Rates by Circuit, 1881–2002

The comparably low pro-alien rates across the three circuits indicates that there were many cases in which the courts were in fact bound by the plainness of the text when rendering their decisions. And clearly there are other statutory and institutional limitations, such as those presented by doctrines that would limit one's pursuit of policy preferences at the Courts of Appeals. Judges are certainly not free to interpret the law however they wish, but the layers of immigration laws, which make immigration regulation more and more complex, as well as the contentiousness of immigration politics, combine to create an opaque statutory regime that courts are routinely asked to interpret and apply. In addition, every new statute brings new purposive opportunities. Indeed, Judge E noted that, specifically in cases of first impression, which raise novel legal issues, judges actually have a clear opportunity to make policy.[56] Adding to the U.S. Courts of Appeals judges' opportunities to pursue their own policy preferences is the growing unlikelihood of Supreme Court reversal. Vague text then creates the necessary conditions for judges to pursue their own policy preferences, while increasing insulation from the Supreme Court magnifies the incentive, even if subconsciously, to do so more often. U.S. Courts of Appeals judges are well aware that the likelihood of reversal or any other kind of sanction is slim to nonexistent.

[56] Interview with Judge E, 7/26/07. Judge E also noted that these types of cases consume a lot of a judge's time.

PURPOSIVE USES OF DISCRETION

In a political system of separate powers, Congress could theoretically legislate rules governing statutory interpretation to limit the range of possible interpretations given certain words or phrases. However, Congress cannot completely, through legislation, close the loopholes on all judges' exercises of discretion. Vague statutory language is only one limit of positive law that creates opportunities for judges to pursue their policy preferences. Positive law cannot be written to anticipate and cover all variations of human experience and existing law must be stretched to cover new and novel situations. Therefore, in some instances, appellate-court judges will be asked to use their own discretion in determining how a fact pattern should be construed and how much latitude to grant the decision makers below the U.S. Courts of Appeals. Courts of Appeals judges are asked to exercise discretion frequently. The cumulative effect of these regular exercises of discretion can be profound. Given the number of times judges are required to use their discretion, Murphy argued that "even where there is no desire to sabotage high policy, the frequent necessity to exercise discretion may have a thwarting effect similar to that of deliberate misunderstanding."[57] The numerous occasions that allow a judge to exercise her discretion in the immigration context alone certainly confirm Murphy's view.

One reason that the power of discretion has been so successfully deployed by purposive judges is because the concept is not clearly understood. As Daniel Kanstroom has indicated, in the immigration context in particular, "we still lack fundamental agreement on what discretion actually means. Discretion is an extremely amorphous concept – a shadow standard, a contentless gapfiller, a euphemism for allocation of authority."[58] Senior Judge Henry Friendly of the U.S. Court of Appeals for the Second Circuit agrees that discretion in the context of appeals courts is difficult to define. He begins with a definition he finds wholly unsatisfying: "The power to choose between two or more courses of action each of which is thought of as permissible."[59] Friendly then offers his own definition of discretion: "The trial judge has discretion in those cases where his ruling

[57] Murphy, *Elements of Judicial Strategy*, 24.
[58] Daniel Kanstroom, "The Better Part of Valor: The Real ID Act, Discretion, and the 'Rule' of Immigration Law," 51 *New York Law School Law Review* 162, 163; and Daniel Kanstroom, "Surrounding the Hole in the Doughnut: Discretion and Deference in U.S. Immigration Law," 71 *Tulane Law Review* 703 (1997).
[59] Henry J. Friendly, "Indiscretion About Discretion" in 31 *Emory Law Journal* 747, 54 (citing Henry Hart and Albert Saks's *The Legal Process*, unpublished text).

will not be reversed simply because an appellate court disagrees. If this be circular, make the most of it!"[60] Friendly may have been being facetious in attempting to pin down the elusive meaning of discretion, but he and Kanstroom both pointed to an important aspect to the exercise of discretion by appellate courts: discretion is about authority, specifically, about whose interpretation should carry the most authority. The hierarchical nature of the appellate process ensures that the one's successful exercise of discretion is, in part, contingent upon one's position in the judicial hierarchy and the sequencing of the immigration appeals process.

Aware of the potential for the manipulation of discretion by judges, Congress has tried to limit the wide interpretive latitude of federal judges. When the Board of Immigration Appeals upholds an order of deportation or removal made by an immigration judge, the alien or the government may appeal to the U.S. Courts of Appeals. However, in some kinds of appeals, the immigration code severely limits the scope of the Court of Appeals' review. The provisions of 8 U.S.C. § 1252 (a)(B)-(D) include a long list of kinds of cases in which the Courts of Appeals do not have jurisdiction to review administrative decisions, including orders against criminal aliens (Section (C)), and also "denials of discretionary relief" (Section (B)). Over the years, Congress has increasingly limited the categories and scope of the review of the federal courts over immigration cases in an effort to streamline the process and reduce the courts' caseload. Another impetus for these reforms is reports of abuses of the system, as aliens have used appeal after appeal to prolong their stays in the United States. In the end, though, congressional attempts to limit the exercise of discretion by the U.S. Courts of Appeals are not meaningful if the Supreme Court is not going to police instances where the U.S. Courts of Appeals have not given sufficient deference to the discretion of another decision maker by reversing the U.S. Court of Appeals' rulings.

The concept of discretion plays a huge role in immigration appeals and it sometimes takes on a purposive cast. Kanstroom noted that, "Due to the harshness and rigidity of our current deportation laws and the powerful historical role placed by discretion in immigration law – often the last repository of mercy in an otherwise merciless system – the issue of discretion is crucially important."[61] It is therefore not surprising that discretion in immigration appeals has become a flashpoint in the Ninth Circuit. As Judge F told me, as the low number of pro-alien decisions in the circuit illustrates,

---

[60] Ibid. at 754.
[61] Kanstroom, "The Better Part of Valor," 163.

there is a remarkable level of agreement, not disagreement, among the Ninth Circuit and the other Courts of Appeals on immigration matters. She confirmed the quantitative findings of the dataset when she indicated that the grant rates for immigration appeals was "about the same" across the twelve circuits, a finding consistent with the data in Figure 4.3. However, she noted that in the Ninth Circuit in particular, the fight over immigration appeals is in regard to "the level of deference" exercised in immigration cases. Judge F indicated that, "In concept, we're not following Congress; we show substantial disrespect to IJs [immigration judges]. We are far more prone to second-guess IJs," even though the statutory and legal standard requires substantial deference to immigration judges.[62] She attributed the second-guessing of immigration judges to the psychological effect on judges of seeing many "bad decisions getting through the system" which in turn "makes it hard to trust the system." She added that the level of confidence of the Ninth Circuit judges in district judges' decisions and competency and in the decisions of administrative law judges outside the immigration policy area is much higher than toward the administrative fact-finders in the immigration system; there is no comparable second-guessing of these other fact finders.[63] The many criticisms of the immigration system offered by Judge F and many of her colleagues that are detailed in the following chapter confirm what Melnick noted about the connection between deference to administrative agencies and agency reputation. Melnick noted that all judges "are likely to give more credence to the interpretations put forth by agencies they consider competent and honest than those they consider bumbling and disingenuous."[64] As Chapter 5 will show, some Courts of Appeals judges do not trust various components of the immigration system. In addition to the incentives created by the small threat of reversal by the Supreme Court, it appears that some of the lack of deference for the determinations of administrative fact finders by U.S. Courts of Appeals judges was being driven by a lack of confidence in the administrative bodies' competence and due diligence in their adjudications.

Part of the ease of using discretion purposively is that it is difficult to detect and police. As Kanstroom and others have pointed out, efforts to regulate the use of discretion have tended to "blur the line between

---

[62] Interview with Judge F, 8/6/07.
[63] Interview with Judge F, 8/6/07.
[64] Melnick, *Between the Lines*, 239–40.

interpretation and discretion."[65] The judges spoke to this very issue about the purposive uses of discretion in our interviews. Several judges stated that the fact that Congress had tried to instruct the U.S. Courts of Appeals through statute to defer to the Attorney General's discretion did not mean that the hands of the Courts of Appeals judges were completely tied; nor did it mean that the judges' review of a case was limited to reviewing the legal issues laid out in the briefs. Judge H stated that if a Court of Appeals judge agrees with the previous decision making body's conclusion, she can simply state that the Attorney General (through the Board of Immigration Appeals) has exercised her discretion and that the case is no longer within the jurisdiction of the federal courts. In other words, a judge could "punt" by citing the Attorney General's discretion. Similarly, Judge E explained that despite the statutory directive that federal courts should not second-guess the Attorney General or his designated entities' exercises of discretion, in fact, cases containing egregious errors "*will* get sent back to the BIA regardless of discretion."[66] Judge E indicated that flagging procedural due process violations or a determination that there was an "abuse of discretion" was a way around statutory and doctrinal directives to respect the Attorney General's discretion. Likewise, Judge F confirmed that the level of scrutiny brought to the case by judges could skew the eventual outcome. She reported, "You get into a case far enough and you start second-guessing the fact finder. We don't show that much deference to the immigration court."[67] In a speech about the Seventh Circuit's experiences with immigration appeals, Judge Richard Posner echoed this point when he stated, "The less deeply you get into a case, the less likely you are to find issues and arguments for reversal."[68] An example of what Judge F and Judge Posner refer to as getting into a case "far enough" or "deeply enough" to result in second guessing the fact finder is found in *Suntharalinkam v. Gonzales* (9th Cir. 2007), where the panel's majority contested eight different conclusions pertaining to the credibility determination that the immigration judge had reached.[69] In response, the dissent by Judge Rawlinson cited a case counseling deference to the BIA and concluded, "I simply cannot agree that we are

[65] Kanstroom, "The Better Part of Valor," 197.
[66] Interview with Judge H, 3/26/07 and Judge E, 7/26/07.
[67] Interview with Judge F, 8/6/07.
[68] Richard Posner, "Judicial Review of Immigration Judges." Speech before the Chicago Bar Association, Chicago, IL, April 21, 2008.
[69] 458 F.2d 1034, 1039.

compelled to find *Suntharalinkam* credible."[70] The Ninth Circuit is aware of the controversy over discretion and the court had called an *en banc* hearing in *Suntharalinkam v. Gonzales* to try to settle once and for all the question of what is the appropriate level of review and discretion in immigration appeals.[71] According to Judge E, it was one judge (she did not indicate which judge) who called for the *en banc* sitting for the purpose of rewriting a body of doctrine because of his or her belief that many of the Ninth Circuit panels had not given enough deference to the immigration judges. As Judge E further stated, she would have no problem with the proposition that the fact finder should be given deference, "if the IJs were well trained" and "not erratic."[72] Aside from the pursuit of one's policy preferences, the lack of deference to IJs' and the federal attorney general's discretion was fueled by Courts of Appeals judges' perceptions that the immigration administrative fact finders did not deserve deference because their adjudications were slapdash.

Kanstroom has written that immigration law has "proven particularly resistant to any consistent definition of discretion." Yet discretion arises in a range of scenarios, ranging from whether bond should be granted, to whether a motion to reopen has been established based on a prima facie case for relief, and to factual determinations by immigration judges.[73] Given the volume of immigration appeals the Ninth Circuit Court of Appeals adjudicates, the judges of that bench have significant influence in this policy area because of the sheer number of cases they adjudicate. Some of the judges' exercise of discretion is explicitly called for in statutes, such as the requirement that many types of Board of Immigration Appeals decisions shall be reviewed under a narrow scope called "abuse of discretion." In other words, the U.S. Courts of Appeals are not to disturb the administrative agency's findings unless there was a clear abuse of discretion. What constitutes an abuse of discretion is less clear. In fact, the cases in this study revealed that U.S. Courts of Appeals have quite a bit of discretion over how much discretion to accord other decision making bodies.

---

[70] Dissenting opinion by Judge Johnnie B. Rawlinson (referencing *Malhi v. Immigration and Naturalization Service*, 336 F.3d 989, 993 (9th Cir. 2003)), 458 F.2d 10324, 1050.

[71] *Suntharalinkam v. Gonzales*, 458 F.3d 1034 (9th Cir. 2006) was granted an *en banc* hearing in the summer of 2007, but the petitioner voluntarily withdrew the petition a few weeks after oral argument and therefore there was no opinion filed. (Email communication with Judge F, 12/31/07.)

[72] Interview with Judge E, 7/26/07.

[73] Kanstroom, "The Better Part of Valor," 169.

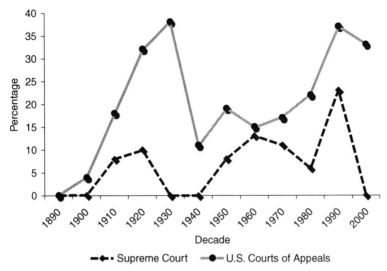

FIGURE 4.4. Use of Fact/Evidence, 1881–2002

Discretion and Judging Credibility

U.S. Courts of Appeals judges do not have an opportunity to exercise discretion only when engaging in statutory interpretation. As the following example will show, a judge may also exercise her discretion by determining how many discrepancies are too many in judging a witness's or an appellant's credibility in oral testimony. Although one thinks of factual review as being the primary duty of the trial courts, the data show that the U.S. Courts of Appeals are engaging in this type of review quite frequently. This kind of close review of facts and evidence was a common approach taken by the Courts of Appeals during the Chinese Exclusion era and still is today. Consistent with the specialized roles of the two courts, the chart below shows that the U.S. Courts of Appeals, much more frequently than the U.S. Supreme Court, have engaged in review of facts and evidence to decide cases. The reason is that these courts' error correction function requires their judges to ask themselves whether the decision making of the previous fact finder is correct, and these determinations often entail *de novo* review. As Figure 4.4 shows, the U.S. Courts of Appeals' use of fact/evidence as a mode of legal reasoning to decide cases far outpaces its use at the Supreme Court. By contrast, Figure 4.0 demonstrated that the Supreme Court's use of statutory interpretation as a mode of legal reasoning far outstripped the use by the U.S. Courts of Appeals. These charts illustrate empirically verifiable correlations between the choices of legal reasoning and the mission and function of each of the courts and also the very distinctive approaches the justices and judges take to legal decision making.

The U.S. Courts of Appeals most frequently use the facts/evidence as a mode of legal reasoning in contemporary asylum cases, but that mode of legal reasoning was also commonly used in many historical cases. Through the 1950s, the Chinese Exclusion Act and its amendments generated many legal challenges. Many of these cases resulted from Chinese aliens' challenging the Chinese Exclusion Act by claiming right of entry based on one of the exempt categories (merchants, students, teachers) or a familial relation to an alien who belonged to one of the exempt categories. Many ethnic Chinese also sued for the right to enter based on their status as a U.S.–born citizen or their relationship to a native-born citizen. These cases took place in an era where procedures and tools to verify the validity of such official documents as birth certificates were extremely limited to nonexistent. In these cases, a reliable paper trail of evidence was not always available to establish the alleged relationship between the principal alien qualified for admission and the immediate family members of the principal alien who were seeking entry to the United States. In lieu of physical evidence, immigration examiners and judges often had only the word of the applicants themselves to prove an alleged familial relationship. The immigration examiners and judges engaged in detailed questioning about the alleged relationship between the two people as well as to ask common knowledge questions of the two about the village or town the applicants were from, common relationships of the two, events from the persons' pasts, and so on. The decision maker then had to ascertain whether the responses were truthful based on the consistency of the responses. In *Siu Say v. Nagle* (9th Cir. 1926)[74] the panel laid out some general criteria for determining the credibility of an applicant's testimony when oral testimony is the only evidence available:

In cases of this character experience has demonstrated that the testimony of the parties in interest as to the mere fact of relationship cannot be safely accepted or relied upon. Resort is therefore had to collateral facts for corroboration or the reverse. If the witnesses are in accord as to a number of collateral facts which they should know if the claimed relationship exists, and probably would not know if the claim of relationship did not exist, there is at least a reasonable probability that the testimony is true. If, on the other hand, the witnesses disagree as to collateral facts which they should or would know if the claimed relationship exists, especially such an important fact as membership in the immediate family of the

74 225 F. 676.

parties, there is a strong probability that the claim of relationship is false and fraudulent.[75]

Sounds simple enough, except that the above directive really requires the U.S. Courts of Appeals judges to make two discrete decisions: first, about the credibility of the witness, and, second, about the accuracy of the previous decision maker.

The *Siu Say* directive first requires judges to determine the degree and extent of discrepancies that are acceptable to them before they conclude that the witness's testimony is fraudulent. Another case, *Gung You v. Nagle* (9th Cir. 1929)[76], raises this very issue. The *Gung You* case involved a 14-year-old Chinese boy who sought entry into the United States based on his alleged relationship to his American-born father. To grant entry based on the derivative citizenship, the court first had to determine whether the relationship between the boy and the native-born father was real. In reviewing the testimony from the district court, the Ninth Circuit wondered how to construe inevitable discrepancies in the testimony of witnesses. They asked, "But what sort of discrepancies will justify such an order? Are we to say that a discrepancy as to the amount of pavement in front of a house is not a sufficient basis for an order of exclusion, and that one concerning the number of houses in a block, or the number of windows in a house, is a sufficient discrepancy to justify an order of exclusion?"[77] What kind of and how many discrepancies in testimony would indicate fraud? The fact of the matter was that judges were left to decide the credibility of witnesses on a case-by-case basis.

Beyond the number and nature of the discrepancies, the *Gung You* court also expressed doubt about the entire exercise of immigration authorities' and courts' judging the veracity of a witness. They pointed to several structural problems of such a determination:

If we have knowledge of the fact, we can weigh the value of evidence at variance with the fact and thus arrive at credibility of a witness. Evidence concerning the town or village of the home is adapted to develop the question as to whether or not the applicant lived in the village and thus in the home from which he claims to come. But discrepancies here must be of the most unsatisfactory kind upon which to base a finding of the credibility of a witness, and when the cross-examiner and the Board of Inquiry know nothing of the actual facts concerning the village, the result is even more unsatisfactory and inconclusive...The difficulty in these cases of "discrepancy" is that there is no standard of comparison. *The immigration*

[75] 225 F. 676.
[76] 34 F.2d 848.
[77] 34 F.2d 848, 853.

authorities know nothing of the actual facts, but match witness against witness and thus develop inconsistencies.[78]

The court raises a valid question. How does one judge credibility if one has no basis to compare the testimony with the facts? In expressing its skepticism of the judgment process itself, the court was laying the groundwork for its eventual reversal of the district court, whose decision it derided as "purely arbitrary."[79]

The requirement to judge a witness' credibility, which falls under the fact/evidence mode of legal reasoning, arises in many different kinds of immigration cases. In the historical era, these types of cases generally arose when aliens seeking entry to the United States alleged they had a relationship to an eligible lawful permanent resident or U.S. citizen that would permit them to enter also. In the contemporary era, the need to determine a witness's credibility, often without corroborating physical evidence, occurs routinely in asylum cases where claimants frequently arrive with no physical evidence, only their story.[80] In all these cases, Courts of Appeals judges must use discretion in accepting or declining to accept any number of discrepancies in testimony. Yet, in judging credibility, each person has his or her own threshold of belief or doubt. It is likely that different judges would render different legal outcomes, based on their own threshold of belief. It is also conceivable that a judge who is sympathetic to an alien will be more flexible in allowing discrepancies to pass while a judge who is unsympathetic to an alien's claim will be more exacting about the number and nature of the discrepancies.

After the initial determination of whether the witnesses' testimony is personally acceptable to the judge, U.S. Courts of Appeals judges are required to exercise a second level of discretion. They must then decide how much deference to accord the administrative agency representative or the district court judge, the decision makers below the Courts of Appeals, especially if the lower court's decision is contrary to their own developing decision. Given that another decision maker has already rendered a judgment on the credibility of the testimony, when should a federal appellate court overturn the determination of the lower court and on what basis should it do so? In *Gung You*, the panel initially began with a deferential view of reviewing the lower court or administrative

[78] 34 F.2d 848, 853–54 (emphasis added).
[79] 34 F.2d 848, 853.
[80] See, e.g., *Singh v. Immigration and Naturalization Service*, 2000 U.S. App. LEXIS 15488 (9th Cir. 2000) and *Shah et al. v. Immigration and Naturalization Service*, 220 F.3d 1062 (9th Cir. 2000).

body's decision. They wrote, "The courts are powerless to interfere with conclusions of the immigration authorities and can only deal with cases where the principles of justice have been flagrantly outraged. The refusal to hear competent witnesses or competent testimony available is a denial of due process of law, as we held in a recent case refusing to permit the taking of a deposition in such cases."[81] So the court will only interfere when an egregious due process violation has occurred. But eventually the *Gung You* court decided not to be so deferential to the immigration authorities, in effect second-guessing these authorities when it reversed their decision.

In another case, *Young Len Gee v. Nagle* (9th Cir. 1931),[82] the appellant tried to establish his relationship to a U.S.–born father in order to gain entry into the United States. The two were questioned at length about numerous aspects of their alleged relationship, including their family life, their home village in China, the age at which the applicant began going to school, and the location of the nearest river to the village. After questioning the son and father separately, the Board of Special Inquiries and district court both denied the appeal, based on three discrepancies in the testimony of the two. One of the discrepancies was over the skylight in the home of the appellant. Although both father and son agreed on the size of the skylight, the son said the skylights were covered with glass, although he was not asked whether he could see through the glass. Meanwhile, the father had stated that the skylights were covered with porcelain, which he apparently said was translucent rather than transparent.[83] After reviewing this alleged discrepancy over the skylight and two others, the court stated:

We think that none of these three [alleged discrepancies], either separately or collectively, are sufficient to warrant the exclusion order of the Board of Special Inquiry. It is not that we are substituting our judgment on the admitted evidence for that of the Board; it is rather that the weight of evidence in support of the claimed relationship is so strong, and is supported by those imponderables of which the Board may take cognizance, that any failure to recognize the claimed relationship is a purely capricious and arbitrary action on the part of the Board.[84]

Despite their protests to the contrary, the appellate judges had indeed "substituted their judgment" in evaluating the evidence for that of the Board of Special Inquiry (the historical predecessor of the Board of

[81] 34 F.2d 848, 851.
[82] 53 F.2d 448.
[83] 53 F.2d 448, 449.
[84] 53 F.2d 448, 450.

Immigration Appeals). When witnesses are questioned extensively about the minutiae of everyday life, it is very possible that discrepancies will occur. It is a judgment call that the Courts of Appeals judges must make in regard to the level of deference to the determination of another decision making body. In this second level of discretion, the court again has room to maneuver completely within the acceptable boundaries of the law and legal norms to reach a decision in line with their own policy preferences.

In contrast to the *Gung You* and *Young Len Gee* cases, *Dong Ah Lon v. Proctor* (9th Cir. 1940)[85] illustrates what happens when a panel does show deference to earlier fact finders. The appellant arrived in Seattle with her three alleged brothers and claimed admission by presenting herself as the daughter of a deceased U.S.–born citizen. The only question before the court was whether Dong Ah Lon had successfully established her relationship to Dong Toy, her allegedly U.S.–born father. Before her *habeas* appeal arrived before the Ninth Circuit, it had passed through the Board of Special Inquiry, Department of Labor, and the district court. On questioning Dong Ah Lon and her three brothers, the Board of Special Inquiry noted numerous inconsistencies and discrepancies that in its view should not have resulted if in fact the applicant did indeed grow up together with her three alleged brothers. When the Ninth Circuit reviewed the case, it deferred to the Board of Special Inquiry, noting:

[T]he discrepancies here shown having been considered sufficient by the Board to warrant the action taken, which was for it to determine, and the determination not being arbitrary or unreasonable, we can not say that applicant was not given a fair hearing by the Board or that the District Court committed error in sustaining the findings of the Board. Reasonable men might readily disagree as to the probative effect of these discrepancies. When there is possibility of such disagreement, the findings of administrative boards will not be disturbed.[86]

Here the Court recognized that different persons may have different interpretations of discrepancies, and instead of seizing on this variance to overturn the fact-finder's decision, they chose to give the other fact finders the benefit of the doubt and affirm the district court's decision.

When U.S. Courts of Appeals judges are required to judge the credibility of a witness or appellant, they face two decision points. The first is whether they themselves find the witness convincing based on her testimony. The second is whether to accept the previous fact finder's

---

[85] 110 F.2d 808.
[86] 110 F.2d 808, 810.

judgment, which is usually that of an administrative official, of credibility, especially if these determinations do not conform to their own. Both decision steps require an exercise of judgment and therefore discretion. One may choose to let discrepancies slide or not. One may also choose to let stand the previous fact finder's determination or not. Both decision steps have consequences for the outcome of the case. Given the volume of cases the contemporary U.S. Courts of Appeals adjudicate, these courts and their judges' individual decisions affect many lives. Strictly in terms of numbers, it could be argued that the U.S. Courts of Appeals have more effect on people's lives than the Supreme Court in this respect.

Discretion: Counting a Single Incidence vs. Cumulative Events

I have already shown that unclear legal terms such as "extreme hardship" and "good moral character" can present interpretative opportunities, as can exercises of discretion in evaluating the credibility of witnesses and evidence. The deportation case of the Hernandez-Cordero family shows another variation of discretion that judges have when dealing with an imprecise term such as "extreme hardship." One can either consider a single incidence of hardship or the cumulative effect of several hardships. In *Hernandez-Cordero v. Immigration and Naturalization Service* (5th Cir. 1986)[87], the court had to determine whether the deportation of Mr. and Mrs. Hernandez-Cordero would result in extreme hardship to them or to their four minor children, who are all native-born U.S. citizens. Mr. Hernandez-Cordero had entered the United States illegally and his wife had overstayed a visitor's visa, so both were deportable. The immigration judge found that although both husband and wife had met the statutory requirements for a suspension of deportation based on their good moral character and their continued seven-year residence in the United States, their deportation would not result in extreme hardship. At the outset, the Fifth Circuit noted that the Court of Appeals review is limited:

The Board of Immigration Appeals, to whom the Attorney General has delegated his authority, has broad discretion to determine what constitutes extreme hardship. Our power of review of its decisions is, as we have repeatedly said, of the most limited kind. We may reverse the Board only if its decision is "arbitrary, irrational or contrary to law," and, therefore, constitutes an abuse of its discretion. The Board's narrow interpretation of what constitutes "extreme hardship"

---

[87] 783 F.2d 1266.

is consistent with the exceptional nature of the relief provided by suspension of deportation.[88]

But like "extreme hardship," "abuse of discretion" is sometimes in the eye of the beholder. The Fifth Circuit recounted that the immigration judge and Board of Immigration Appeals had dismissed one by one the factors that the Hernandez-Corderos had presented in their petition for suspension of deportation including: 1) Mr. Hernandez-Cordero's argument that he would not be able to provide for his family in Mexico because he would not be able to find comparable work as a carpenter; 2) even if he could find comparable work, the family would suffer a drastic reduction in their standard of living in Mexico; 3) the family's having to leave behind friends and family would be emotionally distressing; and 4) the children who could speak but not read or write Spanish would have difficulty adjusting to life in Mexico, where their education would also be at a lower standard. The Fifth Circuit panel did not disagree with each of the single determinations and indicated in fact that many of the conclusions were supported by case law. The court noted that the Board of Immigration Appeals had "Approv[ed] and endors[ed] the careful ticking off of the factors" that the immigration judge had presented. What the Fifth Circuit objected to was that neither the immigration judge nor the Board of Immigration Appeals had considered the factors in cumulative fashion. They wrote:

The judge and the Board apparently considered these matters, since they are mentioned in the psychologist's and teachers' affidavits to be a problem, difficulty, or hardship, but found none of them extreme enough to warrant a suspension of deportation. But just as one more straw may eventually break even the back of a camel, the cumulative effect of these many hardships, each deemed not in itself sufficient, may make their total weight extreme. The board should at least determine, in a deliberate and reasoned manner, whether the straws of hardship here are the kind the statute exacts or whether they are together so onerous that relief should be granted.[89]

The Fifth Circuit argued that even if each one of the factors did not on its own create extreme hardship, cumulatively the suffering might very well be extreme hardship. The end result was that the *Hernandez-Cordero* court reversed and remanded the case to the Board of Immigration Appeals with instructions to consider the cumulative effect of the hardships on the family. Thus, to construe individual hardships discretely or

[88] 783 F.2d 1266, 1267.
[89] 783 F.2d 1266, 1269–70.

to construe them cumulatively is a decision left to the judges. One can see from the *Hernandez-Cordero* case that how one chooses to weigh the hardships, either individually, as the immigration judge and Board had done, or in cumulative fashion, will have implications for the outcome of the case. The issue here is not which approach is correct and which approach the judges of the U.S. Courts of Appeals should take; rather, the case illustrates yet another decisional fork in the road that U.S. Courts of Appeals judges *can* take should they wish to reach a particular legal result. When not bound by clear case law and where the statutes provide any wiggle room based on unclear language, the U.S. Courts of Appeal will defer when they feel like deferring to the lower court or administrative agency.

Discretion: Deciding to Defer

Thus far the chapter has discussed how U.S. Courts of Appeals judges can reach a legal outcome despite congressional limitations on the scope of judicial review by using a variety of creative statutory interpretation techniques and purposive exercises of discretion. One final approach that judges can take is to construe a statute broadly or narrowly to reach a desired legal outcome.

The deportation case of *Tipu v. Immigration and Naturalization Service* (3d Cir. 1994)[90] illustrates how judges can disregard congressional edicts limiting their scope of review in order to reach a desired result. Tipu was an alien from Pakistan who was placed into deportation proceedings because of a narcotics conviction. He applied for a "212(c)" deportation waiver found at 8 U.S.C. § 1182 (c) that would have allowed him to stay in the United States and halt his deportation based on extreme hardship to his family members if he were to be deported. In his application, Tipu presented evidence of his rehabilitation since his narcotics conviction and of his seriously ill brother's dependence on him; his brother had suffered kidney failure and Tipu drove him to weekly dialysis treatment. The immigration judge and the Board of Immigration Appeals denied Tipu's waiver and ordered him deported to Pakistan. Tipu appealed to the Third Circuit Court of Appeals. In this type of case, the normal review standard is "abuse of discretion," which the Third Circuit defined by referring to established case law to mean, "[d]iscretionary decisions of the BIA will not be disturbed unless they are found to be 'arbitrary,

[90] 20 F.3d 580.

irrational or contrary to law.'" In addition, the 212(c) waiver found at 8 U.S.C. § 1182(c) provides that the Attorney General or her delegate (in this case the Board of Immigration Appeals) "as a matter of discretion can determine [whether] to grant a waiver once statutory eligibility is established."[91] The statute is fairly clear that the BIA has to make an error of law or an arbitrary determination before a U.S. Court of Appeals can disturb the findings. Further, the statute granted discretion to the Board to determine whether to award the waiver.

The statutes were constructed to elicit deference from the U.S. Courts of Appeals toward the determinations of the BIA in these instances. However, the statute did not specify how to determine the alien's eligibility for a favorable exercise of discretion so the BIA did what it had done in other cases – it balanced the factors favorable to the alien and those against. After the balancing test, the Board concluded that Tipu's criminal record outweighed the other factors he had presented in his defense. The Third Circuit vacated and remanded the case, saying that the BIA had abused its discretion because it had "inexplicably discounted significant evidence of the hardship that Tipu's deportation would impose on his brother and his family given their financial dependency upon Tipu and the brother's ill health" and not properly weighing his evidence of rehabilitation.[92]

Judge Samuel Alito (then a U.S. Court of Appeals judge) opened his dissent by noting, "The majority has wandered well beyond the limited scope of appellate review that we are permitted to exercise in a case like this."[93] He further noted that 212(c) waivers for deportation are subject to the Attorney General (and her delegate's) discretion and therefore the court's review of these types of decisions is quite restricted. Instead, the majority had decided that the Board of Immigration Appeals had improperly weighed factors for and against the alien's case, an action that Alito thought was impermissible given the limited scope of review. He attributed the actions of the majority purely to the majority's disagreement with the way the BIA had decided the case: "My colleagues in the majority, however, vacate the BIA's decision essentially because they do not like the way the BIA weighed the various factors...In this government of separated powers, it is not for the judiciary to usurp Congress' grant of authority to the Attorney General by applying what approximates de novo appellate review."[94] Call it a balancing of equities, or call it

[91] 20 F.3d 580, 582.
[92] 20 F.3d 580, 587.
[93] 20 F.3d 580, 588.
[94] 20 F.3d 580, 588.

an exercise of discretion, but in the end, the decision of whether to defer to another decision making body is predicated in some cases on whether the U.S. Court of Appeals panel agrees with the determination of the previous decision making body.

Just as the Supreme Court must first decide to grant *certiorari* in a case before the Court can decide the legal outcome, a decision H.W. Perry has dubbed "deciding to decide," the U.S. Courts of Appeals get to decide whether they wish to defer to the Board of Immigration Appeals, to a district court judge, or to statutory intent. One could say the U.S. Courts of Appeals judges have the option to decide to defer.

THE SIGNIFICANCE OF THE VERTICAL STRUCTURE OF THE APPELLATE PROCESS

Given the number of opportunities for purposive behavior that arise, the fact that the appellate process is a hierarchical one becomes very significant to federal litigants, not just in immigration cases but in all types of federal appeals. This chapter identified multiple junctures in the legal decision making process in which a decision maker, whether an administrative official, a judge, or a justice, is confronted with a fork in the road, so to speak; they arrive at a point where they may choose to take one approach over another, which would lead to diverging legal dispositions. In light of the interpretative and discretionary opportunities that arise in immigration cases, the vertical structure of the appellate process takes on added importance, very much as in the childhood game of King of the Hill, where children try to push each other off a hill with the goal of being the last one standing. In a hierarchical appeals system, in effect, the last decision maker's interpretative and discretionary preferences stand. Examination of the 180 pairs of Supreme Court and U.S. Courts of Appeals opinions that had run the length of the federal appellate process and had made it all the way to the Supreme Court yielded the following results (Table 4.1).[95]

---

[95] Although the total number of immigration cases that reached the Supreme Court between 1881 and 2002 was 200, in this particular analysis, I was looking for case "pairs," cases that had both a Courts of Appeals opinion and a Supreme Court opinion that could be compared. Therefore, a number of cases have been omitted from this analysis because there was no corresponding Courts of Appeals opinion or that opinion was too sparse to provide any useable information. In some instances, there was no Courts of Appeals opinion because the case had been appealed directly from the district court (the trial court) to the Supreme Court.

TABLE 4.1. *Analysis of Pairs of Cases that Reached the Supreme Court,*
1881–2002

Categories of Paired Cases	Raw #	Percentage
Cases where the U.S. Supreme Court and U.S. Courts of Appeals used different modes of legal reasoning	113	62
Cases where both the U.S. Supreme Court and U.S. Courts of Appeals both used statutory interpretation as the mode of legal reasoning	55	31
Cases where the U.S. Supreme Court and U.S. Courts of Appeals used the same mode of legal reasoning	67	37

In the majority of these case pairings, the Supreme Court and U.S. Courts of Appeals have used dissimilar modes of legal reasoning. This finding is not surprising in light of the argument of this book that the two courts take dissimilar approaches to deciding cases including using the same set of legal reasoning but to very different extents. The more interesting finding is that in 67, or 37 percent, of these cases, the two courts adopted the same mode of legal reasoning to adjudicate the case, including in 55 cases or 31 percent where both courts used statutory interpretation. In these cases where the two courts agree on the mode of legal reasoning, the salient factor is that given the vertical setup of the appellate process, the Supreme Court's interpretation and judgment is the final one for the simple reason that it is the last stop in the judicial hierarchy. Regardless of whether in any of these 180 total cases the Supreme Court ended up affirming or reversing the decision of the U.S. Courts of Appeals, the high Court's interpretation of a statute or of doctrine is the final one that will stand. The decision making body to handle the appeal last is the one whose judgment stands, regardless of whether that judgment or interpretation is the "correct" one; structure matters and the last court to handle the case is the King of the Hill.

CONCLUSION

This chapter examined the institutional factors that both enable and constrain judges who may wish to act in a purposive manner to pursue policy preferences. There are clear expectations of and constraints on the way federal judges may decide cases. They cannot, for instance, base an outcome purely on their own political or policy preferences, divorced from the requirements stipulated by relevant legal norms, structures, and doctrine that govern the case and of the rule of law. Judges are also bound by rules and norms of professional conduct. But even when operating within these boundaries there is much wiggle room. The power of "mere judgment" turns out to be quite significant when combined with unclear text and many opportunities that either explicitly require or allow judicial discretion. Moreover, due to the hierarchical nature of the appeals process, a higher decision making body can trump and overturn the will of a lower one. Compound these purposive opportunities by the sheer number of cases and the slim possibility of Supreme Court review, and you have an institutional setting that offers ample opportunities for the U.S. Courts of Appeals to become significant policy makers in their own right.

This chapter also outlined some of the interpretative and discretionary strategies and mechanisms available to judges should they desire to reach a particular outcome. First, they may infuse unclear words and text with their own preferred meaning. The words and text at issue may be historically contingent, but this is not true of the interpretative flexibility available to the judges. Second, judges may exercise discretion in a way favorable to the government or the alien that comes down to the level of scrutiny they bring to a case. Finally, given the hierarchical structure of the judiciary and the appeals process, there is a built-in mechanism that favors the will of the last decision making body's preferred interpretation or exercise of discretion. Judges of the contemporary U.S. Courts of Appeals are aware that the chances of reversal are low. Regardless of the motivations, when judges of the U.S. Courts of Appeals render an elucidation of text or statute, it is their determination that trumps the interpretation of other decision making bodies below them, and in almost all instances, their decision is final. The limits of positive law create the conditions for exercises of discretion; the hierarchical structure of the federal judiciary, along with the distinctive docket control mechanisms of each court, create additional incentives for judges of the contemporary U.S. Courts of Appeals to engage in purposive behavior.

5

Institutional Growth and Innovation

The Ninth Circuit Court of Appeals and Immigration

Having examined how institutions originate and some of the factors that cause them to evolve over time, one finds that the U.S. Supreme Court and the U.S. Courts of Appeals, as institutions, developed along parallel but distinct paths. In this chapter, I posit that scholars of institutional development must not only be aware of the important contextual differences between the U.S. Supreme Court and the U.S. Courts of Appeals, but they must also be sensitive to the causes and effects of uneven institutional development within the same level of the federal courts, such as in the U.S. Courts of Appeals system. Beginning in 2002, the Second and Ninth Circuits experienced a sharp and sudden spike in their immigration caseloads. What happens to an institution and its occupants when it is forced to adopt new procedures and processes to cope with a sharply rising caseload? In the set of interviews conducted for this study, several of the Ninth Circuit Courts of Appeals judges insisted that a sharp rise in caseloads does not alter the way they decide cases or otherwise do their jobs, even as the institution must make adjustments and accommodations for the increase.[1] Despite the judges' protestations to the contrary, and consistent with the theory perpetuated throughout this book, a change

---

[1] Judge D stated on 6/13/07 that the increase in volume of immigration appeals "doesn't affect the way she does her job." Similarly, Judge A said on 6/12/07 that she "does not treat the immigration appeals differently" from any other cases f177.11 and Judge E said on 7/26/07 that the increased immigration appeals had not affected the way she personally does her job and that she "handles the cases the same way." As detailed in Chapter 2, the judges' and staff interviews are cited without any identifying information to preserve their anonymity. Throughout the book I refer to judges and staff with feminine pronouns for the sake of avoiding the cumbersome "he/she" and "her/his." The gender of the pronoun used may not match the actual gender of the judges.

in institutional context recalibrated the adjudicative procedures within the Ninth Circuit and reshaped the range and opportunities for purposive behavior available to the judges. Ultimately, the adaptations by the Second and Ninth Circuits altered the way in which most immigration appeals are adjudicated and shifted the very nature of judicial review by moving the Second and Ninth Circuit Courts of Appeals away from their traditional error-correction function and toward the behavior of a *certiorari* court.

This chapter is based primarily on the eight semi-structured, in-person (and one by phone) interviews conducted by the author with eight Ninth Circuit Court of Appeals judges, and in-person interviews with three central staff members of that court. It assesses the impact of the innovations necessitated by the circuit's skyrocketing caseload, which is primarily driven by a dramatic surge in immigration appeals that began in 2002. The case study of the Ninth Circuit and immigration appeals serves two purposes. First, it demonstrates that institutional development within one level of the courts, the U.S. Courts of Appeals, can be uneven. Immigration appeals have had disproportionate effects on several U.S. Courts of Appeals, thereby setting those courts on experiments of reconfiguring existing resources. Second, the case study shows that within each policy area, the federal courts are but one part of a larger system. As a result, when other parts of the immigration system, such as administrative agencies, do not perform their designated functions, the U.S. Courts of Appeals (and individual courts at that), not the U.S. Supreme Court, bear the brunt of the fallout as problems that used to occur earlier in the process are simply shifted further up the appellate chain.

As appeals from alien litigants surged into the federal court system, the structural design of the judicial hierarchy exacerbated the problem in a number of ways. Chief among these problems is that a bottleneck occurs where the cases bunch up at the U.S. Courts of Appeals level, leaving the Supreme Court unaffected. In addition, as two circuits discovered, the institutional adjustments and experimentation they engaged in were very much constrained by the structure, rules, and norms that were already fixed by the Constitution, thereby limiting the options before them.

The swelling caseload at the Courts of Appeals has had very concrete effects. It has affected the way individual judges and staffs adjudicate and process cases and it has also changed the institution itself by necessitating a change in procedures. The broken immigration bureaucracy places psychological pressure on Courts of Appeals judges, who now feel the added pressure to "back fill" for the administrative agencies and other parts of the immigration system that are not fulfilling their duties and functions. Also, as this case study will show, the upshot of the inevitable alterations to the court's processes and procedures to keep pace with the flood of immigration appeals is to force the court to adopt *certiorari-* like functions as it "triages" its cases.[2] This triage process means that some cases get more of the judges' attention while other cases are routed to a track where appeals get far less judicial attention. Their strategy is consistent with the observation, made by Judge Richard Posner of the Seventh Circuit Court of Appeals, that increasing reliance on staff and law clerks and the proliferation of unpublished opinions are two ways that the Courts of Appeals have coped with their increasing caseloads.[3] But, as will become evident, it is not just a matter of who is adjudicating the appeals; it is a shift in the division of labor on the court between the judges and central staff. This division of labor is characterized by qualitative differences between an Article III judge's or a staff member's review of one's appeal, where judges and staff are meant to fulfill specific institutionally designated functions. In the end what is really at issue is the quality and depth of the review an alien litigant obtains.

Chapter 4 described some of the developments outside the federal courts that affected the number and nature of immigration appeals flowing into the federal courts that began in 1980. However, in 2003, the U.S. Courts of Appeals noticed a sudden and very sharp increase in immigration appeals flooding into their courts. The catalyst for the recent wave of immigration appeals can be traced to changes at the Board of Immigration Appeals; the vast majority of these appeals were petitions for review of decisions made by the BIA.

Changes to the operational procedures at the Board of Immigration Appeals were the primary cause of the most recent increase in immigration appeals to the Courts of Appeals. As one will see, the so-called immigration surge had a disproportionate impact on the U.S. Courts of Appeals system, substantially affecting the Second and Ninth Circuits in particular.[4] The *Los Angeles Times* reported, "The growing number of

---

[2] Judge E, Judge F, and the central staff members of the Ninth Circuit I interviewed used the word "triage" to describe the way immigration appeals are sorted and tracked. (Interview with Judge E, 7/26/07; Judge F, 8/6/07; and court staff, 6/11/07.) I also wish to thank Judge D for initially drawing my attention to the implications for judicial review of the court's tracking procedures.

[3] Richard A. Posner, *Federal Courts* (Cambridge, MA: Harvard University Press, 1985), 97, 105, 107.

[4] The term "surge" was used in the article "Immigration Appeals Surge in Courts," *The Third Branch* (e-newsletter produced by the Administrative Office of the U.S. Courts, Office of Public Affairs, Washington, DC), Sept. 2003 (available at http://www.uscourts.

appeals filed in the federal court system has been most severe in the 9th Circuit... So many new immigration appeals pour in – 150 a week in recent months – that the 9th Circuit is automatically issuing stays of all deportation orders, defeating the intent of [Attorney General] Ashcroft's rules to resolve cases more quickly."[5] Cathy Catterson, then Clerk of the Ninth Circuit, confirmed this assessment when she wrote in a 2006 article that the current "caseload challenges" at the Ninth Circuit were due to "two words – 'immigration cases.'"[6]

The surge also presented challenges for the Second Circuit. A study conducted by Second Circuit staff and a law professor stated that the surge has "placed a huge strain on judicial resources, requiring courts to hire additional staff, recruit visiting judges, and schedule extra sessions for hearing cases."[7] In another article, Palmer further observed that the Second Circuit "... has now received more than three times as many immigration appeals since 2002 [through 2006] as it received in the previous thirty years combined."[8] The Second Circuit responded to the immigration surge in a number of ways, including heavier reliance on its mediation system, hiring more part-time attorneys, initiating a non-argument calendar in October 2005, and adding additional panels to process immigration cases, among other strategies. The numerous changes adopted by this circuit are detailed elsewhere so I highlight the circuit's main strategy.[9] The "most significant change" adopted by the

gov/ttb/sept03ttb/immigration/index.html). Subsequent articles and studies picked up the term and started using it as well. See John R. B. Palmer, Stephen W. Yale-Loehr, and Elizabeth Cronin, "Why Are So Many People Challenging Board of Immigration Appeals Decisions in Federal Court? An Empirical Analysis of the Recent Surge in Petition for Review," 20 *Georgetown Immigration L.J.* 1 (2005), 6. See also Claire Cooper and Emily Bazar, "Immigration Appeals Swamp Federal Courts," *Sacramento Bee*, Sept. 5, 2004, A1; Solomon Moore and Ann M. Simmons, "Immigrant Pleas Crushing Federal Appellate Courts: As Caseloads Skyrocket, Judges Blame the Work Done by the Board of Immigration Appeals," *Los Angeles Times*, May 2, 2005, 1; and Tom Perotta, "Immigration Appeals Surge in Second Circuit," *New York Law Journal*, Nov. 4, 2004, at 1.

5 Lisa Getter and Jonathan Peterson, "Speedier Rate of Deportation Rulings Assailed," *Los Angeles Times*, January 5, 2003.
6 Cathy Catterson, "Challenges in Appellate Caseload and Its Processing," 48 *Arizona Law Review* 287–299, 294. In late 2007, Catterson was promoted to Circuit and Court of Appeals Executive and Molly Dwyer is now the Clerk of the Court.
7 Palmer, Yale-Loehr, and Cronin, "Why Are So Many People Challenging Board of Immigration Appeals Decisions in Federal Court?," 6.
8 John Palmer, "Symposium on Immigration Appeals and Judicial Review: The Second Circuit's "New Asylum Seekers": Responses to an Expanded Immigration Docket," 55 *Catholic University Law Review* 965 at 968 (2006).
9 *Supra*, notes 1 and 3.

Second Circuit in response to the immigration surge was the creation on October 3, 2005, of the non-argument calendar where "appeals relating to asylum claims can be decided without oral argument."[10] Therefore, the main effect of the surge on the Second Circuit was to cause that circuit to abandon its long-cherished commitment to provide oral argument in all its cases. Only the Ninth and the Second circuits, among the twelve U.S. Courts of Appeals, were left scrambling for ways to cope with their spiking caseload.

This particularized effect on these two circuits is because of immigration entry and settlement patterns and their correspondence with the geographically defined boundaries of each circuit jurisdiction. Recall that immigration settlement is essentially a regional phenomenon that most affects the metro areas of six states: California, Arizona, New York, Illinois, Texas, and New Jersey.[11] And, in deportation or removal proceedings, an alien's appeal originates in the federal court jurisdiction where they reside. The confluence of immigration settlement patterns and the geographically determined boundaries of the U.S. Court of Appeals system skewed the distribution of immigration appeals when their numbers increased in 2002. Moreover, the Supreme Court, because of its docket control mechanism, was insulated from the immigration surge.

THE ROLE OF BIA STREAMLINING IN THE SURGE

The structural setup of the immigration appeals process and statutory rules that govern the federal judiciary ensured that changes in the BIA were felt in the U.S. Courts of Appeals system, and most strongly in the Ninth Circuit Court of Appeals. (Given the U.S. Supreme Court's docket control mechanism, it felt no particular effect.) Various studies and media reports have attempted to pinpoint the cause for the immigration appeals spike in the Courts of Appeals in 2002; these studies draw the same conclusion: that it was the BIA streamlining procedures, which first went into effect in 1999 and were later more comprehensively instituted in 2002, that were the cause of the surge. Although the steady rise in immigration appeals since the 1990s that is discussed in Chapter 4 could be attributed to a variety of factors, the 2003 surge could be isolated to the reforms at the BIA. In the late 1990s, the BIA was facing a significant and growing backlog of cases. The membership on the Board had increased, "more

---

[10] Ibid. at 974.
[11] Migration Policy Institute Staff, *The New Century: Immigration and the U.S.United States* (available at: http://www.migrationinformation.org/Profiles/display.cfm?ID=283).

than quadrupling" in less than seven years, yet in 2002 the Department of Justice came to the conclusion that enlarging the BIA membership was not helping to reduce the backlog of cases.[12]

The BIA's first attempt to deal with its backlog problem was in 1999, when Attorney General Janet Reno mandated a set of "Streamlining Rules" that became effective on October 18, 1999.[13] In this first round of streamlining, two major changes were implemented. First, the new rules allowed a single permanent[14] BIA member to "act alone in affirming certain decisions of immigration judges and the Service without opinions."[15] Second, the BIA chairman could "designate certain categories of cases as suitable for review [by a single member, without opinion]."[16] These two changes in adjudicative procedures had an impact on the backlog, and when the Executive Office of Immigration Review (EOIR) and the BIA retained Arthur Anderson LLP to evaluate the effectiveness of the measures, Anderson reported that the moves had contributed to a 53 percent increase in the overall number of cases the BIA was able to process between September 2000 and August 2001. The audit agency also reportedly stated its belief that the streamlining had not adversely affected aliens and Anderson deemed the measures "an unqualified success."[17]

In August 2002, Attorney General John Ashcroft again ordered the BIA to clear its backlog of more than 56,000 cases by March 2003.[18] The order resulted in what one study called "a qualitative change in the BIA's decision making."[19] To make headway on its backlog, the Board was ordered by Ashcroft to streamline its procedure further. Previously, panels of three BIA members had decided cases; now a single Board member could decide most cases. This procedure remains current policy. Put differently, current practice is that all cases are decided by a single member, except for the small class of cases that are designated for review by a three-member panel.[20]

[12] Dorsey Report, 15.
[13] Executive Office of Immigration Review, "Board of Immigration Appeals: Streamlining Rules," 64 Fed. Reg. 56, 135 (8 C.F.R. Part 3).
[14] Some of the expansion of Board membership was accomplished with the appointment of "temporary Board members."
[15] Dorsey Report, 17.
[16] Cited in the Dorsey Report, 17.
[17] Cited in the Dorsey Report, 19.
[18] See "Board of Immigration Appeals: Procedural Reforms to Improve Case Management," 67 Fed. Reg. 54, 878 (Aug. 26, 2002).
[19] Palmer, Yale-Loehr, and Cronin, "Why Are So Many People Challenging Board of Immigration Appeals Decisions in Federal Court?," 7.
[20] The move to single-member adjudications might be what prompted Judge C to tell me, "The BIA says that they have stopped streamlining, but they haven't." Interview with Judge C, 6/13/07.

The move to single-member adjudications raised a host of concerns in the immigration advocacy community and among many of the U.S. Courts of Appeals judges I interviewed. A primary concern was that a single BIA member is far more likely to make a mistake than is a panel of three judges and that the benefit of the deliberative nature of a panel discussion that could detect errors would be lost with the move to single-member adjudications.[21] As Stephen Legomsky wrote, "accuracy, consistency, efficiency, and public acceptance" should be four main goals of an administrative process.[22] One current BIA member, who was interviewed by the media and spoke only on condition of anonymity, agreed with the critics' assessment when she stated, "I think we are still providing adequate review…It's just that when only one person decides a case instead of three, there's a lot more potential for errors."[23]

Exacerbating the worry that individual Board member adjudications would lead to more errors than a three-member panel was the increase in summary affirmances of immigration judges' decisions that went against the alien. Summary rulings are those with little more than a few lines and no elaboration of how the BIA member came to the the conclusion that he or she reached. The *Los Angeles Times* found that even before the streamlining was to commence officially, the Board's summary rulings went up to 38 percent from the previous 9 percent.[24] The Dorsey Report, commissioned by the American Bar Association's Commission on Immigration Policy, Practice and Pro Bono, also confirmed the qualitative change of BIA decisions. The report notes that by the end of 2001, "approximately 10% of BIA decisions were summary affirmances. By March 2002, more than half of the BIA's decisions were summary affirmances."[25]

The increase in summary affirmances signaled lower success rates for asylum applicants, and indeed this was empirically verified by several studies. One study done by three law professors, Ramji-Nogales, Schoenholtz, and Schrag, found "a sudden and lasting decline in the rate of success by asylum applicants" after the BIA "changed its mode of

---

[21] See, e.g., Stephen H. Legomsky, "Learning to Live with Unequal Justice: Asylum and the Limits to Consistency," 60 *Stanford Law Review* 413 (2007). Legomsky shows, on pages 423–28, why consistency in adjudication is so important.

[22] Stephen H. Legomsky, "An Asylum Seeker's Bill of Rights in a Non-Utopian World," 14 *Georgetown Immigration Law Journal* 619, 622 (2000).

[23] Quoted in Getter and Peterson, "Speedier Rate of Deportation Rulings Assailed," 4.

[24] Getter and Peterson, "Speedier Rate of Deportation Rulings Assailed," 2.

[25] Dorsey and Whitney, LLP. "Study Conducted for: The American Bar Association Commission on Immigration Policy, Practice, Pro Bono RE: Board of Immigration Appeals: Procedural Reforms to Improve Case Management," October 2003, 40.

decision making."[26] More specifically, the success rate of asylum applicants represented by counsel dropped from 43 percent in FY 2001 (pre-
BIA streamlining), to a low of 13 percent after FY 2005, a decrease of
70 percent. Meanwhile, the unrepresented aliens were "hit even harder,"
with their success rate dropping from 26 percent in FY2001 to 6 percent
in FY2005, a decrease of 77 percent.[27] The nature of BIA opinions had
indeed changed, with repercussions not only for the alien appellants but
also for the U.S. Courts of Appeals system.

The move to single-member adjudication, coupled with the increase
in summary rulings, left many aliens and their lawyers frustrated and
angry. Philip Schrag has outlined the multiple functions fulfilled by written opinions. For one, written opinions go a long way in "helping the los-
ing party to accept the legitimacy of an appellate decision." The opinion
also "ensures that harried adjudicators actually read the parties' contentions and formulate reasoned responses to them," and in cases headed
for further judicial review, the written opinions "give the federal courts
insight into why the agency did not agree with appellant's contentions."[28]
As Judge F was quick to clarify, it was not the streamlining itself that was
the problem: "It was the nonreview rubberstamping" on the part of the
BIA that caused alien litigants and U.S. Courts of Appeals judges anger
and frustration.[29] The summary rulings after streamlining consist of little
more than a few lines stating the disposition of the case without any
explanation or justification of why the appeal was denied.

Another concern raised by the streamlining procedure is the speed at
which the post-streamlined Board seemed to be adjudicating the cases.
This concern has been fueled by a notable increase in the rate of denial
of alien claims. A *Los Angeles Times* review of BIA decisions found that
the denial rate rose from 59 percent in October 2002 to 86 percent in
October 2003 after the streamlining took effect. More striking, the study
found that some Board members were spending only a few *minutes* on
each case. The *Los Angeles Times* reported, for instance, that "On Oct. 31,
Frederick Hess, a member of the Board of Immigration Appeals, signed
more than 50 cases – a decision nearly every 10 minutes if he worked a
nine-hour day without a break...Edward Grant, Hess's colleague, signed

[26] Jaya, Ramji-Nogales, Andrew Schoenholtz, and Philip G. Schrag, "Refugee Roulette: Disparities in Asylum Adjudication," 60 *Stanford Law Review* (2007): 295–408 at 359–60.
[27] Ibid. at 359–60.
[28] Philip G. Schrag, "The Summary Affirmances Proposal of the Board of Immigration Appeals," 531, 534–35.
[29] Interview with Judge F, 8/6/07.

more than 50 cases that same day, the *Times* found. Altogether that day, the board issued nearly 400 decisions, ranging from complex asylum cases to simple jurisdictional matters."[30]

The Department of Justice (DOJ) issued a statement contesting the findings of the *Los Angeles Times*, arguing that the day the cases are signed does not always reflect the day the case was decided. One DOJ official noted that the date on which the Board member signs a decision reflects "the date the case was mailed to the parties."[31] The DOJ's protestations that the *Los Angeles Times*'s statistics may not be completely accurate may well be true, but perhaps the more salient point is the public perception of the legitimacy of this process. This includes not just the perception of the aliens and the lawyers involved in litigating these cases, but also the Courts of Appeals judges, who read the newspapers like everyone else. In fact, Judge E cited that very *Los Angeles Times* article in raising her concern that the BIA was not being conscientious about doing its job and her feeling that the burden had shifted to the U.S. Court of Appeals to rectify errors and abuses.[32] Criticisms about the procedural changes at the BIA have come from a broad range of sources, including "lawyers, scholars, Congresspeople, and even [retired] IJs and a former Board Member" – people that know the immigration system best.[33]

Indeed, because of the confluence of BIA streamlining and changes to the immigration law, immigration appeals have added exponentially to the Ninth Circuit's caseload, as evidenced by a variety of quantitative measures. Tables 5.1 and 5.2 respectively quantify the surge in raw numbers and also show immigration appeals as a percentage of that circuit's overall caseload and as a percentage of all immigration cases filed nationwide.

One can see the disproportionate impact of the immigration appeals on the Second and Ninth circuits and a less dramatic increase in the Third and Fifth circuits, the other two circuits in this study. Also evident is the large impact that immigration cases have on the Second and Ninth circuits, as illustrated by the percentage of those cases that constitute those

[30] Getter and Peterson, "Speedier Rate of Deportation Rulings Assailed," 2.
[31] Getter and Peterson, "Speedier Rate of Deportation Rulings Assailed," 2. Getter and Peterson also add that the Board members "privately did not dispute the *Times's* findings that some members are deciding as many as 50 cases a day."
[32] Interview with Judge E, 7/26/07.
[33] Palmer, Yale-Loehr, and Cronin, "Why Are So Many People Challenging Board of Immigration Appeals Decisions in the Federal Courts?," 38.

TABLE 5.1. *Number of BIA Appeals Filed During 12-Month Periods 2001–2006 and as Percentage of Total Appeals Filed in Circuit*

Year Ending	National	As % Total Cases Filed	Second	Third	Fifth	Ninth
12/31/2001	1,642	(3%)	166 (4%)	90 (2%)	208 (2%)	913 (9%)
12/31/2002	6,465	(11%)	991 (19%)	296 (8%)	398 (5%)	3,672 (30%)
12/31/2003	8,750	(14%)	2,180 (33%)	469 (12%)	383 (4%)	4,035 (32%)
12/31/2004	11,366	(18%)	2,602 (38%)	517 (13%)	501 (6%)	5,964 (40%)
12/31/2005	12,873	(18%)	2,710 (37%)	797 (17%)	653 (7%)	6,625 (41%)
12/31/2006	10,750	(17%)	2,486 (37%)	660 (15%)	585 (7%)	5,166 (37%)

Source: All statistics were provided by the Office of the Clerk of the Court, U.S. Courts of Appeals for the Ninth Circuit (3/29/07). The percentages of the Ninth Circuit appeals reflect only the immigration appeals from the BIA and exclude federal district court and other filings that are also immigration related.

courts' overall dockets. The surge seems to peak in 2005 and then level off by 2006.[34]

Table 5.1 shows a comparison of the numbers of immigration appeals filed nationally and of those filed in the Ninth Circuit and in several other circuits. Table 5.2 is another way to understand how the BIA's streamlining precipitated a surge of immigration appeals that affected the Ninth Circuit Court of Appeals. Consider that the Ninth Circuit experienced from 2000 to 2001, a 180 percent increase in the percentage of immigration cases; from 2001 to 2002 this increase was 58 percent; from 2002 to 2003, 28 percent; and from 2003 to 2004, 19 percent. Put differently, from 2000 to 2005, the Ninth Circuit experienced a 570 percent increase in immigration appeals.[35] Together, Tables 5.1 and 5.2 illustrate the concentrated impact of this on the Ninth Circuit.

[34] On May 30, 2008, Attorney General Mukasey announced the addition of five new BIA members (available at http://www.usdoj.gov/opa/pr/2008/May/08-ag-483.html). Whether the expansion of the BIA will alter its actual adjudications process remains to be seen.

[35] Cathy Catterson, "Changes in the Appellate Caseload," in 48 *Arizona Law Review* 287–299, 295. The percentage increases in the immigration appeals rate in the Ninth Circuit are measured in years, ending September 30 of each year.

TABLE 5.2. *Immigration Cases in the Ninth Circuit and Nationwide, 1994–2005, for 12-Month Period Ending September 30 (Percentage of National Immigration Appeals)*

Year Ending	National	Ninth Circuit
1994	983	431 (44%)
1995	1,180	624 (53%)
1996	1,062	579 (55%)
1997	1,921	1,018 (53%)
1998	1,936	1,102 (57%)
1999	1,731	938 (54%)
2000	1,723	910 (53%)
2001	1,760	954 (54%)
2002	4,449	2,670 (60%)
2003	8,833	4,206 (48%)
2004	10,812	5,368 (50%)
2005	11,741	6,390 (54%)

Source: Catterson, "Changes in Appellate Caseload," 295 (see note 6). These numbers include immigration appeals originating from the federal district courts, not just from the Board of Immigration Appeals.

The Board's streamlining measures, which were aimed at clearing its own logjam, had simply shifted the backlog of cases to the U.S. Courts of Appeals, particularly the Second and Ninth circuits. One unintended consequence wrought by the BIA streamlining, the backlog at the Ninth Circuit, appeared also to be fed by a feedback loop. Judge F speculated that, given the delays in the Courts of Appeals, "people figured out that once you file, it will take a while, years, before they get to me." In Judge F's estimation, immigration lawyers filed appeals at increased rates because, to some extent, they had figured out how to "game the system" and lengthen their alien client's stay in the U.S.[36] From the aliens' perspective, the longer they are able to remain in the country, the more equities they will build up, and perhaps Congress will pass legislation entitling them to some new relief, such as a temporary guest worker program. Not only was the Ninth Circuit staggering under the weight of the immigration appeals, but the very delays in processing caused by the immigration surge were creating incentives for even more aliens to appeal to the U.S. Courts of Appeals. The BIA streamlining and 1996 court-stripping measures did

[36] Interview with Judge F, 8/6/07.

nothing to change the incentive structure for aliens to appeal their cases as far as they could go in the appellate process.[37]

Beyond the immigration appeals' effects on individual staff members and judges is a potentially more serious overall effect on the Ninth Circuit as an institution. The immigration appeals are slowing down all the business in the court. Judge E described it as a "tail wagging the dog" effect. Her sense was that this slowdown was the main effect of the immigration appeals on the Ninth Circuit. She said, "When people complain about delays across the board, from the length of time of a filing to oral argument and the length of time to get a disposition…whether they know it or not, immigration cases are a systemic drag."[38] Cathy Catterson, the Clerk of the Ninth Circuit, confirmed this assessment when she reported that appellate cases (of all kinds, not just immigration) used to take about six months to complete, but now they take nine months.[39] As Judge E stated, "It's not fair to the other litigants."[40] In the instance of the Ninth Circuit, immigration appeals do not just affect the manner in which judges and staff do their jobs; it has affected other U.S. Courts of Appeals litigants and their lawyers who have nothing whatsoever to do with immigration.

EFFECT OF SURGE ON NINTH CIRCUIT PERSONNEL

The effect of the immigration surge on the Ninth Circuit as an institution was one thing, but it also affected the occupants of the institution in a number of ways. One effect commonly experienced by both the central staff and judges was to change the mix of cases on the circuit's docket. Judge B and the staff noted that when they had first joined the court some ten years ago, they had had a much more varied mix of cases. Members of the central staff said that about ten to fifteen years earlier they had had the "perfect mix of cases."[41] Judge G noted that some judges on the circuit resent the large percentage of immigration appeals at the circuit and these judges "don't want to be immigration judges."[42] However, Judge G disputed her colleagues' perception that they were being inundated with immigration appeals. She noted that on the few days that a judge serves

---

[37] See Lenni Benson, "Making Paper Dolls," 64–8, for her suggestions of reforms that might attack the incentives of aliens.

[38] Interview with Judge E, 7/26/07.

[39] Solomon Moore and Ann M. Simmons, "Immigrant Pleas Crushing Federal Appellate Courts," at 1.

[40] Interview with Judge E, 7/26/07.

[41] Interviews with Judge B, 6/12/07, and court staff, 6/12/07.

[42] Interview with Judge E, 7/26/07.

on a screening panel, 60 percent of the cases to be dealt with are immigration cases, and many of the immigration cases are of such low weight that the judges never see them. Therefore, in this judge's estimation, about "20 percent of the [overall] time is the most an average judge deals with immigration appeals. Their [any Ninth Circuit judge's] time is *not* consumed by immigration."[43] In response to the notion that some judges are irritated by the large percentage of immigration cases at the Ninth Circuit, she responded, "I don't know what these people expect when they got to the court. Isn't our job to deal with people's problems?" She added that part of the job of being a judge on a court of general jurisdiction was that one could not select the type or mix of cases arriving at the court.[44]

Another effect experienced by both the judges and staff was that the recent congressional changes to the immigration laws, such as those made by AEDPA and IIRIRA, created difficulties that were only exacerbated by the volume of cases coming in during the surge. Specifically, these laws had changed the nature of the cases flowing to the courts by increasing the overall difficulty because of the more technical and procedural review that became necessary in these cases, as opposed to just concentrating on questions of legal merit. As Posner and others have noted, one's caseload is not the same as one's workload.[45] A heavy caseload does not necessarily mean a heavier workload, just as a lighter caseload does not always mean a lighter workload; the two are not correlated. Especially after the 1996 legislative changes to the Immigration and Nationality Act, highly technical jurisdictional and procedural issues, not questions of legal merit, now largely consume much of the staff attorneys' time. One staff member expressed frustration and a feeling of a lack of efficacy in "helping people" because of the vast number of cases dealing exclusively with technical issues that are nonlegal in nature.[46] Because of the central staff's primary role in screening arriving appeals for jurisdiction, one can see how the changes to the immigration laws would significantly change the nature of their jobs.

To elaborate, the recent legislative changes have had unintended consequences for all the personnel on the Ninth Circuit. Although the goal of these laws was to strip large classes of cases from federal court jurisdiction, presumably to lighten the courts' caseload and to clamp down on aliens abusing the legal system to delay their inevitable deportation or removal, in fact the consequence has been to add to both the staff's and

---

[43] Interview with Judge G, 7/27/07.
[44] Interview with Judge G, 7/27/07.
[45] Posner, *Federal Courts*, 73.
[46] Interviews with court staff, 6/11/07.

the judges' work. One unintended result of the reforms in immigration appeals is to give rise to an array of jurisdictional issues. Currently, instead of just deciding the merits of the case, staff as well as judges must first wade through the diverse requirements for federal court jurisdiction over the case. These determinations are often quite complex; they can turn, for example, on the reading of the federal statute, the meaning of a "conviction" under various states' criminal laws, when an alien was convicted, or on the effective date of the statutes. The central staff as well as many of the judges noted that instead of alleviating the court's caseload crunch and lightening individual workloads, the recent changes in immigration laws have consumed *more* of the staff's and the judges' time. Rather than decreasing the circuits' workload by stripping cases from their jurisdiction, the legislative changes have added to it by requiring a painstaking sorting through jurisdictional issues first. Even when judges end up finding that the court has no jurisdiction to review, they have already sunk a significant amount of time and staff resources into the case. One judge was of the opinion that it would have been easier if the Congress had left the law as it was because now, instead of going "straight to the merits of the cases," the judges spend at least half their time wading through and "figuring out procedural issues" such as jurisdiction before they can even get to the merits of the case.[47] The Ninth Circuit and its personnel were hit with a double whammy beginning in the late 1990s with an increase in both caseload and workload.

Although the interviews with the Ninth Circuit's judges and staff revealed common effects of the surge felt by both groups, there were also more individualized effects. In fact, it was the staff that bore the brunt of the difficulties created by the burgeoning caseload. One of the judges indicated that because a larger percentage of immigration appeals are handled up front by the staff, the caseload crunch does not affect the judges as much as the staff. She surmised that "morale issues are at the staff level" rather than at the judges' level.[48] The staff spoke of the great pressure placed on them with the increased reliance on their role in case management. The court administration has had to develop very precise and careful tracking of cases, not just to keep track of who gets what kinds of appeals and motions, but because there is now a much heavier burden on staff to keep track of which legal issues are sent to which panels, so that no two panels are deciding the same legal issue. The goal

---

[47] Interview with Judge G, 7/27/07.
[48] Interview with Judge A, 6/12/07.

of not sending the same legal issue to more than one panel is not only to avoid duplication of effort, but also to avoid the creation of precedents pointing in opposite directions

Some internal statistics from the court provide an estimation of the staff's workload. In the Ninth Circuit, the name of the author of published opinions is provided, except in cases designated as *per curiam*. These opinions identify the opinion's author and the names of the judges who sat on the panel. These published opinions have gone through the oral argument track. But some decisions that went through the oral argument track may also be signed with the designation "Memo." "Memo" can indicate a case that either went through an oral argument or through a screening panel.[49] In their internal communications, the judges make the distinction between published opinions and unpublished (nonprecedential) memorandum dispositions and they refer to the latter in shorthand as "memodispo" or "memdispo."[50] "Orders" are decisions written by law clerks or motion panels; 61 percent of motions appeals are disposed of in this way. The staff indicated that, in recent years, only 1 percent to 3 percent of immigration appeals resulted in a published opinion that made new law. They concluded that although the volume of immigration appeals may have risen substantially over time, the number of "merit cases" has not gone up.[51]

Although the raw numbers of immigration appeals went up during the surge, the percentages of how the cases were terminated stayed roughly the same (Table 5.3). The numbers do confirm that in terms of raw numbers, more and more cases were dealt with by court staff attorneys (as indicated by "Order"), rather than by Article III judges who have gone through a confirmation process and hold life tenure. There can also be implications for the disposition in a case based on who handles it.

THE NINTH CIRCUIT RESPONDS: BUILDING
ON THE BROWNING ERA REFORMS

Because the the number of judgeships in the Ninth Circuit has not increased in recent years, any institutional adjustments created by the

---

[49] If the "memo-designated" case has gone through an argument panel, then the memo will likely have been written by one of the judge's law clerks. If the case came from a screening panel, the memo was likely written by staff attorneys. The former types of memos would be more reflective of the judge's own views, or, as Professor Stephen Wasby described it, "the judge's fingerprints are likely to be all over it." (Author's email communication with Wasby, February 14, 2008.)

[50] Email communication with Wasby, February 14, 2008.

[51] Interviews with court staff, 6/11/07.

TABLE 5.3. *Terminations of the Ninth Circuit's Immigration Appeals by Calendar Year*

Year	2001	2002	2003	2004	2005	2006
Opinion	38 (3%)	38 (3%)	54 (3%)	112 (2%)	79 (1%)	50 (1%)
Memo	345 (33%)	381 (27%)	703 (33%)	2299 (48%)	1704 (35%)	1904 (38%)
Order	673 (63%)	981 (70%)	1358 (64%)	2394 (50%)	2995 (63%)	3069 (61%)
Total	1061	1400	2115	4805	4778	5023

Source: Statistics provided by the Office of the Clerk of the Court of the Ninth Circuit.

surge in immigration appeals and the rest of the court's caseload have been restricted to the use of innovative case management procedures. Under the tenure of former Chief Judge James R. Browning (1976 to 1988), the Ninth Circuit had already undertaken a number of reforms in order to handle the large circuit's larger caseload. Beginning in 1978, notable reforms included the Ninth Circuit's move to an *en banc* procedure that allowed a panel with fewer judges than the full bench to hear a case; the court's creation of three administrative units located in different cities in the circuit's jurisdiction; and the establishment of a large and structured staff attorneys' office.[52] The office of the staff attorneys is responsible for a case-inventory system that was designed to sort cases by difficulty. This system's purpose is to help the judges balance their workload and maintain consistency in the adjudication of cases.[53] This sorting system commences as soon as a case arrives at the court. The staff first checks that the Ninth Circuit actually has jurisdiction over the case. Then the cases are coded by the legal issues involved, of which the staff must then keep track for the later purpose of assigning the cases to panels. Finally, the staff assigns a numerical "weight" to the case of S, 3, 5, 7, or 10.[54] The higher the number, the more complex and difficult the legal issues involved in the case.

[52] See generally, *supra* note 14, especially Arthur Hellman's chapter, "The Crisis in the Circuits and the Innovations of the Browning Years," 7.
[53] Ibid.
[54] Oakley and Thompson, "Screening and Delegation," in Arthur Hellman, ed., *Restructuring Justice: the Innovations of the Ninth Circucit and the Future of the Federal Courts* (Ithaca, NY: Cornell University Press, 1990), 110.

This weighting system also dictates how the cases are calendared and whether the cases are placed on an oral argument track or on a screening track. The former, which may not literally mean that counsel will engage in oral argument before the judges, nevertheless means that the appeal will receive more attention from judges rather than staff. The latter means that an appeal will receive less judicial scrutiny and is characterized by heavy staff involvement. The oral argument track is intended for cases with more complex and difficult legal issues. The screening track (or non-argument track in the Second Circuit) is meant for appeals that are regarded as straightforward and therefore easy, or appeals that are perceived as frivolous or hopeless. The screening system began in January 1982.[55] The case weight "S" was first introduced in the spring of 1988, toward the end of Browning's term. A case with an S designation is automatically scheduled for a screening panel.[56]

This weighting procedure is similar to the system used at the Board of Immigration Appeals.[57] The lower the number "weight" assigned to the case by staff attorneys, the less contact time the judge will have with the appeal. (The term "contact time" is my own, not the staff's.) An S-weight case might be one in which the alien's counsel files a ten-page brief in which counsel argues, citing the Geneva Conventions, that the alien should be granted extended voluntary departure (an alternative to deportation/removal). Such a case falls under settled law and the brief is relatively short. The "1" weight is also an indicator to the staff attorneys that they should be spending no more than a few hours on the case. An example of a case weighted "7" might be one in which, for example, there is a 30-page brief accompanied by reams of supporting documents, and where there are multiple legal issues, including statutory interpretation and jurisdictional issues. Such a case might take a staff attorney days, if not weeks, to sort through. The higher-weighted cases are eligible to be placed on the oral argument track although not all of them will wind up there.

The designation of a case for oral argument or screening also determines the degree of scrutiny by Article III judges. In an appeal that is set

---

[55] Ibid.

[56] Ibid. at 110–11. The "S" weight designation simply replaced the previous "1" and "3L" classifications that designated low- weighted cases.

[57] The practice of sorting cases by level of difficulty, which is determined by the number and nature of the legal issues involved, is also a practice used at the Board of Immigration Appeals, where the difficulty of cases is "matched to staff attorneys' perceived level of ability." (Michael Heilman, retired BIA member 1986–2001; email communication with author, 12/28/07.)

for oral argument, the judges review the case file in depth. In contrast, screening panel procedures involve a three-judge panel sitting through staff presentations of summaries of the case files, and often the judges will not have read the files.[58] Under the Ninth Circuit's current procedure, staff attorneys "routinely prepare draft dispositions in advance of judicial consideration."[59] In the past, the Ninth Circuit's screening procedure did not require a physical meeting (sometimes virtual meeting via videoconferencing) with the judges; the judges would review the screening cases either simultaneously (the three judges simultaneously review the case in their own chambers), or sequentially (the first judge reviews the file and then passes it along to the second judge, who reviews it and sends it on to the third judge on the panel). Today, the more common practice is to use videoconferencing to cut down on travel.[60]

To gain some sense of how long judges spend on screening cases, one may consider Judge Kozinski's assessment of the judicial time put into these cases. He wrote that there was "an average of five to ten minutes devoted to each case" and during the two or three days each month that a judge sat on a screening panel, the panel "may issue 100 to 150 such rulings."[61] On a screening panel, a decision must be unanimous. If the screening panel cannot reach consensus, a single judge who does not agree to sign on to the opinion, for whatever reason, can "kick" the case back for oral argument.

Approximately 10 percent to 15 percent of the cases on a screening panel (not just immigration cases) get "kicked."[62] Judge E, however, estimated that the percentage of kicked cases to be in the range of 30 percent. She also had recently sat on an admittedly anomalous panel that kicked 80 percent of their cases.[63] Because of the rule that only one judge is necessary to kick a case, several judges indicated that the composition of the screening panel matters greatly and one judge can act strategically

[58] Penelope Pether, "Sorcerers, Not Apprentices: How Judicial Clerks and Staff Attorneys Impoverish U.S. Law," 39 *Arizona State Law Journal* 1, 15 (2007). Sometimes one of the parties on the screening panel will join the discussion via videoconferencing.

[59] Arthur D. Hellman, "The 2005 National Conference on Appellate Justice: Conference Report: The View from the Trenches: A Report on the Breakout Sessions at the 2005 National Conference on Appellate Justice," 8 *Journal of Appellate Practice and Process* 141–205 (2005) at 185.

[60] John B. Oakley, "The Screening of Appeals: The Ninth Circuit's Experience in the Eighties and Innovations for the Nineties," *Brigham Young University Law Review* 859 (1991), at 876, 907.

[61] Ibid. at 11.

[62] Email communication with Judge B and Judge F, 12/19/07.

[63] Email communication with Judge E, 1/8/08.

to slow a case down. Judge E noted that "some judges don't care; they will just rubber stamp the administrative agency."[64] Another judge noted that even though they are pressed for time on a screening panel that is designed to move cases along more quickly than on the oral argument track, "some judges pay attention anyway and kick the case or slow down the screening." She added disapprovingly, "Some judges are willing to let several hundred go through [with little scrutiny], but they would also do this even for oral argument cases."[65] One judge told me she knew of another judge who "would *automatically* kick any cases involving U.S. citizen children" because of her belief that the deportation of an alien parent is the de facto deportation of the citizen children.[66] These comments lend credence to the arguments presented in Chapter 4 that one kind of purposive behavior in the Courts of Appeals takes the form of the judges' exercise of discretion in determining the level of scrutiny a case receives. By kicking a case, a judge can slow the case down and force a higher level of scrutiny of the case.

ATTEMPTS AT INNOVATION AND EXPERIMENTATION

Given the 1978 creation of the Ninth Circuit's staff attorneys' office and their elaborate case inventory system, the institutional infrastructure needed to process a large volume of cases was already in place before the sharp spike in immigration appeals that began in 2002. As Judge C and the central staff reported, the court did not require "*new* procedures for immigration appeals" because the court simply "tweaked the old process" to accommodate the post-BIA streamlining flood of appeals.[67] Indeed, in the end, after a series of experiments, the Ninth Circuit ended up adopting no obviously new procedures to handle the rising immigration caseload. Instead it simply leaned more on the existing screening system.[68]

Even so, the Ninth Circuit had to become creative and undertake a number of additional experiments in judicial administration with the onset of the surge. Realizing the systemic nature of the immigration appeals phenomenon, the Ninth Circuit "sent emissaries" to meet with

---

[64] Interview with Judge E, 7/26/07.
[65] Interview with Judge G, 7/27/07.
[66] Interview with Judge E, 7/26/07. She refers to immigration cases where a "mixed status" family is affected. These families have members of dissimilar immigration statuses. One parent could be a lawful permanent resident ("green card" holder), the other could be an illegal alien, and they could have children who are U.S. citizens.
[67] Interview with Judge C, 7/26/07.
[68] Follow-up phone interview with Judge F, 3/08.

representatives of the Board of Immigration Appeals and the National Association of Immigration Judges to gain a better understanding of what was going on in other parts of the immigration bureaucracy.[69] The court also hosted an "Immigration Brainstorming Session" in San Francisco on May 5, 2006, that lawyers, law professors, and representatives of law schools, legal aid societies, and bar association groups attended either in person or by conference call.[70] The session resulted in a set of new ideas, including recommendations for "greater and more efficient use of pro bono legal services, more mentoring of inexperienced attorneys by veteran immigration counsel, and closer scrutiny of negligent or incompetent immigration attorneys."[71]

The flood of cases that deluged the Ninth Circuit also brought about extensive discussions among the circuit's judges, and a series of experiments followed. In April 2004, the subject of how to deal with immigration appeals was the topic of the judges' annual symposium and retreat where judges and staff get together to discuss the court's administrative business. From that conference came ideas for various experiments, in which many of the judges I interviewed took part. Even before the symposium took place, then-Chief Judge Mary Schroeder had asked an ad hoc committee of four judges to "brainstorm about the court's backlog of immigration cases and to list a variety of proposals for the court's consideration at the upcoming symposium."[72]

The ad hoc committee's memo laid out a number of options, one of which was to maintain the status quo and operate as usual, which was immediately rejected. Several of the judges and the central staff referred to these tests as "experiments," not in the sense that it was a scientific test, but that they were going to try something new and see what happened. The existing screening procedures that were built upon with these options were not new in themselves. What was new was the construction of the panels in terms of the mix of cases they heard, the frequency with which the screening panels would meet, the number of these panels a

[69] Interview with Judge C, 6/13/07.
[70] Andrew P. Gordon, "Special Feature: Ninth Circuit Riding Wave of Immigration Appeals," 14 *Nevada Lawyer* 8–9 (2006), 9 July 2006.
[71] Gordon, "Special Feature: Ninth Circuit Riding Wave of Immigration Appeals," 9.
[72] Internal memo to Ninth Circuit judges from ad hoc committee on immigration case processing, April 9, 2004; henceforth referred to as "ad hoc immigration appeals committee memo." (Memo is on file with author. I am grateful to Professor Stephen Wasby, who passed along the memo after he obtained it through the course of his own research.) In late 2007, Alex Kozinski replaced Mary Schroeder as the Chief Judge of the Ninth Circuit.

judge would have to sit on per year, the staffing of the panels (whether by judges or visiting judges), and the amount of judges' contact time with the case files on these panels. Recall that Judge C earlier noted that the new procedures consisted of "tweaking" existing ones.

The remaining experiments sought to prioritize cases, redeploy existing personnel, add visiting judges (borrowed from other federal courts), maximize the use of existing personnel's time, or some combination of these. Except for the visiting-judge option, the proposed options assumed that panels would be "made up of active judges and senior-judge volunteers, but not visiting judges except [as] otherwise stated."[73] Only one proposal would make use of borrowed personnel. This option would add new judges – "new" in the sense that the Courts of Appeals sometimes have district court or other federal court judges, including retired Supreme Court justices, who are visiting judges and who sit by designation. The "visitor proposal" would establish eight more argument panels in the next year "using visiting judges but reshuffling existing calendars so that our own active judges and senior-judge volunteers will participate in each argument panel. These would be ordinary calendars with the usual mix of cases, only some of which would be immigration cases."[74] This proposal would decide about 240 more cases.

Other options would not borrow personnel, but would simply increase the frequency of both the oral argument and screening panels to process more cases. Option A or the one-week option, for example, entailed a "one-week intensive immigration-case non-argument calendar [screening cases] would occur in San Francisco and Pasadena...Assuming that 24 judges participate (8 panels) and that they decide about 10 cases per day, then about 400 additional cases would be decided."[75] A similar option, the "alternating calendars option," would for six months have half the scheduled argument panels hear the usual mix of Ninth Circuit cases, except immigration cases, and the other half of the argument panels would hear relatively straightforward or low-weighted immigration cases only. The "immigration-only" panels would be expected to decide ten cases a day for a total of fifty cases a week, "because these cases can be 'batched,' sorted by country and/or issue, and given central staff memos to provide an overview."[76] The net result of this option would be to decide an extra 360 cases.

73 Ibid. at 2.
74 Ibid. at 4.
75 Ibid. at 2–3.
76 Ibid.

To minimize the impact of the increased number of panels that judges would be required to sit on and to further the consistency of adjudications, the central staff began grouping cases not only by similar weights, but by other criteria as well. Because of the character of the immigration appeals arriving at the Ninth Circuit, in which half of the cases were political asylum cases, the central staff was able to "batch" or bundle the cases for oral argument and screening panels based on the alien's nationality. An alien who claims political asylum does so by presenting evidence that he or she cannot return to his or her home country based on a well-founded fear of persecution. To adjudicate these cases, the judges must know something about the country conditions and political conditions in, for example, Guatemala, in addition to sorting out the facts specific to that one case. Therefore, it makes sense to group cases that involve aliens who share nationality. For example, panels may be constructed to hear a group of asylum claims from applicants from Guatemala, or asylum applications from a series of Chinese applicants who claimed persecution because they had run afoul of China's one-child policy. The central staff also bundles cases and constructs panels based on a common legal issue. A panel might be constructed to hear "212c" cases, for example. (The waiver, outlined in 8 U.S.C. § 1182, INA § 212(c), was available before changes to the immigration law in 1996 eliminated this form of relief from deportation.) Judges A and G agreed that this grouping of the legal issues together or combining cases in which the same country conditions applied was "helpful rather than boring" because, in their view, it helps increase the consistency in their rulings. The assumption was that a larger number of cases could be processed more quickly and consistently in this manner because bundling the cases would lower mental transaction costs for the judges and help them increase consistency by allowing them to compare like cases.

THE NINTH CIRCUIT'S PRIMARY COPING STRATEGY: THE "SCREENING TRACK"

Although both courts tried other strategies first, the triaging of cases has been the primary means by which both the Second and Ninth Circuits have processed their immigration appeals. According to the interviews with the central staff, the Ninth Circuit, which already had a screening system in place, began routing the majority of its immigration appeals (60 percent) to screening panels, including all *pro se* appeals.[77] This

---

[77] The central staff noted that the majority of immigration appeals at the Ninth Circuit are filed by counsel, not *pro se* appellants. However, a prominent study noted the precipitous

percentage is higher than the "approximately half" of all appeals to the court that are sent to such panels.[78] Along these lines, the internal memo presented a final option, called the "screening proposal," that would maximize the use of existing resources by requiring each judge to take on two more days of screening duty within the next year in addition to the usual two or three days each month. The court's "screening proposal" experiment would increase the number of screening panels. However, "[t]hese days would not be tacked on to existing screening panels (to avoid burnout), and judges would donate the help of their elbow clerks to the effort of carefully reviewing the records, drafting proposed dispositions, and making presentations to the panel [that would summarize each case]."[79] Again, the goal was to process more immigration appeals to draw down the number of accumulated cases.

Judge F noted that there was no "formal decision" or change in policy about how to handle the onslaught of immigration cases, and in fact the memo that had laid out all the experimental options was part of only informal discussion at the Ninth Circuit's spring 2004 retreat. In fact, she noted that *none* of the experiments was adopted because of a "lack of consensus" and general "unhappiness with all the options" that were presented in the memo. Instead, she said the court took an "incremental approach" to the immigration case surge by "picking up the output in expedited methods" of adjudicating cases, including sending more of them to both formal screening (tied to the inventory and weighting system), and informal screening (when the staff attorneys weeded out hopeless and straightforward cases to be placed on the motions calendar instead of on the argument calendar).[80] Judge F noted that about five years earlier all judges would have spent four to five days a year serving on screening panels. In order to accommodate the Ninth Circuit's ever-growing docket, and not directly in response to the immigration cases, now all the judges were required to spend an additional day serving on screening or motion panels, with three days of screening each year and three days on motion panels, a total of six days a year. Senior judges participated in screening panels at their discretion. Therefore, the court never made a formal policy decision to give special treatment to the immigration cases, as the Second Circuit did.

decline in the rate of success from 33% in 2001 (pre-surge) to 5% in 2005 in the asylum grant rates of *pro se* appellants. Ramji-Nogales et al., *supra* note 15, at 360.

[78] Pether, *supra* note 30, at 13.

[79] Internal memo,. *supra* note 32, at 4. "Elbow clerks" are the judges' law clerks that work out of the judges' chambers, not the staff attorneys on the central staff.

[80] Follow-up phone interview with Judge F, 3/08.

COURT PERSONNEL'S ASSESSMENTS OF THE EXPERIMENTS

All the judges' assessments agreed that the experiments were unsatisfactory because these efforts were neither saving energy nor time.[81] As a result, except for the bundling and batching of cases by nationality and legal issue, none of the proposed adjustments was adopted. One judge said the general consensus was that the experiments were "roundly *un*popular" and the reason was because "you have to compromise and cut corners because the number of judges is not getting larger." She added, "it was too hard to cope with twelve cases a day" because "judges wanted to read all the stuff [the full record in the files] and it was getting overwhelming. Many judges wanted to go through the full record…The benefits it was achieving wasn't worth the strain it was causing."[82] Another judge noted that "three weight cases took up as much time as seven or ten weight cases."[83] So there really was no benefit to sorting the case by weight to balance the judges' workload. With regard to her participation on an experimental screening panel, she concluded, "If you are one of the judges that's more careful, you're holding up the screening panel. For those judges [the ones who wish to give more careful review] you're still spending that much time. There is no time savings."[84] These comments suggested that the experiments failed because they ended up frustrating the judges who wished to provide more careful scrutiny of the cases.

Limiting the "innovations" to tweaking procedures and processes, instead of making a more thorough structural overhaul, may have doomed the experiments to failure, because these changes seemed to make no appreciable improvements. The reason for this was that the experiments seemed to work against institutional arrangements that were already in place before the surge. One judge offered a structural reason for why the experiments were unpopular. Judge F's estimation was that the Ninth Circuit has set up a division of labor among the judges and staff attorneys and law clerks, which she described as an "assembly line" and a "certain set way of doing things." She explained that, "staff attorneys process cases a different way from judges." Judges are "inserted into the process at different points depending on whether the case is routed to a screening or oral argument track."[85] She emphasized that the difference between judges and staff, and how they look at cases, is that "judges are

---

[81] Interview with Judge F, 8/6/07.
[82] Interview with Judge F, 8/6/07.
[83] Interview with Judge E, 7/26/07.
[84] Interview with Judge E, 7/26/07.
[85] Interview with Judge F, 8/6/07.

set up to look at each case individually, like hand tailoring," whereas the staff are set up to deal with volume. Simply put, she said, "Judges are set up to do a more thorough review of the cases."[86] The division of labor in the court administration is that judges, by institutional design, are supposed to do a more thorough review of the cases than staff attorneys. The judges' perception that they are doing more thorough review of the cases than the staff may derive from the logic of their triaging procedures. The staff must sort through large numbers of cases to root out those with nettlesome legal issues to save for the judges; the judges might feel that they must necessarily provide more thorough review for these more complex cases. In this sense, the various experiments failed because, in trying to increase the number of cases handled, the experiments were working against the judges' usual level of scrutiny of the cases. Her comments also go right to the heart of the difference between a judge's review of a case versus a staff attorney's review; it is a question of the degree of scrutiny of the record. Whether by structural design or reinforced by personal preference, judges give more scrutiny to cases than staff.

Several judges conveyed the strong sense that they felt rushed and that they feared that a small number of potentially very important cases were slipping through without a thorough review. One of the judges who expressed frustration at not being able to give the immigration appeals the attention she thinks they deserve also noted with dismay that many of her colleagues "don't care...they just want to rubber stamp" the BIA and as a result do not take a closer look at immigration appeals.[87] Another judge stated that the court's immigration appeals are "the most important cases," especially appeals involving asylum, the Convention Against Torture, and suspension of deportation/removal. She singled out as particularly important those cases involving aliens who have resided for a long time in the United States, have children who are U.S. citizens, and "paid their taxes, and played by the rules." She added that in her view, the deportation of the alien parents would in effect be "banishing the children" as well.[88] Judge D found screening panels "objectionable" because, "it's too mechanistic and doesn't give time to judges to think about it."[89] Although the judges expressed confidence that in the vast majority of cases they were getting it right, they worried about the small number of cases with potentially life-or-death implications that might be slipping

---

[86] Interview with Judge F, 8/6/07.
[87] Interview with Judge E, 7/26/07.
[88] Interview with Judge H, 3/26/07.
[89] Interview with Judge D, 6/13/07.

through without careful and thorough review; given the volume of immigration appeals, the system simply could not provide that each and every case got the same level of careful scrutiny.

ALTERNATIVE SOLUTIONS – THE ROADS NOT TAKEN

Experienced Courts of Appeals observers may wonder why the Ninth Circuit tried all these experiments instead of some more obvious reforms that might more directly address the immigration caseload problem. The circuit tried the experiments it did because other options on the table were regarded as completely unworkable and faced widespread opposition among the court's judges and staff. One proposal that originated with Senator Orrin Hatch (R-UT) in the 108th Congress and was later reintroduced by Senator Arlen Specter (R-PA, before he switched parties) would have routed all immigration appeals from all the U.S. Courts of Appeals to the Federal Circuit Court of Appeals in Washington, D.C.[90] When he introduced the provision, Hatch reportedly said, "Immigration is a matter of national security and diplomacy and we must speak with one voice on immigration law. The Federal Circuit is a natural forum for immigration review because it already has experience dealing with specialty areas of law."[91] Similarly, Specter's alleged motivation was to make immigration law uniform and relieve the Second and Ninth Circuits of their deluge of immigration appeals. Immigration lawyers and civil rights activists saw the move as "ill conceived, dangerous and a thinly veiled attack" on the Ninth Circuit.[92] Speaking on behalf of the court, Chief Judge Mary Schroeder's response to the proposal was that, "I don't think this is very constructive...I think it will limit representation" because aliens would have to travel to Washington, D.C., and also to find lawyers who were willing to travel with them. Moreover, Schroeder added that the judges of the Federal Circuit Court of Appeals, being largely patent and trademark specialists, "have no background" in immigration cases.[93]

---

[90] Bob Egelko, "Plan to Unify Immigration Appeals: Senator Specter's Provisions to Centralize Jurisdiction Draws Fire," *The San Francisco Chronicle*, March 13, 2006, A1, and Ralph Linderman, "Federal Circuit/Jurisdiction: Proposal to Shift Immigration Appeals to Federal Circuit Draws Fire," *Patent, Trademark & Copyright Journal*, Vol. 71, No. 1760, March 10, 2006, 488.

[91] Cited in Linderman, "Proposal to Shift Immigration Appeals to Federal Circuit Draws Fire" (available at http://pubs/bna.com/ip/bna/PTC.eh/a0b2m2r2z4).

[92] Egelko, "Plan to Unify Immigrant Appeals," A1.

[93] Cited in Egelko, "Plan to Unify Immigrant Appeals," A1.

The judges interviewed were in agreement with Chief Judge Schroeder about the imprudence of the Federal Circuit proposal. Judge A characterized the proposal as "idiotic" and Judge G called it "ridiculous." When Judge A was asked why she felt this way, she responded that the Federal Circuit "had no expertise" in immigration appeals and that they would structurally and institutionally have to "transform themselves radically to handle the immigration caseload" including staffing up on various kinds of support staff and attorneys. She added that the Federal Circuit would have to be prepared to waive oral argument in the event that lawyers were not willing to travel across the country to Washington, D.C.[94] Similarly, Judge F called the proposal "sort of a laugh" and "peculiar." She echoed her colleagues in pointing out that it "did not make a lot of geographical sense" for the alien litigants and their lawyers to have to travel to the east coast.[95]

In addition to the logistical concerns of the Federal Circuit proposal, some of the judges also contrasted the Ninth Circuit's expertise in immigration appeals with the Federal Circuit's lack thereof. In a March 21, 2006, letter signed by two judges I interviewed sent to Senator Specter and the members of the Senate Judiciary Committee, the judges addressed the Federal Circuit's "narrow expertise." They wrote:

Immigration law is a complex subject, requiring exercises of complex statutory interpretation in deciphering the morass of the relevant and often overlapping statues and regulations, and some degree of empathy for the human beings petitioning for relief. The Federal Circuit has unparalleled knowledge in areas such as patent and trademark law. It has no judicial experience with matters of immigration, nor with habeas corpus, civil rights, or criminal law, issues that are raised in many of the immigration appeals that we hear…We benefit not only from the expertise we have developed in grappling with immigration cases and confronting with the changes in immigration law that have been enacted over the years, but also from our adjudication of questions of law in the broad range of cases before us.[96]

The letter concluded, "This provision would undercut the ability of immigrants to obtain real judicial review."[97] The proposal to route all the immigration appeals to the Federal Circuit was doomed in part because it did

[94] Interview with Judge A, 6/12/07 and Judge G, 7/27/07.
[95] Interview with Judge F, 8/6/07.
[96] Letter signed by two judges of the Ninth Circuit to Senator Arlen Specter and the Senate Judiciary Committee, March 21, 2006 (on file with author). Because I do not know how widely the letter was circulated, I have not identified the two judges who signed the letter.
[97] Ibid.

not take into account the original reason why federal court districts were defined geographically. These concerns are reminiscent of the Federalist and Anti-Federalist debates outlined in Chapter 3 about the ability of everyday people to access federal justice, and therefore the necessity for federal court jurisdictions to be drawn to conform to state lines. The Federal Circuit proposal worked against this basic idea of access to federal justice.[98] What the fate of this proposal indicated is that regardless of the gravity of the problem, in this case the glut of immigration appeals at the Ninth and Second Circuit Courts, proposed solutions are still bound by basic institutional design constraints of the federal courts.

No discussion of reforms to alleviate the Ninth Circuit's caseload crunch would be complete without mention of the seemingly perennial proposals to split the circuit into two or three smaller circuits. The motivations for dividing the Ninth Circuit are diverse.[99] Ostensibly, lawmakers have said that the Ninth Circuit, which is the largest circuit, with twenty-eight active judgeships and twenty senior judgeships (a senior judge has status comparable with that of an emeritus professor), should be divided to ease its caseload and because the circuit has become too large and unwieldy.[100] Some speculate that the move to split the circuit is driven by conservatives who are irate at the Ninth Circuit's perceived liberal rulings.[101] The judges of the Ninth Circuit themselves, who would best know how well the court functions, have voted on this proposal several times, and the number of judges in favor of the split are in a small minority. The politics surrounding the split of the Ninth Circuit are complex and are beyond the scope of this chapter, but the efforts to split the circuit seem not to be driven by immigration appeals. As Judge A stated, the politics driving the split "doesn't have to do with immigration;" it has to do with regional rivalries between the Northwest and California and over unhappiness

[98] Judge C told me about another proposal that would, instead of routing all the immigration appeals to the Federal Circuit, simply evenly divide up all the immigration appeals and distribute them across all the U.S. Courts of Appeals. She indicated that that proposal also suffered many of the same defects as the Federal Circuit proposal. (Interview with Judge C, 6/13/07.)

[99] See discussions in Hellman, *Restructuring Justice*, 228–32 and 356–57.

[100] Jonathan D. Glater, "Lawmakers Trying Again to Divide the Ninth Circuit," *The New York Times*, June 19, 2005.

[101] Glater, "Lawmakers Trying Again to Divide the Ninth Circuit" ("Congressional Republicans are hoping yet again to split the Court of Appeals for the Ninth Circuit, which covers nine Western states and has issued some rulings to the dismay of conservatives, saying a breakup is the best way to reduce the caseload of the circuit's federal judges.").

with the Ninth Circuit's rulings in cases involving Native American law and environmental law.[102] Most important for immigration appeals, the various proposals to split the Ninth Circuit would do little to alleviate the immigration appeals crunch for the simple reason that all these proposals simply divide up the states into different configurations. The plans would not divide the state of California, which contributes the bulk of immigration appeals given the large number of legal and illegal aliens that reside there, into different circuits. Therefore, a circuit split would not help with the immigration caseload.

As the Ninth Circuit judges themselves pointed out, there are not many good options for keeping pace with the immigration appeals except two pragmatic expedients. Many accepted sending more and more cases to screening as a necessary evil to keep up with the immigration caseload because they found these two alternatives even less palatable. One of these is simply to adopt a deferential attitude toward administrative adjudicators and affirm their decisions. Judge G said, "then we wouldn't have to take a hard look at these cases; we'd just process them." This was an approach Judge G strongly disagreed with and she criticized some of her colleagues for taking this line of attack. She stated, "There are no more important cases [than immigration cases] unless they are capital cases. To send someone out of the country and break up their family...Yet so many judges think these [cases] are a nuisance."[103] Yet even as Judge G expressed discomfort with the screening system, she acknowledged that it would be worse to simply "not care how long the cases sit on the docket." The screening process disturbed many judges, but they were resigned to it after the failure of the various experiments and the lack of support for either deferring automatically to the administrative decision makers or leaving the cases to sit on the docket indefinitely.

The upshot of the institutional changes wrought by the immigration surge is that, as Judge D suggested, the increased role played by staff fundamentally has changed the nature of judicial review for these cases. Although she and every other judge expressed great respect and confidence in the court staff's expertise and competence, she noted that staff review of a case is still "different" from the review of an Article III judge. In her view, the court's increased reliance on central staff "weakened" the promise of judicial review.[104] The point of Judge D's comment was not to denigrate the staff as less competent than the judges, but she was

[102] Interview with Judge A, 6/12/07.
[103] Interview with Judge G, 7/27/07.
[104] Interview with Judge D, 7/13/07.

echoing Judge F's observation that in the Ninth Circuit's division of labor, the judges are institutionally designed to provide more thorough review of cases than staff. And there is a correlation between the scrutiny and time spent on a case and the final outcome. Judge D and several other judges suggested that the decision of the case could turn on the amount of contact time and corresponding level of scrutiny provided by the judges. Judge D stated that when the Supreme Court denies a case *certiorari*, they have given the case cursory review: "They haven't had time to read the case." She likened the *certiorari* procedures of the Supreme Court to her circuit's routing cases to screening or oral argument track and observed that, "screening is their [the Ninth Circuit's] way of granting *certiorari*."[105] Just as the grant of docket control to the Supreme Court fundamentally changed and shaped the strategic behavior of the justices of that Court by creating such new opportunities as aggressive grants and strategic denials,[106] changes to Ninth Circuit procedures also may have altered the behavior of the judges by creating purposive uses of kicking a case back to the argument track. The tracking of an appeal along the oral argument or the screening track in the U.S. Courts of Appeals changes the amount of time Article III judges spend on an appeal. It is not so much a matter of who is reviewing an appeal, but the degree of scrutiny that the appeal receives depends on the routing of the case, which may well affect the legal outcome.

THE COURTS OF APPEALS AS PART
OF THE IMMIGRATION SYSTEM

Just as institutional structures and processes constrain institutional innovation, the U.S. Courts of Appeals' caseloads and the mix of cases those courts decide are often dictated by extrajudicial factors that the U.S. Courts of Appeals have no control over. These extrajudicial factors also constrain the agency of the Courts of Appeals in the sense that they reduce the courts to reacting to these developments rather than being able to anticipate them. Another broad theme that emerged from these interviews with the Ninth Circuit's central staff and judges was that the federal courts are really part of a larger immigration system. The fortunes of the U.S. Courts of Appeals are yoked to the administrative agencies

---

[105] Interview with Judge D, 7/13/07.
[106] H.W. Perry, *Deciding to Decide* (Cambridge, MA: Harvard University Press, 1991). See especially chapter 6, "Bargaining, Negotiation, and Accommodation."

and their officials, as well as to the immigration bar; both can affect the nature and number of cases flowing into the federal courts.

Characteristics of the overall immigration system affect directly the manner in which U.S. Courts of Appeals judges do their job. When extra-judicial entities such as administrative agencies do not do their jobs properly or thoroughly, the pressure shifts to the Courts of Appeals, whose judges are cognizant of the fact that they are simultaneously the "first level of real review" and also the "only level of real review" that the aliens are getting, as well as the court of last resort for almost all the litigants.[107] This situation reinforces the error-correction function of the U.S. Courts of Appeal, at least in the immigration policy area. But the Courts of Appeals' judges' perceptions of the deficiencies of the immigration bureaucracy have another effect: it reduces their willingness to defer to administrative agency decision makers. In fact, the perceived defects of the immigration system have implanted the notion that the Ninth Circuit and its staff have to "back fill" to compensate for parts of the immigration system that are functioning at a sub-par level, and part of that compensation entails the frequent challenging of administrative decision makers rather than the deference to administrative agencies that *Chevron v. National Resources Defense Council* (1984) counsels.[108] According to the Ninth Circuit judges (and many immigration law experts), every level of the immigration system, from the immigration bar, to the immigration judges, and then the Board of Immigration Appeals, is plagued by problems of quality and efficiency. The problem that is common to every level of the immigration system, from the immigration judges, to the Board of Immigration Appeals, and now the U.S. Courts of Appeals, can be summed up as too many cases, not enough time.

The deficiencies of the immigration system build cumulatively, beginning with the quality of counsel. Repeatedly I heard from both the judges and the staff that, although they were willing to acknowledge a few standouts in the field, their general observation and estimation of the immigration bar was very poor. A universal and loud chorus of both judges and staff members testified to the poor quality of the lawyers that represent aliens in court proceedings. To quote from the interviews, judges said: "the quality of the immigration bar is terrible," "the immigration bar is so bad," "[there is] no other area of law with a higher risk of fraud

---

[107] Interview with Judge E, 7/26/07. Judge A (6/12/07) and Judge G (7/27/07) also mentioned that they were keenly aware that the U.S. Courts of Appeals had become the court of last resort for almost everyone.

[108] 467 U.S. 837.

and predatory counsel," "to an unusual degree the immigration bar is terrible," and even more strongly, "people who can't make it in practice in another area of law go into immigration law."[109] Another judge explained that "judges are used to good lawyers because of their own years of private practice" or their time as law school professors who come into contact with elite counsel or intellectuals, so it comes as a genuine shock when they see such abysmally bad lawyering in immigration cases.[110] The criticisms of the immigration bar do not come only from Ninth Circuit judges. Judge Richard Posner of the Seventh Circuit, a frequent and vocal critic of the immigration bureaucracy, agreed with his Ninth Circuit colleagues when he stated, "The immigration bar is on the whole, poor."[111] Judge Robert A. Katzmann of the Second Circuit also weighed in on the question when he stated, "The immigrants are also referred to licensed lawyers, too many of whom render inadequate and incompetent service. These attorneys do not even meet with their clients to flush out all the relevant facts and supporting evidence or prepare them for their hearings; these are 'stall' lawyers who hover around the immigrant community, taking dollars from vulnerable people with meager resources. They undermine our trust in the American legal system with damaging consequences for the immigrants' lives."[112] The judges and central staff of the Ninth Circuit also attributed the poor quality of the immigration bar to the vulnerable position of aliens. The population that these attorneys serve is neither familiar with the English language nor with U.S. laws and customs, making its members easy prey for unscrupulous attorneys and those posing as attorneys.

Several judges indicated that the Ninth Circuit has done its share to improve the quality of the immigration bar by offering Continuing Legal Education (CLE) classes in which bad immigration lawyers are "strongly

---

[109] Interview with Judge C on 6/13/07, Judge E on 7/26/07, Judge B on 6/13/07, Judge A on 6/12/07, and Judge F on 8/6/07, respectively.

[110] Interview with Judge B, 6/13/07.

[111] Judge Richard Posner (U.S. Courts of Appeals for the Seventh Circuit), "Judicial Review of Immigration Judges," speech before the Chicago Bar Association, Chicago, IL, April 21, 2008. (Author was in attendance at the speech and took notes.) When asked during Q&A about his views on granting asylum applicants counsel at public expense, he answered that theoretically he thought it a good idea, but in the practical sense, he wondered, allowed, "Who would they get to represent these people?" – an allusion to his critical view of parts of the immigration bar.

[112] Judge Robert A. Katzmann, "The Legal Profession and the Unmet Needs of the Immigrant Poor," Orison S. Marden Lecture of the Association of the Bar of the City of New York, February 28, 2007 (available at: http://www.nycbar.org/pdf/report/marden9.pdf).

urged" or "drafted" to attend what is to some degree a command performance.[113] The circuit has also begun compiling a "watchlist" of those identified by the court that engage in unprofessional conduct in immigration cases. Three violations or one egregious violation will trigger sanctions. By the summer of 2006 more than 100 attorneys had been disciplined under this system.[114] In the CLE classes, the circuit's judges or staff cover basics such as how to write a brief and how to make sure that you have exhausted all your client's claims, issues that were characterized by one judge who actually taught these classes as "fundamentals."[115] This same judge noted that because the immigration bar was so poor, it placed an immense burden on the Ninth Circuit's law clerks to ferret out legal issues that counsel may have missed or neglected to make on behalf of their alien clients. Another judge noted with disapproval the larger role that law clerks had to play in immigration cases. In her estimation, "it hurts the system" when law clerks essentially have to become attorneys for the aliens and "when advocacy moves inside the court, it's a problem."[116]

Judge E also observed that the government's attorneys were not much better prepared than the aliens' attorneys and were "just as incompetent." She attributed the uneven quality of the government attorneys to the fact that the Department of Justice has adopted a policy of prosecuting as many immigration cases as possible, even with a limited number of attorneys trained in immigration law from the Office of Immigration Litigation. Instead, the Department of Justice has pressed into service U.S. attorneys from its antitrust division, its government corruption division, and even attorneys from the Bureau of Measurements and Weights, to argue immigration cases.[117] While most law students and attorneys have had education in criminal law, few have expertise (or even basic working knowledge) in U.S. immigration law, which is complex and quirky. The sometimes-deficient counsel on both sides of the appeal further adds to the burden on the federal judicial system and especially on the Courts of Appeals, which now must often conduct more thorough

[113] Interview with Judge B, 6/13/07.
[114] John T. Noonan, Jr., "Symposium on Immigration Appeals and Judicial Review: Immigration Law 2006," 55 *Catholic University Law Review* 905, 912 (2006).
[115] Interview with Judge E, 7/26/07.
[116] Interview with Judge F, 8/6/07.
[117] Interview with Judge E, 7/26/07, and court staff, 6/11/07. A conversation the author had with an assistant U.S. attorney in Chicago also confirmed that the DOJ had been "farming out" immigration cases to U.S. attorneys around the country whether they had immigration law experience or not (10/24/07).

review of immigration cases compared with other types of administrative law cases.

The nation's 246 immigration judges were the object of both sympathy and criticism from the judges. The immigration courts are the trial-level administrative bodies that adjudicate 65 percent of the asylum seekers' cases that have been referred by asylum officers.[118] The immigration courts also review defensive claims of asylum (a claim raised only after an alien has been placed in removal/deportation proceedings) and all other non-asylum immigration cases. Trials before immigration judges are administrative proceeding with judicial overtones. The immigration judge wears a black robe and the procedures and physical layout of the room resemble that of a judicial proceeding, but neither the Federal Rules of Civil Procedure nor the Federal Rules of Evidence apply.[119]

These immigration courts labor in obscurity and with few resources. One Ninth Circuit judge stated that although she herself did not suffer from mental weariness from the deluge of immigration appeals, she speculated that immigration judges might, given the conditions they must work in. Judge A emphasized that she had "great respect for the work of the IJs."[120] The immigration judges have no law clerks, and no court reporters. They must literally run an antiquated tape recorder themselves to tape a hearing. After a hearing, immigration judges orally dictate their decision into a tape recorder. There is no time for editing or correcting the decision. A *Daily Journal* article similarly characterized the conditions of the immigration courts as "a court system awash in cases yet parched for resources."[121] In this same article, retired immigration judge Bruce J. Einhorn stated, "The immigration court system is the stepchild of the judicial process...Our litigants can't vote. The volume of cases before judges does not allow for the kind of introspection other judges enjoy. And the judges don't get adequate respect from anyone because they can't apply sanctions."[122] Too many cases and too little time to process them is a problem that begins in the immigration judge hearings where the immigration judges must, in all fairness, work with the resources they have. While each immigration judge has a caseload of 1,200 cases a year, federal district judges have 480 criminal or civil cases a year.[123] Immigration

---

[118] Ramji-Nogales, Schoenholtz, and Schrag, "Refugee Roulette" at 326.
[119] Ibid. at 325.
[120] Interview with Judge A, 6/12/07.
[121] Sandra Hernandez, "'LA 8' Judge Steps Down and Speaks Out," *Daily Journal*, February 23, 2007, pg. 1 (available at http://bibdaily.com/pdfs/Einhorn.pdf).
[122] Ibid. at 1.
[123] The Brookings Institution, "Immigration and the Courts," February 20, 2009, 8.

judges do occasionally make mistakes because of the crush of cases and the limited time, and the errors start snowballing as the appeals make their way through the appellate chain.

Although they were sympathetic to the immigration judges, several of the Ninth Circuit judges also criticized the quality of the immigration judges as being highly uneven. This criticism stemmed in part from the knowledge that immigration judges' asylum grant rates vary widely and there is also empirical evidence backing the judges' concerns on this front. A prominent report issued by the Transactional Records Access Clearinghouse (TRAC) based at Syracuse University showed huge disparities in the immigration judges' asylum grant rates.[124] After examining 297,240 asylum cases decided by immigration judges between FY 1994 and the first few months of FY 2005, the TRAC research team found that while the typical judge's asylum denial rate was 65 percent, there were "eight judges who denied asylum to nine out of ten of the applicants who came before them and two judges who granted asylum to nine out of ten cases." Therefore, the asylum grant rate for individual judges varied greatly, ranging from "a low of 10% to a high of 98%."[125] The TRAC report concluded, "Given the broad constitutional hope that similarly situated individuals will be treated in similar ways and the EOIR's [Executive Office for Immigration Review] stated goal of providing uniform application of the immigration laws, the disparities in the aspect of the court's operations are surprising."[126] Even after running further tests of applicants with similarly situated cases, the judge-by-judge disparity persisted. The report concludes with, "It is clear that these findings directly challenge the EOIR's commitment to providing a 'uniform application of the nation's immigration laws in all cases.'"[127]

Another more recent study by Ramji-Nogales, Schoenholtz, and Schrag also confirmed the wide disparity in grant rates among individual immigration judges in asylum cases. Not only did they find differences among grant rates of immigration judges, they found these disparities to exist among immigration judges "on the same court, even holding nationality constant."[128] To illustrate the point, in several cities, the difference in grant

[124] TRAC describes itself as a "data gathering, data research and data distribution organization at Syracuse University." (Their immigration report, henceforth referred to as "TRAC immigration report," is available at http://trac.syr.edu/immigration/index.html.)
[125] TRAC Immigration Report, 2.
[126] TRAC Immigration Report, 4.
[127] TRAC Immigration Report, 5.
[128] Ramji-Nogales, Schoenholtz, and Schrag, "Refugee Roulette" at 332.

rates among judges within the same court was significant. For example, "In Miami, Columbians before one judge were granted asylum at a rate of 5 percent, while those who appeared before another judge, with an 88 percent grant rate, were almost eighteen times more likely to win asylum. The same story was repeated in the New York and San Francisco immigration courts."[129] The judges had reason to be concerned about the quality and consistency of the immigration judges' adjudications.

The TRAC report and the "Refugee Roulette" article by Ramiji-Nogales, Schoenholtz, and Schrag was widely covered in the mainstream media; consequently, many in the immigration field, including practitioners, law professors, and even Courts of Appeals judges, were aware of the report. Indeed, Judge E cited the TRAC report as evidence to support her assertion that, "The immigration judges are very erratic. They are not applying a uniform system of law." Similarly, Judge Posner cited the "Refugee Roulette" study in a speech about the courts of appeals and immigration cases.[130] Judge E also cited Attorney General Alberto Gonzales's memo chastising the immigration judges for being abusive toward aliens.[131] These high-profile studies, and a rare letter of admonishment by the Attorney General to the immigration judges, only served to heighten the concern of the Courts of Appeals judges that the immigration judges were highly inconsistent and that aliens might be suffering as a result of the hostility or indifference of the immigration judges.

Another line of criticism of the immigration judges from the U.S. Courts of Appeals judges stemmed from the immigration judges' observed cultural insensitivity, such as the one Judge B recounted from an East Indian asylum appeal she adjudicated. She noted that the immigration judge had no awareness whatsoever of customs in India, where close family friends are often referred to as "uncle" or "aunt," even if there were no blood relation to the family. The immigration judge in the case had rendered an adverse credibility finding, based on the fact that he

---

[129] Ibid. at 339.
[130] Richard Posner, "Judicial Review of Immigration Judges," speech before the Chicago Bar Association, Chicago, IL, April 21, 2008.
[131] Interview with Judge E, 7/26/07. In a rare memo dated January 9, 2006, and issued to all immigration judges, the federal attorney general wrote, "I have watched with concern reports of immigration judges who fail to treat aliens appearing before them with the appropriate respect and consideration and who fail to produce the quality of work I expect from the Department of Justice. While I remain convinced that most immigration judges ably and professionally discharge their difficult duties, I believe there are some whose conduct can be described as intemperate and even abusive and whose work must improve...Not all are entitled to the relief they seek. But I insist that each will be treated with courtesy and respect." (Memo on file with author.)

could not understand why a non-blood-relation would be referred to as an aunt, and he had drawn the conclusion that the asylum applicant was lying. Although Judge B acknowledged the impossibility of being cognizant of all the cultural nuances of every country that asylum applicants come from, she noted that she witnessed lapses of knowledge among the immigration judges on very basic cultural practices and norms.[132] Similarly, Judge E noted that many of her colleagues wanted to give deference to the opinion of the trial court (which is the immigration judge) because the immigration judge is the fact finder that actually saw the witnesses testify and would be better able to assess credibility than an appellate body two steps removed that was reviewing a cold record. She stated that this was not necessarily a principle with which she disagreed, but the approach assumes that the fact finder is qualified and diligent.[133] Although not every single judge I spoke to expressed qualms about the quality and consistency of the immigration judges, it was evident that many of the Courts of Appeals judges were very aware of the problems in the immigration system.[134]

Concern over the inconsistency of the immigration judges' rulings was also exacerbated by the uneven quality of immigration court interpreters. Indeed this phenomenon was on full display in the 1992 documentary on the asylum process, "Well Founded Fear," where the interpreter's rendering of the applicant's story was much at odds with that of a qualified interpreter.[135] The "Refugee Roulette" study noted, "Court interpreters are of mixed ability."[136] For instance, Judge B recounted from one of the immigration transcripts she reviewed the story of a substandard interpreter in a Chinese asylum case. The Chinese alien was resting his asylum

[132] Interview with Judge B, 6/13/07.

[133] Interview with Judge E, 7/26/07.

[134] Although this chapter is based on interviews with Ninth Circuit Court of Appeals judges, the concern about the immigration bureaucracy is by no means limited to the Ninth Circuit's judges. See, e.g., Adam Liptak, "U.S. Appeals Courts Scold Immigration Judges – Decisions Called Biased and Incoherent," *New York Times*, December 26, 2005, in which Liptak interviews and cites judges from several Courts of Appeals other than the Ninth Circuit who are critical of the immigration judges. Also, Judge Richard Posner of the Seventh Circuit Court of Appeals, a prominent conservative, has been a vocal critic of the personnel in the immigration system. A website is devoted to quotes from legal decisions he has written in which he excoriates the INS and immigration judges for their sloppiness or other incompetence. (See http://everything2.com/index.pl?node_id=1471137.)

[135] "Well-Founded Fear," a documentary film released in 2000. 119 minutes. Directors/producers: Shari Robertson and Michael Camerini. Distributed by The Epidavros Project Inc.

[136] Ramji-Nogales, Schoenholtz, and Schrag, "Refugee Roulette" at 383.

application on the claim that he was persecuted as a practicing Catholic in China. In such cases, it is standard procedure for the asylum officer and the immigration judge to ask basic questions pertaining to the applicant's alleged religion in order to weed out fraudulent applicants. The immigration judge asked the applicant, "What is the significance of the Last Supper?" Judge B reported that that question became literally lost in translation when the interpreter asked the applicant, "What is the significance of the ultimate potluck?"[137] This anecdote illustrates precisely the sort of disastrous errors that Judge F referred to as "the howlers," the egregiously bad decisions that get through the system and land at the U.S. Courts of Appeals. And as Judge F noted, it only takes seeing a few "howlers" for the judges to wonder about the quality and competence of, not just the interpreters, but also the entire administrative bureaucracy. She stated, "The number of howlers is enough" because psychologically it breeds the sense that "We have to look at these [immigration appeals] carefully. 'They [the BIA] aren't doing their job.' is the conclusion/assumption."[138] It seems fair to say that the judges have a heightened state of awareness and indeed may very well be on the lookout for defects that they expect to see in immigration cases.

Compounding the problems with inconsistent immigration judges and bad interpreters and lawyers is the perception among the judges that the BIA, the highest administrative body in the immigration bureaucracy, is not doing its designated job of quality control before these cases get to the Courts of Appeals. The BIA is the last administrative stop before the immigration appeals enter the federal court system, and it is theoretically designed to catch errors made by the immigration judges. In reality, particularly in the post-streamlining environment, the U.S. Courts of Appeals are now often doing *de novo* review of the basic facts in the case.

Judge E noted that the Courts of Appeals had had to "pick up the slack even before the BIA streamlining," but the situation got much worse after streamlining, and now the immigration appeals "require more attention."[139] Judge A made clear how the BIA streamlining had altered the flow of cases to the Courts of Appeals. She acknowledged that although the backlog at the BIA was a real problem that required a real solution, she did not agree that streamlining was the correct response. In fact she stated, "Streamlining was a mistake." The BIA streamlining

---

[137] Interview with Judge B, 6/13/07.
[138] Interview with Judge F, 8/6/07.
[139] Interview with Judge E, 7/26/07.

resulted not just in an increase in the number of cases flowing to the Courts of Appeals, but also in "a decrease in the quality of the adjudications in the BIA. IJ mistakes are not corrected." She further noted that the net effect of the BIA streamlining was "a higher percentage of mistakes now and more of them."[140] Judge B reiterated this point when she said, "Previously the BIA used to catch immigration judge errors; now many errors pass through and the U.S. Courts of Appeals are the error correctors."[141] The view among the judges that the BIA was now much less likely to catch errors had the effect of strongly reinforcing their role perception of the Courts of Appeals' original error-correction function; they repeatedly expressed the belief that immigration appeals demanded closer scrutiny because the possibility of mistakes in those cases was high.

The BIA streamlining decreased the confidence among both the aliens and the U.S. Courts of Appeals judges in the quality and accuracy of the administrative adjudications. With cursory two-sentence affirmances issued by the BIA after streamlining, many aliens felt that they had not received their day in court. Judge E added, "This is life or death for some people and to get one-line summary affirmances from an IJ who is biased leaves people with a sense that there is no justice."[142] Indeed, the theme that alien litigants felt that they were unfairly treated by not being given a thorough review by the BIA was repeated in many media reports about the Board of Immigration Appeals.[143]

Many of Judge E's colleagues agreed that litigants were not getting thorough review of their appeals at the BIA. Judge C believed that the immigration appeals "were not getting any meaningful administrative review by the BIA" and that the Courts of Appeals now had to "review raw IJ decisions. Now the Courts of Appeals have to look at the IJs' hearing transcripts. And now you have to review [the IJs'] credibility determinations."[144] Another judge stated that she had "totally lost faith in BIA discipline" or its ability to do quality control since they were just doing what she termed "summary affirmations." In fact, she stated that the streamlining had "eviscerated the BIA's ability to carry out its administrative functions. It virtually required members to affirm IJs." As a result there were "no reasoned decisions from the BIA" and now the Courts of

---

[140] Interview with Judge A, 6/12/07.
[141] Interview with Judge B, 6/13/07
[142] Interview with Judge E, 7/26/07.
[143] See *supra*, note 18.
[144] Interview with Judge C, 6/13/07.

Appeals "got into the business of reviewing IJs' decisions."[145] Judge D indicated that she "resented [former Attorney General] Ashcroft for the streamlining." In her view, after the streamlining, the BIA was "affirming the IJs without the opinion of the Board." This means that the Courts of Appeals are actually "reviewing the decisions of the IJs, *not* the Board." She noted that because immigration judges are working under time constraints, and usually render a decision after a hearing by dictating into a microphone, with no chance to edit the decision, these decisions "are not really thoughtful statements of the law." The transcripts from the immigration judges' decisions as well as the transcripts from the hearing itself are "sometimes really bad" with many transcription errors. Because of the immigration judges' lack of resources, "now the Courts of Appeals [*sic*] has to do a lot more of the sorting out of the facts."[146] Judge B added, "The resulting transcripts are a mess. There is no discipline at the BIA."[147] And as Judge C summed it up, the law in these cases is not very difficult; "the volume is difficult because of the intensive record review required."[148] These judges stated over and over again that they were dismayed by the lack of quality control at the BIA and the routine summary affirmances the Board issued. Moreover, the results of the BIA appeals were also changing. With regard to immigration cases in general at the BIA, the "Refugee Roulette" study found that "the grant and remand rates declined significantly" and that there was also a "steep drop in remand rates favorable to asylum applicants" once the BIA moved to single-member adjudications.[149] As a result, many Ninth Circuit judges felt an obligation to look more carefully at the immigration judges' decisions and hearing transcripts since the BIA had not done so even in a cursory way. This situation also explains why such a high number of immigration cases at the Courts of Appeals level are decided based on the facts/evidence mode of legal reasoning when one would expect trial courts to use that mode of legal reasoning.

Several of the judges went out of their way to point out that the problems with the lack of administrative review by the responsible administrative agency were immigration specific. They noted that the Ninth Circuit, being a court of general jurisdiction, deals routinely with many other kinds of appeals from administrative bodies, including cases regarding

---

[145] Interview with Judge B, 6/13/07.
[146] Interview with Judge D, 6/13/07.
[147] Interview with Judge B, 6/13/07.
[148] Interview with Judge C, 6/13/07.
[149] Ramji-Nogales, Schoenholtz, and Schrag, "Refugee Roulette" at 355 and 358.

Social Security, taxes, the National Transportation and Safety Board, and veterans' benefits. The parallel administrative bodies to the BIA, such as the appeals board within the Social Security Administration and the Board of Veterans Appeals within the Veterans Administration, do not have the same problems as the BIA.[150] Judge E stated, "There are no competency problems with these [other administrative agencies] and these [appeals] don't take much time."[151] Appeals deriving from administrative agencies per se were not the problem; appeals deriving from the immigration administrative bureaucracy were a major problem. Therefore, immigration cases, but not all administrative law cases, trigger heightened review.

Not only were the U.S. Courts of Appeals no longer getting the benefit of real BIA review, but the REAL ID Act, passed in 2003, had routed many immigration appeals straight to the U.S. Courts of Appeals, bypassing the district courts altogether; the district courts had been stripped of *habeas* review in these cases. The comments by the Ninth Circuit judges criticizing the immigration system (and even each other) go to the heart of a set of questions that were insufficiently addressed by recent legislative changes. These questions are, "How much review is an alien entitled to?" and "Which institution should provide that review?" In a removal case from the district court of Massachusetts, in which a *habeas* case was being transferred to the First Circuit, Chief Judge William Young suggested in an advisory opinion that the U.S. Courts of Appeals might not be the best institutional body to review immigration appeals because those courts are not institutionally designed to review evidentiary and factual records as are the district courts, which are trial courts. In *Enwonwu v. Chertoff* (2005)[152], Chief Judge Young wrote:

Persuant [*sic*] to Section 106(c) of the REAL ID Act, the executive has already filed motions to transfer several of those actions to the First Circuit. These petitioners are now without the benefit of the district courts' experience in conducting searching evidentiary hearings and listening to their first-hand narratives...Instead, they will each now be afforded their "one day in the court[s] of appeals," Committee Report at H2873, judicial bodies more accustomed to reviewing "cold record[s]" for legal error than hearing testimony and evaluating evidence.[153]

Rather than increasing the efficacy in adjudicating cases, Judge Young speculated that one of the real motivations for the REAL ID Act was

[150] Interviews with Judge B, 6/13/07 and Judge E, 7/26/07.
[151] Interview with Judge E, 7/26/07.
[152] 376 F. Supp. 2d 42.
[153] 376 F. Supp. 2d 42, 98.

Congress' mistrust of the district courts when he wrote, "The REAL ID Act imposes a chokehold on the free and proper exercise of the writ of habeas corpus. But it does more. It reveals the drafters' deep distrust of the district courts, the nation's sole jury trial court."[154] Whether Judge Young's charge is correct or not, the Courts of Appeals are now adopting many of the traditional functions of the trial courts, particularly those courts' close scrutiny of evidence and facts.

For better or worse, the U.S. Courts of Appeals are part of a larger immigration system, and indeed are a part of the system of many other policy areas. When one part of the system breaks down, the effects can radiate to the U.S. Courts of Appeals and necessitate changes and reforms that will in turn affect the way cases are processed and even the way judges think of the cases. Judge H summed up the sentiments of many of her colleagues when she said of the immigration bureaucracy, "The system is a disgrace!"[155] Every judge and staff member that I interviewed was keenly aware of the shortcomings of the immigration system and all had a number of "howlers" to relay to me – instances of egregious violations in procedure and protocol by some actor in the immigration bureaucracy. They were equally aware of the life-and-death implications of some of the immigration appeals and the possibility that their decisions might also tear families apart. Judge C reported that she personally found immigration appeals to be "emotionally draining" and that these appeals were "a source of a great deal of emotional distress" for the institution of the Ninth Circuit as a whole.[156] The psychological stress referred to by Judge C derives not only from the volume of the immigration appeals that hit the Ninth Circuit, but also to the judges' and staff's concomitant concern that some important cases might be slipping through the cracks; they worried that some cases were not getting enough attention. The stress Judge C referred to also derives from the awareness of how the immigration appeals surge has affected the Ninth Circuit as an institution. By having a "tail wagging the dog" effect in which these appeals affect all the other business on the court's docket by slowing everything down, immigration policy and its bureaucracy does indeed have broad, system-wide effects. What has happened is that with the streamlining, the backlog of problems and time crunch issues have simply shifted from the BIA to the U.S. Courts of Appeals. These courts have had to adopt many of the time

---

[154] 376 F. Supp. 2d 42, 99.
[155] Interview with Judge H, 3/26/07.
[156] Interviews with Judge G, 7/27/07 and Judge C, 6/13/07.

and case management strategies used by the BIA, including the procedure of weighting cases and bundling cases by country of origin of the alien or legal issues.[157] Moreover, it is not at all clear that the U.S. Courts of Appeals are the best institutions to be conducting detailed review of these administrative cases. Many of the Ninth Circuit judges stated that the best solution to the U.S. Courts of Appeals immigration caseload was to "reinvigorate the BIA" – not to create a special immigration court or to try exotic plans like routing the appeals to other federal courts.[158]

CONCLUSION

As the immigration example shows, the federal courts are a part of a broader bureaucracy, and as such, the federal courts can be directly affected by changes in any part of the immigration bureaucracy. The negative effects caused by the BIA streamlining are many. Not only did a snake-swallowing-a-mouse effect occur, in which backlogs and case overload simply moved further down the litigation chain, but the other effect was to alter the way many of the judges approached immigration cases. Many of the Ninth Circuit judges simply did not trust the adjudications of the BIA and as a result felt obligated to give immigration cases much closer scrutiny than they would another type of administrative case. This tendency to look for errors and abuses was further reinforced by the error-correction mission of the U.S. Courts of Appeals.

The Ninth Circuit as an institution also had to make adjustments to respond to the BIA streamlining and the subsequent surge in cases coming to the court. Scholars who study institutional development must be sensitive to the effect of exogenous pressures on development within the same institution. It is not enough to merely draw distinctions between the institutional contexts of the U.S. Supreme Court and the U.S. Courts of Appeals when studying the judiciary. One must make even finer distinctions among the different U.S. Courts of Appeals. As the case study of the Ninth Circuit and immigration illustrates, exogenous developments

---

[157] Email communication with Michael Heilman, retired BIA member, 12/28/07.

[158] Judge B said "reinvigorate the BIA" (6/13/07); Judge D said, "Make the BIA do its job and give them the resources to do its job" (6/13/07); Judge E suggested that what needs to happen is that "Congress and the Department of Justice [should] put the resources in to hire and train qualified IJs and roll back streamlining" (7/26/07); and Judge G noted that the best thing that could happen would be that the cases reaching the Courts of Appeals "were properly decided by the IJs and BIA…If the DOJ acted properly, we wouldn't get many cases." (7/27/07)

in immigration law and politics can unevenly affect the U.S. Courts of Appeals system, sometimes producing isolated institutional innovation and development. The immigration surge has driven the Second and Ninth Circuits to triage their cases to produce segmented levels of review corresponding to different degrees of judicial scrutiny. That these two courts were forced to find new methods to speed processing while the other federal circuits and the Supreme Court were minimally affected, and did not have to engage in experiments, shows that the immigration tide did not lift all boats.

From the standpoint of reform, the institutional defects in the immigration system require system-wide and simultaneous reforms that must occur at every level of the appeals process, beginning with the immigration bar and including the immigration judges, the BIA, and the U.S. Courts of Appeals. Currently, the problems that originate at the beginning of the appellate chain become magnified and start snowballing as the appeal progresses through the hierarchy. Additionally, any reforms must be applied to all parts of the system, and they must take place simultaneously, so that gains in one area are not erased by backsliding in another area, which is precisely what happened with the BIA streamlining reforms. Although the BIA was able to clear its docket, the cases and problems simply shifted to the U.S. Courts of Appeals. Moreover, many of the problems that the BIA had experienced also migrated to the Courts of Appeals, including the reality that, given the volume of cases, no institutional body can provide each appeal with the same level of attention. The blame game that has commenced among all the parties ultimately does not get to the two fundamental questions: How much attention and scrutiny should an alien's appeal receive? What institution or agency can best provide that review?

The findings of this study also suggest that the U.S. Courts of Appeals are not institutionally designed to conduct the intensive review of facts and evidence that characterizes many immigration cases. It is untrue that the Courts of Appeals cannot perform these functions, because surely they have been left with little choice but to do so, but the consequence is that the strain caused by the immigration appeals have had ramifications for the rest of the business in these courts' docket and for all the personnel of the court.

6

Continuity Amid Change

The Federal Courts' Commitment to Due Process

> Procedural due process is more elemental and less flexible than substantive due process. It yields less to the times, varies less with conditions, and defers much less to legislative judgment. Insofar as it is technical law, it must be a specialized responsibility within the competence of the judiciary on which they do not bend before political branches of the Government, as they should on matters of policy which comprise substantive law.
>
> Justice Jackson, dissenting in *Shaugnessy v. United States ex rel. Mezei*, U.S. 206, 224 (1953)

Two of the recurring modes of legal reasoning that characterize immigration law are plenary power and national sovereignty. Given the expansive ability of these two ideas to provide great leeway for federal action and for correspondingly limited judicial review, what if anything, limits congressional and federal exercise of immigration power over aliens? An examination of the doctrinal development of immigration law reveals that the most significant checks on federal action in immigration have been and continue to be judicial applications of procedural due process protections for aliens. The overwhelming majority of aliens' successful challenges to the exercises of federal power in both the Supreme Court and U.S. Courts of Appeals over immigration have not taken the form of equal protection, substantive due process, or separation of power challenges – it has been due procedural process challenges.[1] Recognizing the form of the judicial limits to federal immigration power is significant in furthering one's

[1] There are, of course, a number of exceptions; see, e.g., *Zadvydas v. United States*, (2001), 533 U.S. 678 (2001) (a rare substantive due process victory for aliens: The detention of an alien, even a nonreturnable one, may not exceed 90 days or a reasonable period); and *Immigration and Naturalization Service v. Chadha* (1983), 469 U.S. 919

understanding of institutional development and evolution. Even as these judicial institutions evolve, certain institutionally based attributes, such as the commitment to due process of the U.S. Supreme Court and U.S. Courts of Appeals, remain constants.

Due process, and especially procedural due process, is not just a mode of legal reasoning; the idea also represents a value that derives directly from the role and mission of legal institutions. This chapter argues that the fact that successful challenges to federal immigration power manifest most often as procedural due process legal reasoning is evidence of the endurance of this idea as a part of the institutional context of both the Supreme Court and U.S. Courts of Appeals. Moreover, it is this particular institutional element of the federal courts' institutional setting that persistently distinguishes the federal appellate courts from the federal executive-branch bureaucracy and the elected branches of government. Chapter 3 examined some of the rationales for the creation of institutions such as the Supreme Court and the U.S. Courts of Appeals and the factors that caused these institutions to change over time. Yet, when one studies institutional development, one must also be mindful of the factors that remain constant even in the face of institutional evolution. A legal norm or value such as due process can be construed as a point of "deep equilibria," or strong continuity in the face of institutional evolution.[2] These deep equilibria occur "when the various factors contributing to the resilience of a particular institution or set of institutions are so considerable that once arrangements settle on that point they are highly likely to endure for an extended period of time."[3] An entrenched judicial value such as due process is part and parcel of the institutional context of the federal courts. Although the commitment to and content of due process doctrine has evolved over time in public law broadly and in immigration law itself, the idea has been a consistent commitment at both the Supreme Court and the Courts of Appeals—albeit to different degrees. This value goes directly to the heart of the role of the federal courts in the American political system, which is to ensure that the rule of law triumphs over the rule of men.[4]

(1983) (a separation of powers victory for aliens). The Immigration and Nationality Act was unconstitutional in authorizing the ability of one house of Congress to veto the decision of the Attorney General.

[2] Paul Pierson, *Politics in Time: History, Institutions, and Social Analysis* (Princeton, NJ: Princeton University Press, 2004), 157–60.

[3] Ibid. at 157.

[4] *Marbury v. Madison*, 5 United States (1 Cranch) 137, 163 (1803).

Although the levels of commitment to due process of the U.S. Supreme Court and U.S. Courts of Appeals vary, the fact that it exists at all in the area of immigration law is quite significant. As Peter Schuck has noted, this is an area of law in which government power is at its "zenith" while "individual entitlement" is at its "nadir."[5] Additionally, the doctrinal influence of plenary power and national sovereignty, ideas that advocate judicial deference to the elected branches of government, are strong. The early foundational immigration cases appeared to provide for no due process to be granted to aliens in exclusion proceedings and even in deportation proceedings. Over time, the Supreme Court came to relax its stance toward long-time lawful permanent residents who were returning to the United States after an overseas trip and also toward aliens in deportation proceedings who were already inside U.S. borders.[6] That the Supreme Court was willing to extend any due process protections at all in an area of law that is most doctrinally inhospitable to due process is testament to the power and viability of the due process idea in the judicial context. The influence of the judicial commitment to due process is witnessed in the idea's ability to trump individual judges' and justices' personal biases against aliens and also to limit the scope and harshness of the plenary power doctrine and the national sovereignty idea on aliens.

ORIGINS AND PURPOSE OF DUE PROCESS GENERALLY

Of course the concept of due process is a mainstay in American jurisprudence generally and not just in immigration law. The idea of due process appears not only in the Constitution's Fifth and Fourteenth Amendments, but occupies an important place in many state constitutions as well. The concept has changed in meaning over time while correlating with the rise and decline of societal interests and changing perceptions of the meaning of what is fair and just.[7] Because due process is invoked in a line of cases in our legal system that is governed by precedent, one can trace the evolution of this concept across time and across a broad range of cases. When examining these cases, whether immigration cases or cases from any

---

[5] Peter Schuck, "The Transformation of Immigration Law," 84 *Columbia Law Review* 1–90 (1984), 1.

[6] See *Yamataya v. Fisher* (1903), 189 U.S. 86 (1903), *Kwong Hai Chew v. Colding*, 344 U.S. 590 (1953), *Landon v. Plascencia*, 459 U.S. 21 (1982), and Justice Jackson's dissenting opinion in *Shaughnessy v. United States ex rel. Mezei*, 345 U.S. 206 (1953).

[7] Charles A. Miller, "The Forest of Due Process of Law: The American Constitutional Tradition," in *NOMOS XVIII: Due Process* (New York: New York University Press, 1977), 3.

other area of law, naturally the fact patterns from one case will not be exactly like any other. However, as one observer indicated, "Although the first links may not closely resemble the last, first and last are connected in a continuous series...the standard of due process is not formulated anew at each judicial generation; it is connected, for better or worse, to what went before."[8] In this sense, its continuity is evidence of its longevity and continued influence in judicial institutions.

Due process more generally is not premised on a historically established practice or on even a practice that is fair, but it is based instead on an adherence to "a *legal* process, one that conforms to the idea of law, government by rules, nonarbitrariness."[9] As Thomas Grey noted, the objectives of due process, and procedural due process protections in particular, were twofold: to produce correct decisions, in terms of the impartiality and accuracy of the legal evaluations, and to provide "a natural counterweight" to the interests of decision makers.[10] These concerns, which arose out of fear of the arbitrary and unchecked nature of a potentially tyrannical monarchy in England, and these two central tenets of due process continue to inform U.S. jurisprudence today. Questions of due process involve not only where and when due process is required, but what constitutes due process and how much of it is required in a given situation.[11] There have been numerous volumes written about the history of due process and its centrality in American jurisprudence.[12] Instead of duplicating that effort here, save the briefest history, this chapter's discussion focuses primarily on the evolution and operationalization of the due process idea in the immigration context.

Due process came to the United States by way of England and the Magna Carta. King John signed the Great Charter in 1215 to appease his

---

[8] John Orth, *Due Process of Law: A Brief History* (Lawrence, Kansas: University of Kansas Press, 2003), 102.

[9] J. Roland Pennocock, "Introduction," in *NOMOS XVIII: Due Process* (New York: New York University Press, 1977), xvi.

[10] Thomas C. Grey, "Procedural Fairness and Substantive Rights," in *NOMOS XVIII: Due Process* (New York: New York University Press, 1977), 184, 187.

[11] J. Roland Pennocock, "Introduction," xxix.

[12] Grey, "Procedural Fairness and Substantive Rights," 182–205; Rodney L. Mott, *Due Process of Law – A Historical and Analytical Treatise of the Principles and Methods Followed by the Courts in the Application of the Concept of "The Law of the Land"* (Indianapolis: The Bobbs-Merrill Company Publishers, 1926); and Hannis Taylor, *Due Process of Law and the Equal Protection of the Laws – A Treatise Based, in the Main, on the Cases in Which the Supreme Court of the United States Has Granted or Denied Relief upon One Ground or the Other* (Chicago: Callaghan and Company, 1917); and more recently, John Orth, *Due Process of Law.*

barons, who were not happy about the king's dispute with the Pope and an unfavorable peace with France. In the Magna Carta, King John promised that "no free man shall be taken or imprisoned or disseised or outlawed or exiled, or in any way ruined, nor will we go or send him against him, except by the lawful judgment of his peers or by the law of the land." Sir Edward Coke, a renowned jurist of the 1600s, explained that the "law of the land" referred to the common law tradition in Britain and "the common law required due process."[13] Due process became a synonym for the law of the land. This idea from the Great Charter was first incorporated into the American colonies' and eventually many states' bills of rights, which preceded the first ten amendments to the U.S. Constitution, the national Bill of Rights. Many of the colonies' constitutions referred to the "law of the land;" the national Constitution prefers Coke's phrase, "due process." For example, Maryland's constitution in 1776 said, "that every freeman, for any injury done him in his person or property, ought to have remedy by the course of law of the land, and ought to have justice and right freely without sale, freely without denial, and speedily without delay according to the law of the land."[14] There were similar phrases in the Massachusetts, Connecticut, North Carolina, South Carolina, and Pennsylvania constitutions by 1778. Legal opinions from these states reflected the influence of the Magna Carta as well as the states' widened application and understanding of due process.

In England, the Magna Carta's due process guarantees were intended to limit the powers of the sovereign as embodied by the King. In the colonies, due process limits were expanded to cover not just executive power but also the legislative power of the state legislatures. In the United States, due process is intended to constitutionally restrict both legislative and executive exercises of power.[15] Eventually the idea of due process was incorporated into the federal Constitution via the Fifth and Fourteenth Amendments. The Fifth Amendment guarantees were applied only to the federal government, but the Fourteenth Amendment made due process guarantees applicable to state actions as well.[16] Taylor reports that from that starting point, "the circle has widened until in our system [in the

---

[13] Orth, *Due Process of Law*, 8.

[14] Taylor, *Due Process of Law and the Equal Protection of the Laws*, 14–15.

[15] Orth, *Due Process of Law*, 8.

[16] For more thorough accounts of the incorporation of due process into the federal constitution in the Fifth and Fourteenth Amendments; see Hannis Taylor, *Due Process of Law and the Equal Protection of the Laws*, 19–48, and Rodney L. Mott, *Due Process of Law*, 143–67.

United States] it has been made to embrace all state power, Executive, legislative, and judicial." The U.S. Supreme Court also held this expanded understanding, as evidenced by the following statement: "Applied in England only as guards against Executive usurpation and tyranny, here they have become bulwarks also against arbitrary legislation."[17] As conceived in the context of restraining King John's power and upon its initial migration to the American colonies, due process was about ensuring one's right to the land and the fairness of procedures. As due process migrated to the United States, it grew to cover many other kinds of concerns of society beyond just land and property. Eventually, the concern over the fairness of procedures became infused with substance – or, as Orth describes it, "beginning as the history of proper procedure, the history of due process became the history of substantive guarantees as well."[18] Thus due process split into two distinct types: substantive due process and procedural due process. Substantive due process is about a set of rights that all persons possess inherently and that cannot be infringed upon by any state. Procedural due process rights, by contrast, stipulate that the state may not take away a person's liberty without first following a set of predetermined procedures that must be consistently applied; the reason for putting these processes in place is to ensure that state curtailment of a person's rights or liberty is not arbitrary.

DUE PROCESS IN THE IMMIGRATION CONTEXT

Since an alien's entry and stay in this country has been described by the Supreme Court as "a matter of permission and tolerance" rather than a right, how do due process protections translate in the immigration realm?[19] Understanding due process in the immigration context requires examination of two other aspects of institutional development: whether deportation is a form of punishment (and why it matters), and how the rise of the administrative state has complicated the application of due process in immigration. The earliest immigration cases did not seem to provide any due process protections for aliens in exclusion proceedings, in part because of the majority's insistence on construing the deportation as not a form of punishment, a distinction that is crucial in the kinds and extent of due process owed to aliens.

[17] *Hurtado v. California*, 110 U.S. 516, 531–2 (1884).
[18] Orth, *Due Process of Law*, 13.
[19] *Harrisiades v. Shaughnessy* (1952), 342 U.S. 580, 586 (1952).

Chae Chan Ping v. United States, and *Nishimura Ekiu v. United States*, two of the earliest exclusion cases, were strong statements about plenary power and national sovereignty.[20] In these classic exegeses on the ideas of plenary power and national sovereignty, the Supreme Court appeared quite adamant that no due process protections extended to aliens in exclusion proceedings because the plenary power doctrine barred it. In *Chae Chan Ping v. United States* (1889), which spelled out the idea of plenary power and laid out the national sovereignty and national security rationales for the congressional control over immigration, the Court stipulated that regardless of whether the nation was at war or not, the "legislative decisions [about the admission of aliens] are conclusive upon the judiciary."[21] Furthermore, immigration questions were "not questions for judicial determination."[22] Just a few years later in *Nishimura Ekiu v. United States* (1892), the Court elaborated that not only was the federal judiciary to be passive in its scrutiny of congressional actions, but it added that the Court would accept decisions of the elected branches as sufficient to meet due process requirements. Justice Gray's majority opinion stated:

It is not within the province of the judiciary to order that foreigners who have never been naturalized, nor acquired any domicile or residence within the United States, nor even been admitted into the country pursuant to law, shall be permitted to enter, in opposition to the constitutional and lawful measures of the legislative and executive branches of the national government. As to such persons, the decisions of executive or administrative officers, acting within powers expressly conferred by congress, are due process of law.[23]

The Court's policy of minimal to no judicial scrutiny in exclusion cases was emphatically reiterated in *Knauff v. Shaughnessey* (1950), in which the majority option written by Justice Minton stated, "Whatever the procedure authorized by Congress is, it is due process as far as an alien denied entry is concerned."[24] This quartet of exclusion cases illustrates the Supreme Court's harshest stance regarding judicial scrutiny of due process for aliens in exclusion proceedings and threw into doubt the availability of *any* due process protections for aliens in entry/exit proceedings.

---

[20] 130 U.S. 581 (1889), 142 U.S. 651 (1892), and 149 U.S. 698 (1893), respectively.
[21] 130 U.S. 581, 606.
[22] 130 U.S. 581, 609.
[23] 142 U. S. 651, 659.
[24] 338 U.S. 587, 544.

IS DEPORTATION PUNISHMENT?

The first consideration of due process in an immigration context appears in the three dissents in *Fong Yue Ting v. United States* (1893),[25] which was a deportation rather than an exclusion case. The dissenters, who had voted unanimously to exclude the alien in *Chae Chang Ping*, changed their vote in *Fong Yue Ting* because they saw a clear distinction between exclusion and deportation. Their view was that aliens should be entitled to more procedural protections in deportation proceedings. *Fong Yue Ting* is a landmark case in both U.S. immigration law and U.S. constitutional law. The case is mostly remembered as another example of the harshness of the plenary power doctrine and the extension of that doctrine to encompass deportation, not just exclusion. And it has often been stated that only the majority opinion creates law. However, *Fong Yue Ting* is arguably most interesting for its three dissenting opinions, where the dissenters laid out their understanding of the due process owed to aliens in deportation proceedings. The dissenters' detailed objections in the case, especially those of Justices Field and Brewer, laid the groundwork for future applications of due process and especially procedural due process protections for aliens. Although the dissents in *Fong Yue Ting* raise the possibility that the Supreme Court would begin to police due process violations, it is not until *Kwong Hai Chew v. Colding* (1953) and *Landon v. Plascencia* (1982), that the Court seemed to soften its stance and make an exception for long-time lawful permanent residents who were returning to the United States from overseas.[26]

Fong Yue Ting v. United States was decided in an era where racial animus against the politically unpopular Chinese was both commonplace and at an all-time high. The Chinese were resented as racially foreign and inassimilable; both "native" Americans and other immigrant groups also reviled them because they presented economic competition, especially in the far western states.[27] One may wonder how it is possible that anyone considered giving due process protections to Chinese aliens in this kind of political atmosphere. Part of the answer is found in the quixotic nineteenth century interpretation of equality. As Christian Fritz explains in his biography of District Judge Ogden Hoffman:

[25] 149 U.S. 698.

[26] 459 U.S. 21 and 344 U.S. 590, respectively.

[27] For accounts of this period, see Alexander Saxton, *The Indispensable Enemy: Labor and the Anti-Chinese Movement in California* (Berkeley: University of California Press, 1995); Elmer C. Sandmeyer, *The Anti Chinese Movement in California* (Urbana, IL: University of Illinois Press, 1991); and Stuart C. Miller, *The Unwelcome Immigrant* (Berkeley: University of California Press, 1969).

One paradox in the nineteenth-century understanding of equality was that it easily accommodated racism. Most of those who embraced the ideal of equality
drew a distinction between civil or legal equality and social, economic, or political equality. All people were theoretically entitled to protection of their person,
property, and liberty. Consequently, racial distinctions that deprived individuals
of their property or their liberty and denied them access to the legal system were
eventually perceived as violations of broadly understood notions of equality.[28]

Indeed, in the 1893 Chinese exclusion case *Fong Yue Ting v. United States*,
due process became an issue not because the dissenting judges felt that
the Chinese were being singled out for mistreatment because of their race,
but because they were incarcerated (deprived of their liberty) and about
to be expelled from the United States under procedures that were unfair –
their rights to *legal* equality were being violated. And as illustrated by the
three dissenting opinions, the very notion of legal equality derives from
the idea of due process.

Recall that in 1892 Congress had passed an act amending the Chinese
Exclusion Act of 1882. This Act required Chinese aliens to possess certificates of residence issued by the U.S. government before they could reenter
the United States from travel abroad. The 1892 Act also required that
resident aliens within the United States carry this certificate with them
to prove that they could legally reside in the United States because they
had entered the country before 1892. In order to obtain the certificate,
applicants had to apply to the tax collector and present evidence that
he or she was eligible to receive the certificate because of U.S. residence
before 1892. The only way to verify the residence date was to produce a
white witness, or an affidavit from a white witness, who would attest to
the Chinese alien's time of residence in the United States.[29]

Fong Yue Ting v. United States involved three Chinese aliens who were
arrested in separate incidents for not having in their possession the requisite certificate of residence. One of the aliens argued that he had applied
to the tax collector for the certificate but had been denied it because
he could produce only a Chinese witness, not a white one, to verify his
residence dates in the United States. All of the three petitioners argued
that they had been arrested and detained without due process of law.
Although the majority opinion ruled against the Chinese aliens, three

---

[28] Christian G. Fritz, *Federal Justice – The California Court of Ogden Hoffman, 1851–
1891* (Lincoln: University of Nebraska Press, 1991), 224.
[29] At the time, a common racist stereotype of the Chinese was that they were compulsive
liars who did not respect the taking of an oath or understand the notion of perjury. In
many legal proceedings, the word or testimony of a white witness was required.

dissenting opinions enumerated the many procedural problems with the treatment of the Chinese. The dissenters also questioned the constitutionality of the 1892 Act.

The majority opinion by Justice Gray was a strong statement of congressional plenary power over immigration and the Court's corresponding adoption of deference in an area that was properly the province of the political branches. The majority opinion also provided a lengthy statement about national sovereignty and how it granted the nation the right not only to exclude aliens from entering the country, but also the right to "expel" or deport aliens deemed inimical to the public good. An often-quoted section from the case on this point is in the majority opinion, "The right of a nation to expel or deport foreigners [derived from the concept of national sovereignty], who have not been naturalized or taken any steps towards becoming citizens of the country, rests upon the same grounds, and is as absolute and unqualified as the right to prohibit and prevent their entrance into the country."[30] The case goes a step further than the *Chae Chan Ping v. U.S* (1889)[31] case by extending the national sovereignty and plenary power doctrines to justify deportation, not just exclusion.

Fong Yue Ting is also significant in immigration law because, beginning with this classic immigration case and continuing through contemporary immigration law, the majority in *Fong Yue Ting* perpetuates the legal fiction that deportation does not constitute punishment.[32] The majority opined:

The proceeding before a United States judge…is in no proper sense a trial and sentence for a crime or offense. It is simply the ascertainment, by appropriate and lawful means, of the fact whether the conditions exist upon which Congress has enacted that an alien of this class may remain within the country. The order of deportation is not a punishment for crime. It is not a banishment, in the sense in which that word is often applied to the expulsion of a citizen from his country by way of punishment. It is but a method of enforcing the return to his own country of an alien who has not complied with the conditions upon the performance of which the government of the nation, acting within its constitutional authority and through the proper departments, has determined that his continuing to reside here shall depend.[33]

[30] 149 U.S. 698, 707.

[31] 130 U.S. 581.

[32] Stephen Legomsky, "The New Path of Immigration Law: Asymmetric Incorporation of Criminal Justice Norms," in 64 *Washington and Lee Law Review* 469, 511 (2008): ("From the Supreme Court's 1893 landmark decision in *Fong Yue Ting v. United States* through the modern era, no court has ever deviated from this principle [that deportation is not punishment].")

[33] 149 U.S. 698, 1028–29.

There are a number of very serious legal implications that flow from construing deportation as "civil rather than punitive."[34] Scholars have attacked this construction as a falsehood.[35] Judges and justices of the federal courts themselves in various opinions have also disagreed with this classification. For example, Judge Garth, in his dissent in *Jacobe v. Immigration and Naturalization Service* (3rd Cir. 1978) wrote, "Deportation is a drastic measure and at times the equivalent of banishment or exile... It is akin to punishment."[36] Perhaps most famous was Justice Brandeis' succinct description of deportation in *Ng Fung Ho v. White* (1922) as "loss of both property and life, or of all that makes life worth living."[37] For the purposes of the argument presented in this chapter, I will focus on the main consequence that flows from treating deportation as a civil proceeding; namely, that the panoply of constitutionally mandated procedural protections available in criminal proceedings are severely curtailed in the civil setting. Among some of these curtailed rights are the right to a *Miranda* warning; protection against double jeopardy; the right to trial by jury; privilege against self-incrimination; prohibition of *ex post facto* laws; and the right to counsel at public expense.[38] Further, formal rules of evidence do not apply in civil settings; therefore, hearsay evidence is admissible.[39] The dissents in *Fong Yue Ting* spotlight the first time the Supreme Court attempted to deal with the disagreement over whether deportation should be classified as punishment or not.

The dissenting opinions in *Fong Yue Ting* also further one's understanding of the relationship of due process and immigration by illustrating the potential of due process as an idea and judicial commitment to counteract even the strong personal biases and racial antipathy held by some of the justices against the Chinese. The majority opinion was followed by three separate dissents. It is noteworthy that Justice Field and Chief Justice Fuller, who had both supported the unanimous opinion in *Chae Chan Ping v. United States*, parted company with the majority when

---

[34] Legomsky, "The New Path of Immigration Law," 512.

[35] See ibid. at 511–15, offering historical and functional evidence challenging the construal of deportation as not punishment; Daniel Kanstroom, "Deportation, Social Control, and Punishment: Some Thoughts about Why Hard Cases Make Bad Laws," 113 *Harvard Law Review* 1890, 1893–1894 (2000).

[36] 578 F.2d 42, 47 (note 14) (3rd Cir.1978), citing in part, *Fong Haw Tan v. Phelan*, 333 U.S. 6, 10 (1948).

[37] 259 U.S. 276, 285 (1922).

[38] Legomsky, "The New Path of Immigration Law," 515–16.

[39] Won Kidane, "Revisiting the Rules of Procedure and Evidence Applicable in Adversarial Administrative Deportation Proceedings: Lessons from the Department of Labor Rules of Evidence," 57 *Catholic University Law Review* 93 (2008).

it came to stretching the doctrines of plenary power and national sovereignty to apply to deportation proceedings. Brewer, the third dissenter, was not on the *Chae Chan Ping* court. Given the national anti-Chinese mood at the time, it is a fair guess that none of the three dissenting justices was personally favorably disposed toward the Chinese as a group. An example of the justices' antipathy toward the Chinese is evidenced by Field's personal correspondence with friends. Field's biographer, Paul Kens, wrote that, "Field felt strongly that Chinese immigration should stop." Field also wrote to John Norton Pomeroy that the presence of the Chinese caused racial conflict and that he believed the Chinese would never assimilate with "our people." And if there were any further doubt about his views about who was entitled to the legal rights and protections of the United Sates, he also wrote that the United States was reserved "I think for our race – the Caucasian race."[40] Similarly, Justice Brewer's own ambivalence toward the Chinese was evident in his references to the "obnoxious Chinese" as a "distasteful class" in his *Fong Yue Ting* dissent.[41]

The judges' personal views toward the Chinese aside, common to all three dissents was a concern for due process. The *Fong Yue Ting* majority had insisted deportation to be civil rather than criminal by claiming that deportation was not punishment. The majority had written: "He [the alien] has not, therefore, been deprived of life, liberty or property, without due process of law; and the provisions of the Constitution, securing the right of trial by jury, and prohibiting unreasonable searches and seizures, and cruel and unusual punishments, have no application."[42] Justice Brewer first raised the issue in his dissenting opinion when he said that as a resident lawfully residing in the United States, Fong Yue Ting and the other two Chinese aliens were entitled to constitutional protections. He continued by saying that section six of the 1892 act "deprives them of liberty, and imposes punishment, without due process of law, and in disregard of constitutional guaranties, especially those found in the Fourth, Fifth, Sixth, and Eighth articles of the amendments."[43] All of these amendments relate to the protection of the accused and the procedures that the government must undertake before a person is deprived of his life, liberty, or property. On the question of whether deportation

[40] Cited in Paul Kens, *Justice Stephen Field: Shaping Liberty from the Gold Rush to the Gilded Age* (Lawrence, KS: University of Kansas Press, 1997), 212.
[41] 149 U.S. 698, 743.
[42] 149 U.S. 698, 1028–29.
[43] 149 U.S. 698, 733.

is punishment, Brewer pointedly rejected the majority view that deportation was not punishment. He wrote, "It imposes punishment without a trial and punishment cruel and severe. It places the liberty of one individual subject to the unrestrained control of another."[44] Brewer added that not only is deportation a kind of punishment, but also it was imposed without due process, "Deportation is punishment. It involves – First, an arrest, a deprival of liberty; and, second, a removal from home, from family, from business, from property...But punishment implies a trial."[45] He unequivocally concluded that deportation required procedural protections to be followed.

On the matter of procuring a certificate of residence, Brewer was equally troubled about the due process violations. He wrote, "It can not be due process of law to impose punishment on any person for failing to have that [the certificate] in his possession, the possession of which he can obtain only at the arbitrary and unregulated discretion of any official."[46] In stark contrast to the statements of plenary power and national sovereignty in other immigration cases of the era, Brewer took the position that the court system, including the Supreme Court, does have an important role in this area of law to scrutinize government action undertaken against aliens. He wrote, "It is the duty of the courts to be watchful for the constitutional rights of the citizen, and against any stealthy encroachments thereon."[47] Although he used the term "citizen," the context of the quote indicates that Brewer understood procedural protections to extend to all persons within U.S. territory, regardless of their immigration status. He rejected the idea that the Supreme Court should suspend all judgment in immigration cases and bow to Congress, as the plenary power and national sovereignty modes of legal reasoning suggested.

Justice Field's dissenting opinion also was focused on due process. Like Brewer, Field believed in a territorially defined application of constitutional rights and protections. In other words, he thought that due process guarantees should be extended to all persons within the jurisdiction of the United States. Field made clear that multiple aspects of the government action troubled him:

The act provides for the seizure of the person without oath or affirmation or warrant, and without showing any probable cause by the official mentioned. The

44 149 U.S. 698, 740.
45 149 U.S. 698, 740.
46 149 U.S. 698, 742.
47 149 U.S. 698, 744.

arrest, as observed by counsel, involves a search of his person for the certificate which he is required to have always with him. Who will have the hardihood and effrontery to say that this is not an "unreasonable search and seizure of the person." Until now it has never been asserted by any court or judge of high authority that foreigners domiciled in this country by the consent of our government could be deprived of the securities of this amendment [the fourth amendment]; that their persons could be subjected to unreasonable searches and seizures, and they could be arrested without warrant upon probable cause, supported by oath or affirmation.[48]

Field was particularly concerned with the absence of warrants for the searches of the Chinese and their subsequent arrests without a demonstration of probable cause that they were in violation of any laws, immigration or otherwise. He also believed that an arrest and removal of a person for deportation "without trial or examination" was "not a reasonable seizure of the person, within the meaning of the fourth article of the amendments of the constitution. It would be brutal and oppressive."[49] He agreed with Brewer that the Chinese aliens' immigration status was not grounds for ignoring or weakening constitutional pledges that should apply to all who reside within the territorial boundaries of the United States.

Chief Justice Fuller's dissent echoed the procedural objections raised in the other justices' dissents. Fuller agreed with the two other dissenters that due process protections should apply to aliens. He wrote, "I entertain no doubt that the provisions of the fifth and fourteenth amendments, which forbid that any person shall be deprived of life, liberty, or property without due process of law, are…universal in their application to all persons within the territorial jurisdiction, without regard to any differences of race, of color, or nationality."[50] The crux of the dispute between the dissenters and the majority was about whether due process protections were available to aliens, or whether those protections were reserved only for citizens.

Chae Chan Ping v. United States hinged on the question of the exclusion of aliens; *Fong Yue Ting* is one of the richest sources of evidence about the Supreme Court's earliest thinking concerning the rights of aliens already residing in the United States. What one learns from this classic immigration case is that deportation is civil in nature, thereby limiting the array of due process protections to aliens. One also learns that,

[48] 149 U.S. 698, 756.
[49] 149 U.S. 698, 756.
[50] 149 U.S. 698, 761–62.

at least in the case of the dissenters, due process commitments trumped any personal biases of the justices' against the Chinese. The dissenters in *Fong Yue Ting* were not so much great supporters of the Chinese as they were believers in requiring the federal government to ensure procedural fairness before they took away a person's rights. This belief derived from their perceptions of their institutional role as federal judges and guardians of constitutional protections.

The influence of the *Fong Yue Ting* dissenters' ideas is observable only a few years later in *Wong Wing v. United States* (1896), a criminal case with immigration elements.[51] But later in another case squarely about immigration entry/exit policy, *Yamataya v. Fisher* (also known as The Japanese immigration case) (1903), the Supreme Court majority for the first time seriously entertained and responded directly to a due process challenge raised by an alien in deportation proceedings.[52] Writing for the majority, Justice Harlan agreed with the alien's due process claim even though he was one of the justices who had voted affirmatively in the *Chae Chan Ping* cases a few years earlier. He noted that although the Court recognized the plenary power of Congress to designate which aliens shall be excludable, the Court had not given a blank check to the government for the treatment of aliens beyond excluding them. He wrote, "But this court has never held, nor must we now be understood as holding, that administrative officers, when executing the provisions of a statute involving the liberty of persons, may disregard the fundamental principles that inhere in 'due process of law' as understood at the time of the adoption of the Constitution."[53] His view is unequivocal about the due process owed to aliens and deserves to be quoted at length:

One of these principles is that no person shall be deprived of his liberty without opportunity, at some time, to be heard, before such officers, in respect of the matters upon which that liberty depends – not necessarily an opportunity upon a regular, set occasion, and according to the forms of judicial procedure, but one that will secure the prompt, vigorous action contemplated by Congress, and at the same time be appropriate to the nature of the case upon which such officers are required to act. Therefore, it is not competent for the Secretary of the Treasury or any executive officer, at any time within the year limited by the statute, arbitrarily to cause an alien, who has entered the country, and has become subject in all respects to its jurisdiction, and a part of its population, although alleged to be illegally here, to be taken into custody and deported without giving

---

[51] 163 U.S. 228.
[52] 189 U.S. 86 and Motomura, "Procedural Surrogates," 1637.
[53] 189 U.S. 86, 100.

him all opportunity to be heard upon the questions involving his right to be and remain in the United States. No such arbitrary power can exist where the principles involved in due process of law are recognized.[54]

Long before the rise of the administrative state and the growth of the sprawling and complex immigration bureaucracy, the majority in *Yamataya v. Fisher* underscored the importance of a fair and independent hearing and the belief that administrative officers may not disregard fundamental due process protections by behaving arbitrarily. Although the alien lost his appeal in the case, another victim of the plenary power doctrine, *Yamataya v. Fisher* has subsequently been cited in a long line of immigration and other cases for the proposition that aliens in U.S. territory are entitled to due process protections. On the idea of the availability of due process (including notice and hearing) to aliens, *Yamataya v. Fisher* has been consistently and affirmatively cited in a line of Supreme Court immigration (and other) cases dating from 1905 and stretching to 2003, the date of the most recent positive citation of the case.[55] Although the alien lost in *Yamataya v. Fisher*, the case is most significant in the sense that it illustrates that congressional plenary power doctrine is not all encompassing; rather, the ideas of plenary power and due process are not mutually exclusive. That the *Yamataya v. Fisher* majority made such a strong statement and prescription about the availability of due process to aliens while being mindful of the plenary power doctrine also illustrates the deeply entrenched nature of the due process ideal in American jurisprudence. There can be no mistake that the majority was using due process to limit the scope of the plenary power doctrine.

---

[54] 189 U.S. 86, 101.

[55] The following cases cite *Yamataya v. Fisher* affirmatively as authority for the idea that an alien (or anyone else) is entitled to due process. Some of these are not immigration cases. In reverse chorological order: *Denmore v. Kim,* 538 U.S. 510, 539 (2003); *Reno v. Flores,* 507 U.S. 292, 306 (1993); *Burns v. United. States,* 501 U.S. 129, 138 (1991); *Landon v. Plascencia,* 459 U.S. 21, 34 (1982); *Abel v. United States,* 362 U.S. 217, 234 (1960); *Greene v. McElroy,* 360 U.S. 474, 507 (1959); *Marcello v. Bonds,* 349 U.S. 302, 315 (1955); *Galvan v. Press,* 347 U.S. 522, 531 (1954); *Shaunessey v. United States,* 345 U.S. 206, 212 (1953); *Kwong Hai Chew v. Colding,* 344 U.S. 590, 598 (1953); *Carlson v. Landon,* 342 U.S. 524, 537 (1952); *Joint Fascist Anti-Refugee Committee v. McGrath,* 341 U.S. 123, 162 (1951); *Johnson v. Eisentrager,* 339 U.S. 763, 771 (1950); *Wong Yang Sung v. McGrath,* 339 U.S. 33, 48 (1950); *Ludecke v. Watkins,* 335 U.S. 160, 181 (1948); *American Power and Light Company v. Securities and Exchange Commission,* 329 U.S. 90, 108 (1946); *Lloyd Sabaudo Societa Anonima Per Azioni v. Elting,* 329 U.S. 90, 108 (1932); *St. Louis SR Company v. Arkansas,* 235 U.S. 350, 370 (1914); and *United States v. Ju Toy,* 198 U.S. 253, 261 (1905).

Some of the earliest immigration cases wrestled with the question of the availability of the Constitution's due process protections for aliens in exclusion and deportation proceedings. Although the federal courts continue to make a distinction between exclusion and deportation, offering aliens who are within U.S. territory more protections than aliens who seek to enter U.S. territory for the first time, after *Yamataya v. Fisher*, both the Supreme Court and U.S. Courts of Appeals recognized that due process protections extended to aliens in deportation proceedings. Contemporary immigration law now treats long-time residents who are returning from abroad differently from an alien who is seeking to enter the United States for the first time. *Shaughnessey v. United States ex rel. Mezei* (1953), for example, stated, "It is true that aliens who have once passed through our gates, even illegally, may be expelled only after proceedings conforming to traditional standards of fairness encompassed in due process of law. But an alien on the threshold of initial entry stands on different footing."[56] Later, in *Leng May Ma v. Barber* (1958), the Supreme Court noted "our immigration laws have long made a distinction between those aliens who have come to our shores seeking admission ... and those who are within the United States after an entry."[57] In short, U.S. immigration laws provide a higher level of procedural protection to long-time residents who are involved in deportation proceedings or are seeking readmission to the United States than to aliens seeking initial entry.

DUE PROCESS AND THE ADMINISTRATIVE STATE

In the area of immigration law, due process issues may arise long before an alien's appeal ever reaches the federal courts. To briefly recap the process by which an alien's appeal reaches the federal courts: an alien's immigration appeal originates in an administrative hearing before an immigration judge. If either the alien or the government is unhappy with the decision of the immigration judge, either party may appeal to the Board of Immigration Appeals (BIA), the highest administrative tribunal in the immigration bureaucracy. Both the immigration judges and the BIA are housed in the Executive Office of Immigration Review (EOIR) and EOIR is under the jurisdiction of the Department of Justice (not the Department of Homeland Security).[58] Although the immigration judges

---

[56] 345 U.S. 206, 212 (1953).

[57] 357 U.S. at 187 (1958).

[58] Lavita Strickland LeGrys, former counsel to Senator Dianne Feinstein on the Senate Judiciary Committee, reported that, during the debate surrounding the creation of

and the BIA members (when the BIA allows oral argument in a case) adjudicate cases wearing black robes and in quasijudicial settings, these personnel are not Article III judges with life tenure; they are administrative agency personnel and not independent adjudicators, because they are accountable to the attorney general. After the BIA, aliens may appeal their cases to the federal courts.

The database for this study reveals that 54 percent of the 2,005 cases appealed to three U.S. Courts of Appeals originate from the Board of Immigration Appeals (as opposed to a federal district court). The Board of Immigration Appeals reviews the decisions of immigration judges and some district directors, and its decisions are binding unless overturned by a U.S. Court of Appeals. Either the alien or the government may appeal the decision of an immigration judge. For a variety of reasons, including a lack of funds to obtain legal counsel for an appeal to the U.S. Courts of Appeals, aliens' appeals often end at the Board of Immigration Appeals.[59] Therefore it is vital that the BIA's decisions be fair and not arbitrary. In a letter to Representative George Geckas (R-PA), Chair of the House Judiciary Committee, a representative of the American Bar Association underscored the important role played by the BIA in immigration appeals:

Nearly all of the cases before the Board involve individuals who are not familiar with U.S. laws or our judicial system, and who often do not speak English. A significant portion of these cases, moreover, involve indigent individuals with little education who have no legal assistance and represented themselves below in an adversarial proceeding where the government was represented by an experienced trial lawyer. At the same time, the interests at stake for these individuals are great – the potential separation of family and loss of all that makes life worth living. In this context, the quality of the administrative appeal is crucial.[60]

the Department of Homeland Security (DHS) following the 9/11 terrorist attacks, she asked the creators of the DHS how the BIA, located in the Department of Justice, would be able to oversee and sanction the actions of immigration officials located in an entirely different department, the Department of Homeland Security. The DHS proponents were at a loss to answer her question and seemed not to have anticipated this situation. (Phone conversation with author, circa June 2005.)

[59] At the conclusion of the administrative hearing before an immigration judge, aliens are provided with a piece of paper advising them of their right to appeal to the BIA. Because immigration proceedings are civil and not criminal in nature, an alien is not entitled to legal counsel at public expense. For the vast majority of aliens, filing with the U.S. Courts of Appeals is prohibitively costly unless they are lucky enough to find *pro bono* counsel through a nongovernment or community-based organization.

[60] Letter from Robert Evans, Director of the Governmental Affairs Office of the American Bar Association, to Representative George Geckas, Chairman of the House Judiciary Committee regarding the proposed reforms to the Board of Immigration Appeals,

The potential life or death consequences of the BIA decisions and the
fact that this agency adjudicates literally tens of thousands of appeals a
year raises the uncomfortable reality that the officials of the BIA, who
are unelected and have not been through the rigorous appointment and
confirmation processes that Article III judges must undergo, nevertheless wield substantial power over so many people's lives. How does one
reconcile the existence of administrative agencies such as the BIA with
our democratic system? What, if any, due process protections are aliens
entitled to in the administrative context and who will ensure that these
protections are actually adhered to?

As immigration law illustrates, the incorporation of the ideas of due
process, including ones relating to procedural due process, has been complicated by the rise of the administrative agencies that often perform
functions akin to the judiciary. In reconciling these quasi-judicial agencies, staffed by unelected officials, with our democratic form of government, administrative agencies have been popularly conceptualized as a
"transmission belt." In this view, the existence of administrative agencies
is indirectly accountable to the people because citizens elect members of
Congress and the president, and these elected officials appoint the leaders
of and oversee the administrative agencies. Therefore, the actions of the
administrative agencies are legitimate because they are merely implementing the desires of the elected officials who oversee these agencies.[61] The
transmission belt model works in theory, but in reality, the administrators
are given wide berth to maneuver as illustrated by the sorts of shirking
and discretionary policy making opportunities described in the previous chapter. The problem with the transmission belt model is, as Jerry
Mashaw has noted, "much administrative decision making, at the micro
as well as the macro level, invites the exercise of judgment concerning not
only the technical means of the implementing policy, but also the priorities to be accorded relevant and competing social values."[62] Mashaw's
description of decision making appears to refer to the same phenomenon
Judge B termed the "interstitial policy making" of the U.S. Courts of
Appeals that was described in the last chapter.[63] In reality, much like

February 6, 2002 (available at http://www.abanet.org/poladv/letters/107th/immigra-
tion020602.html).

[61] Richard Stewart, "The Reformation of American Administrative Law," 88 *Harvard
Law Review* 1667–1813 (1985), 1671–76.

[62] Jerry L. Marsaw, *Due Process in the Administrative State* (New Haven, NJ: Yale
University Press, 1985), 18.

[63] Interview with Judge A, 06/18/07.

judges and justices, administrative officials have ample opportunity to create policy. But who holds the administrative agency officials accountable for their decisions?

A further difficulty with the transmission belt model arises as it is applied to the immigration context. The model is predicated on the indirect supervision of citizens over administrative officials who have been appointed by elected officials. But how do aliens, even indirectly, ensure the accountability and integrity of administrative officials such as those in the BIA when aliens are legally barred from voting? Where along the transmission belt process do aliens get their input into the staffing and operations of administrative agencies?

One could argue that illegal aliens are not entitled to participation in our democratic institutions to begin with, since the polity has not consented to their presence, but this argument would not hold up for aliens who have been lawfully admitted into the country and whom Hiroshi Motomura has urged us to think of as "Americans in waiting" rather than aliens and foreigners.[64] Motomura argues that lawful permanent resident status (held by those with "green cards") is a legal transition point to U.S. citizenship. If one adopts Motomura's conception of lawful permanent residents as pre-citizens, then lawful permanent residents have legitimate grounds for demanding fair treatment from administrative bodies – but someone still has to enforce these protections. As evident in many of the interviews with Ninth Circuit judges in Chapter 5, many of these judges view themselves and their court as the first real review and last line of defense against incorrect administrative decisions or abuses of power.

When federal courts determine the proper level of discretion to be accorded to administrative decision makers, some have argued that judges should defer to these administrative officials because they are "experts" in that policy area, whereas Article III judges are generalists. Each circuit has its own case law governing the degree of judicial scrutiny that should be employed towards administrative agency adjudications of fact and statutory interpretations, both of which are owed deference.[65]

---

[64] See generally Hiroshi Motomura, *Americans in Waiting: The Lost Story of Immigration and Citizenship in the United States* (Oxford: Oxford University Press, 2006).

[65] See, e.g., *Marcello v. Immigration and Naturalization Service*, 694 F.2d 1033 (5th Cir. 1983): "Under accepted standards, on judicial review we cannot disturb the exercise of administrative discretion to deny relief unless the denial was arbitrary or capricious, not in accord with law, or in violation of procedural due process"; *Paul v. Immigration and Naturalization Service*, 521 F.2d 194, 197 (5th Cir. 1975); and *Cortez-Acosta v. Immigration and Naturalization Service*: "We are bound to give the IJ the normal deference owed to an adjudicator, such as sustaining his findings when supported by

But along with the claims of expertise come charges of tunnel vision. An agency may become too insulated from public concerns, too accustomed to doing things its way, and too engrossed in focusing on the proverbial trees that the staff begins to miss the wider view of the forest. There is concern that specialized expertise breeds insularity and promotes bad habits and bad decision making processes that become continually reinforced rather than corrected. Moreover, these administrative agencies, staffed by human beings, are equally susceptible to the kind of mental fatigue described in the previous chapter by the Ninth Circuit Court of Appeals' staff and judges who review thousands of immigration appeals. The reality of the wide discretion of administrative officials, combined with the potential problems of administrative review when considered in conjunction with the legal provisions barring aliens from the franchise, raises the specter of government errors or abuses of power.

Exactly how does one apply notions of due process to the actions of administrative agencies and how much scrutiny should federal courts exercise over administrative agency decisions? As Marsaw describes it, "administrative law became in substantial part law describing the barriers to judicial review of administrative action."[66] As immigration law demonstrates, administrative law has become the battleground for political institutions such as the federal judiciary and administrative agencies contesting whose statutory interpretation and interpretations of facts and evidence should reign supreme. The idea of due process then plays a political role in arbitrating this conflict between administrative agencies and the federal courts, a role it has historically played in "mediating conflict about the appropriate form of American government."[67] The phenomenon of aliens in immigration proceedings taking their grievances against administrative agencies to the federal courts is merely the latest incarnation of this role. Filing a legal challenge in the federal courts is often the only vehicle by which aliens can demand accountability of administrative

substantial evidence. But this deference is owed only when the judge acts in the context of the adjudicatory process and his findings are effectively reviewable on appeal. When the IJ acts outside this process, we treat his findings as the observations of an ordinary witness. Here, the master hearing fell short of what we expect in an adjudicatory proceeding, and so we must treat the IJ's report of what Mr. Cortez-Acosta said as evidence rather than as findings of fact. This subtle, but important, distinction is outcome-determinative in this case. When an adjudicator acts without the minimal trappings of an adjudicatory proceeding, such as in the absence of a contemporaneous recording, he is no longer entitled to the deference normally owed to a judicial officer." 234 F.3d 476, 482–83 (9th Cir. 2000).

[66] Marsaw, *Due Process in the Administrative State,* 25.
[67] Ibid. at 30.

agency actions via judicial scrutiny and oversight. As well, due process calls upon federal appeals courts to exercise their duty to serve as error correctors in the American judicial and political systems.

DUE PROCESS IN THE IMMIGRATION CONTEXT

Due process doctrine has evolved from its early conception in the classical immigration cases. It is understood today that aliens, regardless of their legal or illegal method of entry, are owed certain due process protections in deportation or removal proceedings. As Legomsky has indicated, because the contemporary doctrine is clear that aliens in deportation are entitled to due process, "most of the due process battles in the deportation setting have concerned only the context of the process that is due," rather than whether due process protections exist at all for aliens.[68]

It is true that the Supreme Court granted few alien claims between 1881–2002. To be exact, in 67 cases out of 194 immigration appeals, or 34 percent of the cases, the alien won the legal contest. However, the Supreme Court justices, beginning with the three vigorous dissents in *Fong Yue Ting*, followed by the reasoning in *Yamataya v. Fisher* and in a long line of subsequent cases, have held that government agents, and especially bureaucratic administrators, cannot behave arbitrarily and must conform to due process requirements. It is worth noting that the Supreme Court, albeit in dissenting opinions, contemplated extending due process protections to aliens in *Fong Yue Ting v. United States* as early as 1893, and in the administrative context in *United States ex rel. Arccardi v. Shaughnessy* in 1954. Both cases appeared long before the rise of the administrative state and preceded some of the seminal cases in administrative law, such as *Board of Regents v. Roth* (1971),[69] *Mathews v. Eldrige* (1976),[70] and *Goldberg v. Kelly* (1970).[71] The idea of procedural due process not only successfully made the transition from the British to the American legal traditions; it was integrated into the rise of the administrative state, even in areas such as immigration law where individual rights and entitlements are severely circumscribed by political considerations and existing legal doctrine.

---

[68] Stephen Legomsky, *Immigration and Refugee Law and Policy* (4th ed.) (New York: Foundation Press, 2005), 162.
[69] 404 U.S. 989.
[70] 424 U.S. 319.
[71] 397 U.S. 254.

The Supreme Court's initial solution to applying due process to administrative agencies was to require that these agencies follow applicable rules and where there are no rules governing a situation they must provide minimum procedures.[72] The Court has held that if a government agency or administrative agency has laid out a set of general rules and procedures, the agency is bound by those rules and procedures in adjudications. If an administrative agency has not laid out such rules, it is bound by "minimum procedures."[73] Of course what "minimum procedures" entails is not crystal clear and continues to be defined on a case-by-case basis in the courts, primarily in the U.S. Courts of Appeals.

This formulation of due process as an administrative agency following applicable rules or minimum procedure is illustrated in the immigration context in the deportation case *United States ex rel. Arccardi v. Shaughnessy* (1954).[74] In this case, the Supreme Court ruled that the Attorney General could not establish procedures for deportation and then circumvent his own procedures to reach a desired result. The case also illustrated the move away from the distinction between rights and privileges and instead relied on "limits derived from the rules the agency itself had adopted" in restricting the agency.[75] The Court held that just because immigration cannot be conceived of as a "right" did not mean that the federal courts had no role in ensuring proper procedures were followed even as the government sought to deport an alien.

The contemporary test for due process in administrative proceedings was further refined based on the Social Security benefits case, *Mathews v. Elbridge* (1976).[76] In regard to granting administrative benefits, *Mathews v. Elbridge* calls for the courts to balance three factors: "1) the private interest at stake of the individual, 2) the risk of an erroneous deprivation of such interest through the procedures used and the probable value of substitute procedures and safeguards against error, and 3) the fiscal and administrative costs to the government's interest in requiring additional or substitute procedures."[77] The Supreme Court's ruling in *Mathews v.*

---

[72] Ibid. at 1131.
[73] See, generally, E. Rubin, "Due Process and the Administrative State," 1132, where Rubin lays out in detail both the minimum procedure requirements, including the case law on the subject of procedural due process requirements in administrative proceedings, and also the idea of the rule of obedience, which stipulates that administrative agencies must obey preexisting rules and norms, including the pertinent case law on procedural due process.
[74] 347 U.S. 260.
[75] Rubin, "Due Process and the Administrative State," 1056.
[76] 424 U.S. 319.
[77] 424 U.S. 319, 335.

Eldrige also governs U.S. Courts of Appeals cases. As Legomsky wrote, "Applying *Eldridge*, courts have developed an elaborate body of case law that defines constitutional due process in removal proceedings."[78] In addition, the existence of cases such as *Yamataya v. Fisher* and *Mathews v. Eldridge* provided the inferior courts with a doctrinal basis to apply procedural due process analysis to immigration if they wished to. As a result of these cases, lower courts cannot be accused of "disregarding the teachings of the Supreme Court".[79]

WHEN WOULD PROCEDURAL DUE PROCESS ARISE?

Procedural due process issues can arise on a range of matters in immigration appeals. The most common procedural due process issues in immigration are based on questions of whether the INS, the BIA, and other administrative agencies followed the general procedures that those agencies themselves laid out. Examples of these scenarios include the administrative agencies not following their own rules, an incompetent interpreter assigned to the proceedings, and the BIA or immigration judge producing a "boilerplate" decision that does not seem to take seriously or address thoroughly the existing circumstances in the particular case before them. In addition to the three-part test laid out in *Mathews v. Eldridge*, due process primarily means that an agency must follow its own rules and provide minimum procedures.[80] There are further procedural due process issues that arise in immigration cases that also involve a criminal law element, such as questions about the manner in which evidence is obtained and whether the INS may compel an alien to incriminate himself or herself. In these two latter instances, the U.S. Courts of Appeals' doctrine has been inconsistent and the standards of procedural due process protections are not at the same level as provided in criminal cases. The cases in this study did show that the three Courts of Appeals studied here, regardless of their ideological reputations, held administrative decision makers to standards of procedural fairness in immigration proceedings. Given the small number of cases the Supreme Court grants *certiorari* to each year, it is effectively the Courts of Appeals that must police procedural guarantees for aliens.

[78] Thomas Alexander Aleinikoff, David A. Martin, Hiroshi Motomura, and Maryellen Fullerton, *Immigration and Citizenship Process and Policy* (6th ed.) (New York: Thomson West Publishing Group, 2003), 1046.

[79] Stephen Legomsky, *Immigration and the Judiciary: Law and Politics in Britain and America* (Oxford: Oxford University Press, Clarendon, 1987), 212.

[80] Rubin, "Due Process and the Administrative State," 1055–56.

An example of a Court of Appeals applying the standard that administrative agencies must follow their own rules is found in *Lionel G. F. Panchevre v. Immigration and Naturalization Service* (5th Cir. 1991).[81] In this case, the Fifth Circuit ruled that the BIA's decision should be vacated because the INS withdrew its appeal to the BIA, thus making the immigration judge's decision final and rendering the BIA lacking in jurisdiction to hear the appeal. In reaching this conclusion, the Fifth Circuit wrote, "Courts do not look favorably upon the INS's failure to follow its own regulations."[82]

A due process violation can also arise when a Court of Appeals finds an abuse of discretion by the BIA, the INS, or another government entity in processing or adjudicating an immigration case. In another case from the Fifth Circuit, *Diaz-Resendez v. Immigration and Naturalization Service* (1992),[83] the court ruled that the judgment should be vacated and remanded because the BIA had abused its discretion and did not follow precedent set in a previous case. The case involved a lawful permanent resident placed in deportation proceedings after he was arrested for possession of marijuana. The alien, Diaz-Resendez, applied for section 212c relief that would have suspended deportation if he could show that his deportation would result in undue hardship to himself or his family. In this particular case, such circumstances were present. Diaz-Resendez had been married for 25 years and was the primary provider for his wife and six children, who were U.S. citizens. His wife and youngest child had medical conditions that required the care of specialists. The panel noted that in a previous case where the facts were far less compelling, the BIA had granted 212c relief. The Fifth Circuit panel concluded, "The Board abused its discretion by inexplicably departing from established precedent and failing to actually consider and meaningfully address the positive equities and favorable evidence when reaching its decision."[84] The panel also found unacceptable the BIA's failure to explicitly balance the equities in such a case or to carefully weigh Diaz-Resendez's guilt against the extenuating circumstances of his situation.

The U.S. Courts of Appeals also routinely rule on procedural due process violations by immigration judges, who are administrative agency

[81] 922 F.2d 1229 (1991).
[82] 922 F.2d 1229, 1232, citing *Duran v. Immigration and Naturalization Service*, 756 F.2d 1338, 1342 (9th Cir. 1984); and *Ramon-Sepulveda v. Immigration and Naturalization Service*, 743 F.2d 1307, 1310 (9th Cir. 1984).
[83] 960 F.2d 493 (1992).
[84] 960 F.2d 493, 498.

personnel. For example, in the case *Cortez-Acosta v. Immigration and Naturalization Service* (9th Cir. 2000),[85] Cortez-Acosta was accused of helping to smuggle aliens and was in deportation proceedings because of that charge. The Ninth Circuit concluded that normally the court owed deference to the immigration judge, because the immigration judge is better equipped to ascertain the facts in a trial situation than is an appellate court that is several layers removed. However, in this case the immigration judge did not provide clear and convincing enough evidence that Cortez-Acosta had admitted his guilt of the crime of smuggling aliens and was deportable:

We are bound to give the immigration judge the normal deference owed to an adjudicator, such as sustaining his findings when supported by substantial evidence. But this deference is owed only when the judge acts in the context of the adjudicatory process and his findings are effectively reviewable on appeal. When the immigration judge acts outside this process, we treat his findings as the observations of an ordinary witness. Here, the master hearing [before an immigration judge] fell short of what we expect in an adjudicatory proceeding, and so we must treat the immigration judge's report of what Mr. Cortez-Acosta said as evidence rather than as findings of fact. This subtle, but important, distinction is outcome-determinative in this case. When an adjudicator acts without the minimal trappings of an adjudicatory proceeding, such as in the absence of a contemporaneous recording, he is no longer entitled to the deference normally owed to a judicial officer.[86]

The Ninth Circuit panel found that because Cortez-Acosta had admitted his guilt during a master calendar hearing (which was to schedule a trial date), and not at the actual administrative hearing, this was "not an adjudicatory process" and the information was inadmissible.[87] Without this alleged admission of guilt, the Ninth Circuit found that the circumstances did not show that Cortez-Acosta had "an overwhelming probability of guilt."[88] They also stated that, "There is a real possibility that this man is not deportable, and never admitted that he was."[89] Even though the Ninth Circuit's own doctrine called for deference to the immigration judge's factual determination (because these judges are often the ones who have had the opportunity to question the alien at length), in this case the panel was unwilling to defer when a procedural due process violation had taken place.

[85] 234 F.3d 476, 482 (2000).
[86] 234 F.3d 476, 482.
[87] 234 F.3d 476, 483.
[88] 234 F.3d 476, 483.
[89] 234 F.3d 476, 483.

One final example of a due process violation often flagged by the Courts of Appeals involves the availability and competence of interpreters and the larger issue of whether aliens who often do not speak English are sufficiently informed of the charges against them. As the court in the case of *Tejeda-Mata v. Immigration and Naturalization Service* (9th Cir. 1980) wrote "[T]his court and others have repeatedly recognized the importance of an interpreter to the fundamental fairness of such a hearing if the alien cannot speak English fluently."[90] The importance of an alien being able to understand the legal actions taken against him or her is discussed in *Hernandez-Garza v. Immigration and Naturalization Service* (5th Cir. 1989), a deportation and 212(c) waiver case where the immigration judge denied the alien's attorney's request to cross-examine the border patrol agents to test their fluency in Spanish. Hernandez-Garza found himself in deportation proceedings after being charged with aiding and abetting the entry of an undocumented alien named Arnulfo. At the hearing, the INS attorney presented two affidavits, signed by Hernandez-Garza and Arnulfo, showing that Hernadez-Garza was entering a guilty plea for aiding and abetting the illegal entry of Arnulfo. The INS claimed that the contents of the affidavit were sufficiently explained in Spanish to Hernandez-Garza and that he understood that he was pleading guilty to smuggling. Hernandez-Garza's attorney countered that his client was not cognizant of the charges and did not understand the document he was signing because the agents' Spanish language ability was insufficient. The court explained why the language ability of the agents was key to the case:

The language skills of the agents were critical if the judge was to admit and give credence to the contents of Arnulfo's affidavit. Accordingly, the attempt by Hernandez' counsel to test the agents' fluency in Spanish was appropriate and reasonable, and may have been the only meaningful way to measure the testimony used to corroborate Arnulfo's affidavit…Denying cross-examination on the agents' fluency in Spanish, and relying on the Arnulfo affidavit as proof of the gain element denied Hernandez a fair hearing, to his obvious prejudice. Without Arnulfo's affidavit the evidence of record falls far short of the required clear and convincing level of proof.[91]

The issue at stake was not just the ability of the alien's attorney to cross-examine the government's witnesses (the border patrol agents), but specifically to cross-examine them to assess their Spanish language ability.

---

[90] 626 F.2d 721, 726.
[91] 882 F.2d 945, 948.

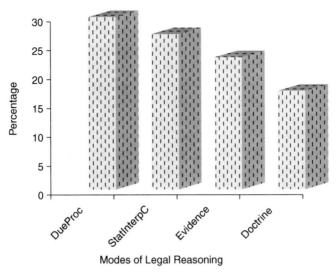

FIGURE 6.1. Modes of Legal Reasoning in Courts of Appeals Cases in which the Alien Prevailed, 1881–2002

The eventual outcome of the case was that the court granted the petition for review, vacated the BIA decision, and remanded to the BIA.

Compared with its infrequent appearances at the Supreme Court, where due process concerns have materialized mainly in egregious situations of government excess and error, procedural due process plays a more prominent role in many of the immigration appeals in the Third, Fifth, and Ninth Circuit Courts of Appeals cases that were surveyed for this book. Moreover, the use of due process as a mode of legal reasoning by the Courts of Appeals is motivated and reinforced not just by a general judicial commitment to fair process but by the specific institutional role expectation of these courts to continue their function as error correctors.

In U.S. Courts of Appeals cases where aliens won their appeals, the most common mode of legal reasoning used was procedural due process (Figure 6.1). Additionally, although there is a grand total of twenty-three references to plenary power and zero references to national sovereignty in the Third, Fifth, and Ninth Circuit Courts of Appeals between the years 1881 and 2002, the procedural due process mode of legal reasoning plays a prominent role in the majority of decisions that found in favor of the alien. Even in the many cases where the alien did not prevail, procedural due process is often the analytical lens by which the Courts of Appeals evaluate their claims, thus indicating the Courts of Appeals continue to perform their role as error-correction courts.

As argued in Chapter 3, the U.S. Courts of Appeals are more naturally inclined toward a procedural focus than the Supreme Court because such an approach dovetails with the prescribed role of the Courts of Appeals as error correctors. And as illustrated in Chapter 5, many of the judges of the contemporary U.S. Courts of Appeals spoke of their obligation to review cases carefully because they were the last line of defense against bureaucratic and administrative error or abuse. These roles are contrasted with the contemporary Supreme Court's role as primarily a policy court and political court.

The cases presented in this chapter are but a small sample of the many cases in which the Third, Fifth and Ninth Circuit Courts of Appeals repeatedly intervened to overturn the decisions of the Board of Immigration Appeals, an immigration judge, or a district court's findings in order to correct government error or abuses. Given the extensive problems that plague the immigration bureaucracy that were described in the last chapter, the error-correction role of the federal courts becomes all the more important. The Supreme Court rarely rendered pro-alien decisions using the procedural due process mode of legal reasoning; it only did so in cases where egregious procedural violations occurred. It is as if only a very severe breach of fundamental fairness could jolt the Supreme Court into action in immigration cases. Meanwhile, the U.S. Courts of Appeals, consistent with their designated mission to be error-correction courts, much more actively use procedural due process to monitor and check administrative agency personnel.

Immigration entry/exit decisions are an area of law where one would least expect to find aliens winning due process claims, given a non-citizen's lack of entitlement to immigrate and remain in this country and the influences of the plenary power and national sovereignty modes of legal reasoning. Yet both the U.S. Courts of Appeals and the Supreme Court have insisted on evaluating the legality of the federal government and its administrative agencies' decisions on immigration. A passage from *United States ex rel. Schachter v. Curran* (1925) summarizes the approach taken by the federal appellate courts in immigration. After acknowledging Congress's expansive and plenary power to regulate immigration, Judge Davis indicated:

[T]his power must be exercised fairly and in good faith with an earnest effort to discover the truth in accordance with the traditions and principles of free government, applicable where the fundamental rights of men are involved, and in accordance "with the fundamental principles of justice embraced within the conception of due process of law." While federal courts may not inquire whether or not on the evidence a decision of a Board of Special Inquiry is right or wrong, they may, nevertheless, inquire whether or not the alien had a fair hearing and whether or not the evidence was disregarded or adequately supports the decision.[92]

This quote neatly encapsulates the thinking of the federal appellate courts on immigration. The plenary power doctrine and national sovereignty idea do not preclude the federal courts from performing their error-correction role, which prompts them to evaluate the legality of the procedures used to deport or exclude someone.

Indeed, Table 6.1 shows that, although procedural due process is never the most frequently used mode of legal reasoning in any decade, that mode of legal reasoning has maintained a consistent presence in both courts and more impressively, across time that includes national periods of restriction and liberal policies toward immigrants.

In immigration cases between 1881 and 2002, the Supreme Court used procedural due process in 9 percent of its majority decisions. Although these cases did not all result in the alien's victory, as I argued in Chapter 4, the selection of procedural due process as a mode of legal reasoning orients the judges or justices toward an individualized approach, as opposed to a group approach, to adjudication. The significance of the Supreme Court's use of procedural due process in 9 percent of its cases is not in the unimpressive percentage of its frequency; the true importance in that figure is that the Supreme Court considered due process protections for aliens at all in light of the ostensible prohibition against doing so by the plenary power doctrine and that Court's sensitivity to the political and policy implications of its rulings. The Supreme Court justices, beginning with the three vigorous dissents in *Fong Yue Ting*, followed by the reasoning in *Yamataya v. Fisher*, and in subsequent cases, have held government agents and especially bureaucratic administrators to procedural due process requirements. That the Supreme Court justices have done so in contravention of their own clear doctrinal directives to defer and to minimize judicial scrutiny of government action in immigration is testimony to the deeply embedded nature of the idea of due process as one of the essential essences defining a judicial institution.

---

[92] 4 F.2d 356, 358.

TABLE 6.1. *Three Most Frequently Occurring Modes of Legal Reasoning by Frequency, Percentage of Usage, and Decade, 1881–2002*

Decade	Supreme Court	%	Courts of Appeals	%
1890	NationalSov 2	33	StatInterpC 2	40
	StatInterpA 1	16	AdminDis 2	40
	PlenaryPow 1	16		
	Doctrine 1	16		
1900	StatInterpC 6	40	StatInterpC 12	52
	Doctrine 5	33	Doctrine 5	22
	Plenary Pow1	7	PlenaryPow 2	9
	AdminDis 1	7		
1910	StatInterpC 10	71	Doctrine 15	21
	PlenaryPow 1	7	Fact/Evidence 13	18
	ProcDueProc 1	7	**ProcDueProc** 12	17
	Facts/Evidence 1	7	StatInterpC 12	17
1920	StatInterpC 13	65	StatInterpC 49	33
	ProDueProc 5	25	Fact/Evidence 49	33
	Fact/Evidence 2	10	**ProcDueProc** 15	15
1930	StatInterpC 6	67	Fact/Evidence 47	38
	Doctrine 3	33	StatInterpC 25	20
			Reasonable 18	14
1940	StatInterpC 8	67	StatInterpC 25	20
	StatInterpB 1	8	Doctrine 14	11
	ProcDueProc 1	8	**ProcDueProc** 8	17
1950	StatInterpC 20	50	StatInterpC 49	30
	ProcDueProc 6	15	**ProcDueProc** 34	21
	PlenaryPow 4	10	Doctrine 33	20
	Doctrine 4	10		
1960	StatInterpC 12	80	StatInterpC 59	36
	Fact/Evidence 2	13	Doctrine 34	21
	ProcDueProc 1	7	Evidence 24	14
1970	StatInterpC 4	44	StatInterpC 86	35
	PlenaryPow 2	22	**ProcDueProc** 47	19
	Doctrine 2	22	Fact/Evidence 42	17
1980	StatInterpC 10	56	Doctrine 49	26
	Doctrine 3	17	StatInterpC 43	23
	AdminDis 2	50	Fact/Evidence 41	22
1990	StatInterpC 6	46	Evidence 224	37
	Evidence 3	23	Doctrine 147	24
	PlenaryPow 1	7	**ProcDueProc** 86	14
	ProcDueProc 1	7		
	Doctrine 1	7		
	AdminDis 1	7		
2000	StatInterpC 3	75	Fact/Evidence 33	37
	StatInterpB 1	25	Doctrine 29	32
			ProcDueProc 15	10

PROCEDURAL DUE PROCESS AS A "PHANTOM NORM"
OR "SURROGATE"

It is also the specific idea of procedural due process that has driven jur-isprudential innovation at both the Supreme Court and U.S. Courts of Appeals in the area of immigration law. Hiroshi Motomura has written extensively about very curious behavior in the federal courts; he observes that real jurisprudential innovations seem to be occurring, not through dramatic constitutional pronouncements from the bench, but through more incremental and mundane sorts of creative interpretations that are not constitutional in nature.[93] He has argued that the dominance of the plenary power doctrine (and to a lesser extent the idea of national sov-ereignty in the classical immigration cases) has occasionally elicited con-scious and purposive "subconstitutional" judicial decision making on the part of the Supreme Court and the lower courts.[94] He defines "constitu-tional immigration law" as "the application of constitutional norms and principles to test the validity of immigration rules in subconstitutional form, including statutes, regulations, and administrative guidelines."[95] "Subconstitutional immigraton law" by contrast means "the interpre-tation and application of those statutes, regulations, administrative guidelines, and the like."[96] More important, he indicates "the principal decisions that have contributed to this expansion of judicial review in immigration cases have not been decisions of constitutional immigration law. Instead, they reached results favorable to aliens by interpreting stat-utes, regulations, or other form of subconstitutional immigration law."[97] Motomura argues that federal judges are circumventing the restrictions of the plenary power doctrine that is the governing constitutional doc-trine in this area of law, by using what he calls "phantom norms" or creative statutory and rule interpretations to reach pro-alien rulings. He considers these norms "phantoms" in a sense that "they do not serve in the first function of 'constitutional' norms – namely, direct applica-tion to constitutional issues raised in immigration cases."[98] Judges use the

---

[93] Please refer to Chapter 5 for examples of the kinds of creative interpretations he refers to.

[94] Hiroshi Motomura, "Immigration Law After a Century of Plenary Power: Phantom Constitutional Norms and Statutory Interpretation," 100 *Yale Law Journal* 545, 547 (1990); and "The Curious Evolution of Immigration Law: Procedural Surrogates for Substantive Constitutional Rights," 92 *Columbia Law Review* 1626–1704 (1992).

[95] Motomura, "Immigration Law After a Century," 560.

[96] Ibid.

[97] Motomura, "Immigration Law After a Century," 548.

[98] Motomura, "Immigration Law After a Century," 565.

phantom norms to "produce results that are more sympathetic to aliens" rather than apply the plenary power doctrine, which would require a result that would have gone against the alien.[99]

As Motomura and the judges interviewed in the previous chapter suggested, there are several ways to circumvent the plenary power and national sovereignty directives, such as the use of statutory interpretation strategies and other types of purposive behavior discussed in Chapter 5. But it was clear from a close reading of the cases for this database that due process as a mode of legal reasoning is also used to undercut modes of legal reasoning that may lead to a legal result not favorable to aliens. In a separate law review article, Motomura notices that judges use procedural due process rulings as "a 'surrogate' for the substantive judicial review that the plenary power doctrine seems to bar."[100] He explains that judges use these surrogates when they have "constitutional misgivings about an immigration decision by the government" and also to "ameliorate the harshness of the plenary power doctrine by first construing the constitutional challenge as 'procedural,' and then invalidating the decision on procedural due process grounds."[101] In other words, judges may sometimes engage in creative jurisprudence to arrive at pro-alien results by shifting from one mode of legal reasoning to another, and procedural due process is almost always the mode of legal reasoning to which they move to reach a pro-alien result.

I agree with Motomura's analysis about the use of phantom norms and procedural surrogates, but it begs the question of why judges might want to reach pro-alien results in the first place. What is the motivation for judges to use phantom norms and procedural surrogates? Motomura does not argue this, but it cannot be that it is a matter of the judges' personal sympathy for the aliens; there are numerous hard-luck cases where the judges did not engage in the kind of phantom norms or procedural surrogate decision making described by Motomura to reach a pro-alien result. Indeed, pro-alien results even at the U.S. Courts of Appeals are not the norm; aliens' victories in the federal appellate courts remain rare. Nor is this a matter of the judges pursuing their policy preferences by using procedural due process as a subterfuge. Instead, it appears that the judges' attention to due process, and its persistence in immigration law, which is an area of law that would seem the most inhospitable to it,

[99] Motomura, "Immigration Law After a Century," 564.
[100] Motomura, "The Curious Evolution of Immigration Law," 1628.
[101] Ibid.

points to the deep entrenchment of due process and its fundamental role in defining the role and mission of an independent judiciary.

Motomura hints at some institutional motivations for this behavior when he writes about "judicial self-image," a version of what public law scholars would call "role perception." According to role perception theory, judges make decisions based on their normative beliefs about what they perceive to be the role of the court and the kind of behavior that is appropriate for a judge as an official of the court.[102] Motomura speculates, for example, that judges have preferred procedural review over substantive review of immigration cases because they may feel more "competent" to review procedural matters, since "the judiciary constantly wrestles with questions of process, particularly questions related to the values of accuracy, participation, and predictability" as opposed to the political branches of government, which focus on "weighing competing political and economic interests."[103] No doubt a judge's perception of his or her duty to review cases for procedural errors is at work here, but this duty derives from the institutional setting a judge works in. Members of Congress, the president, and administrative agency personnel do not feel so strongly compelled to evaluate their actions by these standards. The dissimilar institutional contexts of the elected branches of government provide an entirely different set of incentives and guiding principles of behavior from those that influence judicial institutions.

The impetus for federal judges, including the Justices of the Supreme Court, to engage in decision making that deviates from the requirements of the plenary power and national sovereignty modes of legal reasoning and corresponding doctrinal directives is motivated by deeply ingrained commitment to due process and procedural fairness that is rooted in the *raison d'être* of courts of law. Additionally, the judges' and justices' commitment to due process is separate from and irrespective of their personal views toward aliens and immigration policy generally. Therefore, it is not so much that judges are being creative in reaching pro-aliens because they are somehow sympathetic to the aliens, but they are doing so because their job description requires them to flag due process violations. In addition to serving as a check on bureaucratic error or abuse, the idea of due process can be an alternative to the plenary power, national sovereignty, and administrative deference modes of legal reasoning that otherwise dominate this area of law.

[102] James Gibson, "Judges' Role Orientation, Attitudes and Decisions: An Interactive Model," *American Political Science Review* 72:911–24 (1978).
[103] Motomura, "The Curious Evolution of Immigration Law," 1646.

PRESERVING *HABEAS CORPUS* REVIEW POST IIRIRA AND AEDPA

Further evidence of the staying power and continuing influence of due process can be found in examining how the U.S. Courts of Appeals and the Supreme Court responded to the 1996 congressional attempts to strip the federal courts of jurisdiction over a class of immigration cases, mainly deportation and removal cases involving criminal aliens. In 1996, Congress passed the Antiterrorism and Effective Death Penalty Act (AEDPA) and the Illegal Immigration Reform and Immigrant Responsibility Act (IIRIRA) within several months.[104] Both contained provisions that dramatically streamlined judicial review in immigration cases, and in some instances, bar *habeas* review, especially in cases involving aliens with criminal convictions. Like procedural due process, *habeas corpus* review is intended to safeguard an individual's rights from overzealous persecution or prosecution by the state by allowing an individual to challenge her detention.[105] The impetus for these changes was the belief among some that many aliens were abusing the judicial review procedures by filing frivolous claims for the sole purpose of delaying deportation. As a result, Congress sought to cut out layers of judicial review and eliminate access to *habeas corpus* for certain classes of aliens even though many of the congressionally mandated changes in AEDPA and IIRIRA were at odds with judicial norms and basic notions of fairness. Many of the provisions were roundly criticized by prominent immigration law specialists.[106] Indeed, both pieces of legislation precipitated a flurry of litigation that sought to challenge and clarify various requirements.

The response of the Courts of Appeals to AEDPA and IIRIRA are instances of interstitial decision making. Even as rising caseloads create pressures for the circuit judges to adopt certain types of legal reasoning, the independence from the Supreme Court created by the caseload situation also facilitates the circuit judges' use of creative noncompliance when they find themselves in disagreement with congressional statutes. In the face of the court-stripping measures passed by Congress, the U.S.

---

[104] AEDPA, Pub. Law No. 104–132, 110 Stat. 1214, and IIRIRA, Public Law No. 1-4-208, 110 Stat. 3009–546. AEDPA was intentionally passed in time to mark the one-year anniversary of the Oklahoma City bombing.

[105] See Duker, *A Constitutional History of Habeas Corpus*, and Freedman, *Habeas Corpus: Rethinking the Great Writ of History* (2001) for an historical overview of *habeas corpus* in American law.

[106] Aleinikoff, "Detaining Plenary Power" (2002) and Neuman, "Jurisdiction and the Rule of Law After the 1996 Act," 113 *Harvard Law Review* 1963–98 (2002).

Courts of Appeals used highly technical, procedural arguments to preserve some judicial review and to ease some of the severity of the 1996 reforms. These resistance tactics could be construed as the judiciary engaging in turf battles with Congress, or under Motomura's "phantom norms" theory, as the circuits attempting to mitigate the harshness of federal immigration policy by using procedurally based arguments to preserve judicial review in some cases. It is also quite plausible that the U.S. Courts of Appeals (and some members of the Supreme Court in dissenting opinions) engage in this kind of defiant behavior because their professional sensibilities as judges have been offended by congressional attempts at stripping judicial review and perceived violations of basic notions of fairness by the 1996 legislation. These judges could have simply acquiesced to congressional will, but their commitment to judicial principles of procedural fairness and to judicial review itself caused them to interpret AEDPA and IIRIRA in sometimes highly creative ways that produced less harsh outcomes for aliens. The U.S. Courts of Appeals in these cases seemed to go the extra mile to delve into minute technicalities that could have been overlooked or taken for granted instead of following the Supreme Court doctrine by citing national sovereignty or plenary power.

As mentioned, AEDPA and IIRIRA were motivated in part by the belief that many aliens were taking advantage of the legal procedures in place to file frivolous claims to delay their inevitable deportation. Toward these ends, efforts to streamline judicial review began with targeting section 212c of the Immigration and Nationality Act, which was perceived as a loophole that granted relief for aliens in deportation proceedings. This provision, before it was significantly curtailed by the 1996 reforms, provided aliens who were long-term permanent residents with relief from deportation by allowing them to present mitigating factors (considerations of equity) to argue against their deportation. In many cases, aliens would point to the severe hardship caused to their U.S. citizen or lawful permanent resident spouses or children if they were deported. Prior to the 1996 legislative reforms, the only bar to 212c eligibility was if the alien had committed aggravated felony and served a five-year sentence for it. Then AEDPA was passed on April 24, 1996, and barred 212c relief for any aggravated felony regardless of the sentence imposed. AEDPA also added some crimes to a list of what crimes constituted an aggravated felony, including any controlled substance violation. This move vastly expanded the group of aliens who are now ineligible for 212c relief and it repealed the provision that had provided for *habeas corpus* review for aliens in deportation proceedings. Specifically, the Act stated, "Any final order of deportation against an alien who is deportable by reason of [certain enumerated criminal grounds] shall not be subject to review by any court."[107] This language eliminated the statutory grounds for habeas corpus relief for all aliens in deportation proceedings and denied judicial review for those with certain criminal convictions.[108]

Several months later, Congress passed the IIRIRA, which erased the long- held distinction between exclusion and deportation, rolling the two into what is now called a "removal" proceeding. IIRIRA also completely repealed section 212c of the INA and replaced it with a procedure called "cancellation of removal." In addition, IIRIRA created a set of transitional rules for cases initiated before April 1, 1997, and a different set of permanent rules for cases initiated on or after that date. As the following examples will demonstrate, the more multilayered and complex the rules were, the more wiggle room the Courts of Appeals had in deciding how to implement the law. The permanent rules further streamlined the appeals procedure for deportation by attempting to cut out U.S. district court review of cases and channel all review of final orders of deportations to the U.S. Courts of Appeals. Access to *habeas corpus* was also modified by AEDPA and IIRIRA, with further restrictions added. Together, AEDPA and IIRIRA, especially the attempts to restrict judicial review, raised serious concerns for the U.S. Courts of Appeals and the U.S. Supreme Court. The question was, did Congress have the right to shield the removal of a large class of criminal aliens from all judicial review? The federal courts were being stripped of their traditional power of reviewing aliens' challenges of their apprehension, detention, and removal, thus raising serious separation of power issues.[109] The responses of the federal courts indicated that they believed Congress had overreached in its court stripping. Much has been written by legal analysts on the questions of whether aliens retained the right to *habeas corpus* after the 1996 reforms and under what conditions they retained that right after the passage of AEDPA and IIRIRA, but what did the federal judges and justices themselves believe?[110] Although many portions of IIRIRA and AEDPA were

---

[107] Codified at 8 U.S.C. § 1105a (1996).
[108] David Cole, "No Clear Statement: An Argument for Preserving Judicial Review of Removal Decisions," 12 *Georgetown Immigration Law Journal* 427 (1998), 429.
[109] Neuman, "*Habeas Corpus,* Executive Detention and the Removal of Aliens," 1988.
[110] For a history of how *habeas corpus* has been used in immigration cases, see Gerald Neuman, "Habeas Corpus, Executive Detention and the Removal of Aliens," 98 *Columbia Law Review* 961–1066 (1998); and "Jurisdiction and the Rule of Law

challenged in the courts, I focus here on the availability of *habeas corpus* review. The response of the U.S. Courts of Appeals and even the Supreme Court indicated that the federal courts believed that Congress had impermissibly crossed a line. At first, some of the Circuits dismissed many cases for lack of jurisdiction and agreed that Congress had the right to divest their review of these cases. Then something more interesting began to happen. The majority of the twelve circuits, not just the allegedly liberal Ninth Circuit, adopted a "we have jurisdiction to determine whether jurisdiction exists" approach.[111] By the end of 1999, ten of the U.S. Courts of Appeals (including the Fifth, Ninth, and Eleventh) had adopted the position that they, and not Congress, had the right to determine the appellate courts' jurisdiction in these cases.[112] In so doing, most Circuits declined to make sweeping statements about the availability of *habeas corpus* review while noting the substantial nature of the claims being raised by the aliens. See, for example, the Eleventh Circuit case, *Mayers v. Immigration and Naturalization Service* (11th Cir. 1999), where the panel wrote:

It is important to emphasize...that in exercising habeas corpus jurisdiction in this case, we do not decide whether every statutory claim raised by an alien is cognizable on habeas...the Petitioners' claims in the present case, however, affect the aliens' substantial rights and are of the nature that courts have enforced through judicial review even when Congress has attempted to limit the courts' jurisdiction in immigration matters as far as constitutionally permitted.[113]

Here, the Eleventh Circuit panel especially noted that some judicial review has always been available to aliens even when Congress had tried to limit it, and that the two aliens were unable to obtain any judicial review in other venues, to justify the circuit's intervention in the matter.

After the 1996 Immigration Act," 113 *Harvard Law Review* 1963–98 (2000). For a discussion of the connection between *habeas corpus* and due process, see David Cole, "Congress and the Courts: *Habeas Corpus* and Due Process as Limits on Congress's Control of Federal Jurisdiction," 86 *Georgetown Law Journal* 2481 (1998). See also the special issue of the *Georgetown Law Journal* for the collection of articles published as part of the "Symposium: Congress and the Courts: Jurisdiction and Remedies," July 1998, Volume 86.

[111] *Aragaon-Ayon v. Immigration and Naturalization Service*, 206 F.3d 847, 849 (9th Cir. 2000).

[112] See the Fifth Circuit case *Requena-Rodriquez v. Immigration and Naturalization Service* (1999), 190 F.3d 299, 304, noting that the Fourth, Sixth, Eighth, Tenth, and Eleventh Circuits had found that *habeas* jurisdiction continues to exist under the IIRIRA transitional rules.

[113] 175 F.3d 1289, 1301.

They suggest that to close off all avenues of judicial review would be contrary to past practice and therefore unacceptable. In contrast, the Tenth Circuit was the only circuit that has held that even the question of deportability is beyond the power of its review.[114] On the question of whether habeas corpus review remained available under the permanent IIRIRA rules, where the statutory language was more explicit than under the transitional rules, the circuits were divided.

While ostensibly determining their jurisdiction over these cases, the U.S. Courts of Appeals engaged in three kinds of behavior that challenge and undermine the AEDPA and IIRIRA restrictions on judicial review.[115] First, most of the circuits insist on making highly technical and in-depth determinations about whether the person is an alien under the immigration law, and whether the alien is deportable under any of the grounds specified in the Immigration and Nationality Act (INA). These inquiries often involve parsing the language of state and federal statutes about what crimes are considered aggravated felonies for deportation purposes and what the person's legally determined immigration status is. For example, in one case the Eleventh Circuit stated that that court retains jurisdiction only if the Eleventh Circuit itself (not the Congress or the administrative agency) determined whether judicial review is barred in each case. They would do this by determining whether the alien is indeed an alien *and* has committed a criminal offense that renders him or her deportable.[116] See also the example in *Santos v. Reno* (2000), from the Fifth Circuit, on whether burglary of a vehicle is considered an aggravated felony for deportation purposes, and *Lujan-Armendariz v. Immigration and Naturalization Service* (2000), where the Ninth Circuit ruled that the "conviction" did not count for deportation purposes.[117]

The second kind of behavior the circuits use to circumvent the 1996 reforms involves decisions on how to apply the effective date of the AEDPA and IIRIRA reforms, specifically whether the new rules should apply to cases already in the pipeline – the retroactivity question. In

---

[114] Neuman, "Jurisdiction and the Rule of Law After the 1996 Act," 1963–1968, 1977–1978, notes 88, 89; see also *Requena-Rodriquez v. Immigration and Naturalization Service* (1999), noting, "the Seventh Circuit is the only circuit arguably maintaining that there is no habeas jurisdiction in cases under transitional rules." 190 F.3d 299, 304.

[115] When asked about the motivation of the judges to undertake this kind of detailed review of jurisdiction, several judges responded that the determination of jurisdiction is consistent with the role of any court before it begins review of the substance of the cases.

[116] *Mayers v. Immigration and Naturalization Service*, 175 F.3d 1289, 1294.

[117] 228 F.3d 591, 222 F.3d 728.

Letterman v. Reno (1999), from the Eleventh Circuit, the panel ruled that Letterman was not deportable because the murder he committed predated the AEDPA effective date.[118] Therefore, the panel concluded, the district court retained jurisdiction in the case. Similarly, in the Fifth Circuit case *Beltran-Resendez v. Immigration and Naturalization Service* (1999), the panel dismissed Beltran-Resendez's petition for review but still held that the Fifth Circuit had jurisdiction to review the case.[119] In deciding the effective dates of the new legislation and whether it could apply retroactively, the U.S. Courts of Appeals could preserve or deny judicial review in these cases. The key was that they retained the right to decide their jurisdiction by deciding which legal regime the cases fell under by interpreting that statute written by Congress.

A third strategy employed by some of the U.S. Courts of Appeals to retain *habeas* review was to second-guess Congress. These Courts of Appeals opined that if Congress did not clearly state that *habeas corpus* was to be abolished, then Congress could not have meant that it be abolished. For example, the Fifth Circuit panel in *Requena-Rodriguez* (1999) wrote, "As both hoary and recent Supreme Court cases explain, Congress must be explicit if it wishes to repeal *habeas* jurisdiction. Yet the alleged jurisdiction-stripping provisions here are simply not explicit."[120] In another Fifth Circuit case, the panel took a similar position: "It is well-settled that Congress must be explicit if it wishes to repeal *habeas* jurisdiction."[121] Similarly, the Ninth Circuit in *Flores-Miramontes v. Immigration and Naturalization Service* (2000), cited cases from the Second, Third, Fourth, Sixth, Eighth, and Tenth Circuits on the point that IIRIRA did not repeal or limit existing *habeas corpus* because there was no clear or explicit statement that Congress intended to repeal it.[122] These Courts of Appeals were unwilling to let Congress abolish the writ of *habeas corpus* by implication.

Why were the U.S. Courts of Appeals behaving this way? Viewed in light of their crushing caseloads, they seemed to be making more work for themselves when they could have simply pointed to the relevant statute and concluded that they had no jurisdiction. Indeed many Courts of Appeals panels took that very approach. Part of the explanation of why many other panels did not go that route hinges on the continuing

[118] 168 F.3d 463.
[119] 207 F.3d 284.
[120] 190 F.3d 299, 305.
[121] *Max-George v. Reno*, 205 F.3d 194, citing *Felker v. Turpin*, 518 U.S. 651, 660–661.
[122] 212 F.3d 1133, 1137.

influence of the institutional norm of due process. The opinions indicated that many of the judges of the U.S. Courts of Appeals believed that Congress had impermissibly crossed a line by curtailing the due process rights of a class of aliens. In fact, for much of immigration legal history and before Congress authorized the Courts of Appeals to hear deportation appeals in 1961, *habeas corpus* was the "usual method for obtaining judicial review of deportation orders."[123] The response of the U.S. Courts of Appeals to the court-stripping measures in the 1996 acts was very similar to the response of the early Supreme Court in the late 1880s and 1890s, in which the Supreme Court initially deferred to, and seemed to take literally, the congressional stipulation that the decision of the administrative agency personnel were final. Gradually, that initial judicial deference gave way to a more assertive posture that administrative power and executive power cannot be arbitrary and therefore must be subject to some judicial oversight.[124] As Henry Hart, Jr. indicated, "The very existence of a jurisdiction of *habeas corpus*, coupled with the constitutional guarantee of due process, implied a regime of law."[125] And a regime of law implies judicial review, which takes one right back to the initial argument of this book regarding the role of the federal courts, particularly the "province and duty of the judicial department to say what the law is," and to assess whether a statute is in comportment with the Constitution.[126] The majority of the U.S. Courts of Appeals that weighed in on the question of whether *habeas* review for criminal aliens survived the 1996 legislative reforms were deeply influenced by their perception of the role the federal courts should be playing in a system of government with separated branches.

Perhaps the most interesting development on the question of *habeas* review and AEDPA and IIRIRA was the reaction of the Supreme Court, which finally had to step in to settle the inter-circuit conflict spawned by the numerous legal challenges to AEDPA's and IIRIRA's limits of judicial review. On this question the Court majority sided with the alien and concluded that the 1996 reforms did not preclude *habeas corpus* review. This was one of the very few victories for aliens at the Supreme Court. Daniel Kanstroom commended those who tirelessly litigated the *St. Cyr* case and stated that they deserved a "Nobel Prize for against-the-odds litigation"

---

[123] Legomsky, *Immigration and Refugee Policy* (4th ed.), 741.
[124] Henry M. Hart, Jr., "The Power of Congress to Limit the Jurisdiction of Federal Courts: An Exercise in Dialectic," 66 *Harvard Law Review* 1362, 390 (1953).
[125] Ibid.
[126] *Marbury v. Madison*, 5 U.S. 137, 177 (1803).

because of the enormity of what they had achieved. They had pushed the Court to affirm propositions that "many had thought fundamental," including affirming the right of *habeas corpus* review for aliens.[127]

In so doing, the Supreme Court took a similar approach to that taken by some of the Courts of Appeals in pointing out that "[i]mplications from statutory text or legislative history are not sufficient to repeal *habeas corpus* jurisdiction; instead, Congress must articulate *specific and unambiguous* statutory directives to effect a repeal."[128] The majority also adopted a standard method of statutory interpretation that directs the courts to interpret statutes, if it all possible, in such a way as to avoid constitutional problems.[129] Writing for the majority, Justice Stevens noted, "A construction of the amendments at issue that would entirely preclude review of a pure question of law by any court would give rise to substantial constitutional questions [of the availability of *habeas corpus* as provided by the Constitution's Artic I, § 9, cl. 2]."[130] The majority was very concerned that in foreclosing *habeas* review for this class of aliens, "[i]f it were clear that the question of law could be answered in another judicial forum, it might be permissible to accept the INS' reading of § 242. But the absence of such a forum, coupled with the lack of a clear, unambiguous, and express statement of congressional intent to preclude judicial consideration of *habeas,* strongly counsels against adopting a construction that would raise serious constitutional questions."[131] En route to reaching its final disposition, the majority indicated several times that to conclude that the writ of *habeas corpus* would no longer be available to some aliens would be "a departure from historical practice in immigration law. The writ of *habeas corpus* has always been available to review the legality of executive detention."[132] Congress could attempt to limit judicial review, but the federal courts succeeded in wresting some of their power back by insisting that the courts (not Congress) would determine jurisdiction.

---

[127] Daniel Kanstroom, "*St. Cyr* or Insincere, the Strange Quality of Supreme Court Victory," 16 *Georgetown Immigration Law Journal* 413 (2002).

[128] *Immigration and Naturalization Service v. St. Cyr,* 533 U.S. 289, 299 (2001) (emphasis added).

[129] *Immigration and Naturalization Service v. St. Cyr,* 533 U.S. 289, 299: "If an otherwise acceptable construction of a statute would raise serious constitutional problems, and where an alternative interpretation of the statute is 'fairly possible,' we are obligated to construe the statute to avoid such problems."

[130] *Immigration and Naturalization Service v. St. Cyr,* 533 U.S. 289, 300.

[131] *Immigration and Naturalization Service v. St. Cyr,* 533 U.S. 289, 314.

[132] *Immigration and Naturalization Service v. St. Cyr,* 533 U.S. 289, 305.

CONCLUSION

Although the plenary power doctrine implies that Congress has full, complete, and absolute control over immigration, this has not been the understanding of the federal courts. Similarly, the fact that the national sovereignty idea prescribes expansive congressional and executive power in regulating the nation's borders has not meant the federal courts have faded away in this policy area. Although the Supreme Court in the earliest immigration cases appeared to cede total control over immigration to Congress as the plenary power demanded, the Court over time came to find that a returning long-time resident alien, and any alien in deportation proceedings, was entitled at least to a minimum of procedural due process protections, even as substantive due process arguments almost never gained traction in this area of law.

Based in part on some of the precedent created by the Supreme Court's procedural due process rulings, however few and far between, the U.S. Courts of Appeals were also able to make similar due process rulings. The increasing independence of the U.S. Courts of Appeals from the Supreme Court also bred innovation among the Courts of Appeals in their use of statutory interpretation techniques. The U.S. Courts of Appeals' response to the 1996 court stripping measures in AEDPA and IIRIRA was initially passive, but eventually the Courts of Appeals asserted themselves and pushed back against congressional and statutory attempts to limit the judicial role in this area of law. Congress may indeed have plenary power over immigration and the notion of national sovereignty conveys sweeping power to the state to police its borders, but the federal appellate courts have carved out their own role in immigration to ensure that government follows proper procedures while exercising its powers in immigration. And of course a determination of whether due process has been met implies judicial review, which might explain why both the Supreme Court and the U.S. Courts of Appeals so strenuously objected to the 1996 court stripping attempts.

7

Conclusion

For generations of aliens coming to America, the Statute of Liberty was the first figure they saw as their ships sailed into New York Harbor. For many other aliens fighting their deportation or removal in the federal courts, the image of Lady Justice was the last thing they saw as they headed into a federal courtroom. Yet neither of these two iconic figures of American life conveys the full story of the federal courts' treatment of immigration. The welcoming and majestic symbol of Lady Liberty elides the dark chapters of exclusion and bias in United States immigration history, in which the United States has blatantly discriminated against races, nationalities, and ideologies of "undesirable" aliens by preventing them from entering or outright expelling them from the United States. Similarly, the representations of Lady Justice belie the very complex interactions of the multitude of influences that affect and shape judicial decision making.[1]

Judicial decision making, in addition to being influenced by the ideology and individual characteristics of the judges, is very much circumscribed by the institutional settings and contexts of the courts. Some formal or informal norms, such as the constraining influence of stare decisis and doctrine, are indigenous to legal institutions, as opposed to the elected branches of government. But the analysis of other aspects of institutional context, such as the manner in which the federal judiciary is structured, or the limitations posed by formal and informal rules of operation, can be applied to studying other political institutions. The salient point is that

---

[1] See Dennis E. Curtis and Judith Resnik, "Images of Justice," 96 *Yale Law Journal* 1727–72 (1987), for an exploration of the ambiguities in the symbolism represented by images of justice.

institutional settings influence legal decision making and outcomes and therefore must be a focus of research in their own right, not a secondary or incidental consideration to other foci of analysis.

Although this book used the federal courts' treatment of immigration appeals as a case study to investigate judicial decision making and institutional development, the findings are generalizeable to judicial decision making in other areas of law. The set of modes of legal reasoning that appear in immigration law will not be the same as the modes of legal reasoning in other areas of law, although there will be some overlap. Similarly, the judges' interview questions for this book focused on their views on immigration cases. The findings that are transferable to help scholars understand judicial decision making in other areas of law are the processes and mechanisms that characterize the decision making of the U.S. Supreme Court and the U.S. Courts of Appeals vís a vís their distinctive institutional settings. More specifically, this study helps scholars better understand the linkages and interactions between extrajudicial variables, each court's institutional setting, and justices' and judges' selection of particular types of legal reasoning, as well as their varying degrees of commitment to types of legal reasoning.

With regard to immigration studies, this book confirms a conclusion reached by other scholars that "the state" does not act in a cohesive fashion and is far from being a monolithic actor in immigration policy.[2] Moreover, not only is the state fractured, even actors within the same institution have dissimilar goals and motivations. Immigration is characterized by the tension between the imperatives of national sovereignty and equal protection of the laws. The value with which the federal courts side depends on where the court is located in the judicial hierarchy.

Beyond immigration, this book has also been about the institutional evolution of the two highest appellate courts in the land. Formal rule changes to the U.S. Supreme Court's and the U.S. Court of Appeals' jurisdictions and abilities to control their dockets, combined with the pressures of a growing caseload, drove institutional development in each court and eventually led to a divergence in mission and function between them. Ultimately these transformations altered the institutional settings of both institutions, which had implications for the way justices and judges conceived of their jobs. The U.S. Supreme Court rose to prominence at the top of the federal judicial hierarchy, as it became primarily a policy

---

[2] See, e.g., Kitty Calavita, *Inside the State: The Bracero Program, Immigration, and the INS* (New York: Routledge, Chapman and Hall, 1992); and Gil Loescher and Jon Scanlon, *Calculated Kindness: Refugees and America's Half-Open Door, 1945 – Present* (New York: Free Press, 1998).

and political court. For this reason, the Supreme Court, far more than the lower federal courts, is very sensitive to the political dimensions of issues such as immigration. As a result, the Supreme Court found politically based ideas such as plenary power and national sovereignty persuasive. However, although the Supreme Court produced a clear line of doctrine based on the ideas of plenary power and national sovereignty, these ideas (and the attendant doctrine) were hardly referred to in the U.S. Courts of Appeals.

The Supreme Court's influence and its ability to create change derive from its ability to set policy and law with just one case, which will then serve as binding precedent for a much larger number of similarly situated cases. In the vast majority of cases, the Supreme Court engaged in statutory interpretation as it became the final arbiter in interpretative disputes and the tiebreaker in disagreements among the U.S. Courts of Appeals. However, given the vertical structure of the federal judicial hierarchy, the Court's influence is felt only in the small number of cases where it has granted *certiorari*, leaving large numbers and categories of cases to the U.S. Courts of Appeals to decide, such as the contours of the definition of assessing "persecution" in the context of asylum claims. And even in cases where the U.S. Courts of Appeals have either incorrectly applied or strategically circumvented established Supreme Court precedents, there is only the slimmest possibility that these cases will be granted *certiorari*, much less be reversed by the Supreme Court.

The U.S. Courts of Appeals evolved from courts intended as a mere way station on the way to the Supreme Court into courts that gained tremendous policy making power. Over time, these courts became effectively the "courts of last resort for all people," as Judge A described them.[3] Indeed, the U.S. Courts of Appeals' main power derived from the fact that they were often the final stop in the litigation chain for all federal appellants, not just alien appellants. And because they were almost always the last court to handle many appeals, it is their preferred interpretation of statutes, doctrine, or evidence and fact that trump those of the district courts or of the administrative agency personnel. In insulating itself from mundane cases and enhancing its importance by the very selective use of *certiorari*, the Supreme Court has ceded large portions of doctrine and policy making authority to the U.S. Courts of Appeals. In areas, such as immigration law, that generate tens of thousands of appeals annually, the U.S. Courts of Appeals, and the Ninth Circuit in particular, create the operative doctrine – not the Supreme Court.

[3] Interview with Judge A, 6/12/07.

The evolving institutional landscape of the federal judiciary has had a number of consequences for alien litigants. For one thing, alien litigants cannot assume that the Supreme Court will be as vigilant and aggressive about protecting their individual rights in the immigration context as the rights of other kinds of discrete and insular minority groups, such as racial minorities. This situation is not because of the Court's xenophobia or any personal animus of the justices against aliens; rather it derives from the unique combination of specific elements of immigration law and the function and mission of the Supreme Court as a policy and political court. Immigration policy and law are both characterized by a political division of labor, as embodied in the plenary power doctrine. The Supreme Court, being a policy court, is very sensitive to the political dimensions of this policy area and will often abide by the plenary power doctrine in deferring to Congress. By the same token, because the U.S. Courts of Appeals retain much of their error-correction mission and function, these courts find political arguments less relevant and persuasive. Whether the Supreme Court will offer close scrutiny of a case in order to protect the rights of an unpopular minority is dependent on what kind of minority it is and the political dimensions relevant to that particular area of law. One may not assume that the Supreme Court will always provide greater scrutiny of the treatment of a minority group.

The differentiated roles and missions of the U.S. Supreme Court and the U.S. Courts of Appeals affect the degree of scrutiny the justices or judges bring to the cases, which can affect final outcomes. When justices and judges take an individualized approach to adjudicating cases and carefully analyze the evidence and procedures in the case by using the fact/evidence and procedural due process modes of legal reasoning, aliens stand a better chance of winning their appeals. By contrast, when the justices or judges use an approach that conflates an individual alien's situation into an abstract and larger group, or if they defer to the previous administrative decision maker, the alien is unlikely to fare well. The degree of scrutiny brought to bear on a case is far greater when justices and judges use fact/evidence or procedural due process as a mode of legal reasoning than in cases in which they select plenary power, national sovereignty, or administrative deference as the mode of legal reasoning to decide the case. Yet whether a justice or judge takes an individualized approach toward immigrants or a generalized approach is very much predicated on the institutional setting and context in which he or she works.

Even as the Supreme Court and the Courts of Appeals have changed over time and become specialized in different functions, both institutions still remain courts of law and are clearly distinguishable from the elected branches of government. The two courts continue to be bound by *stare decisis* or doctrine and both courts continue to be concerned with due process protections, albeit to different extents. Due process is a judicial value that cannot be dislodged by politics or institutional development, even as the due process concept itself has evolved. The main difference between the two courts' commitments to due process in immigration law is that it takes a fairly egregious due process violation to jolt the Supreme Court into action, or the case must contain elements of the violation of substantive due process for the high Court to intervene on behalf of the alien and in contravention of another branch of government or the administrative decision makers. Meanwhile, the U.S. Courts of Appeals have taken over most of the error-correction function as well as the role of checking for bureaucratic abuses and errors.

The best-laid plans of the Constitution's framers did not play out exactly as intended or expected, but neither did their aspirations for the role of the federal judicial branch fail completely. They envisioned the judiciary as an independent branch of government that would balance and check the elected branches and the government bureaucracy and ultimately would further democracy. In his recent book, Paul Frymer concluded that in the labor arena, "The role of [federal] courts remains distinctively judicial in that courts not only enforce legislative acts, they rewrite them to fit within notions of rights and democracy."[4] In other words, Frymer found much evidence that the federal courts were indeed upholding their *Carolene Products* Footnote Four promise to protect those who cannot protect themselves. I would slightly modify Frymer's conclusion; in the immigration context, certain courts, particularly the U.S. Courts of Appeals, have rewritten laws and legislative acts to further the notions of rights and democracy for aliens. It is not that the Supreme Court has completely declined to do so; it is a matter of degree. Aliens in immigration cases can expect more vigorous and vigilant protection of their individual rights from the U.S. Courts of Appeals than from the Supreme Court. Because of the intercurrent development of the federal judiciary, in which the U.S. Supreme Court and U.S. Courts of Appeals have over time diverged in their mission and function and become specialized, it is the Courts of Appeals that now have primary responsibility for scrutinizing administrative and bureaucratic decisions for error and abuse.

[4] Paul Frymer, *Black and Blue: The Labor Movement and the Decline of the Democratic Party* (Princeton, NJ: Princeton University Press, 2008), 129.

Increasingly, the question that court scholars and concerned citizens ask is not, "Can minority groups count on federal court protection?" Instead, the question has become, "*When* and *under what conditions* can minority groups count on federal court protection?" With Footnote Four in the *Carolene Products* decision, the Supreme Court took on a mission to protect vulnerable minority groups that would not have recourse to other parts of the political system. However, Gerald Rosenberg has charged that the Court's promise has been "hollow" in light of the Court's necessary reliance on the other branches of government for the enforcement of its decisions.[5] John Dinan pointed out that in periods of "social and political foment," judicial institutions did a superior job to the elected branches of securing the rights of citizens.[6] This book has spotlighted one more variable that one must take into consideration in assessing when and under what conditions federal courts will intervene to protect politically weak minorities: the distinctive institutional context of the court or courts. It would not be correct to say that the Supreme Court has no interest in protecting aliens in immigration cases. Rather, the Supreme Court and its justices are guided by a different set of institutional directives that lead them to weigh sometimes-competing concerns differently from the way judges of the U.S. Courts of Appeals might. Even judges' or justices' ideology and political pragmatism are bound by their courts' institutional context.

In a nation of immigrants, the highest court in the land is not hostile or indifferent to aliens' immigration claims. The Supreme Court will intervene only when a constellation of political and institutional variables align, but unfortunately those variables do not often include the consideration of whether justice will be served in an individual alien's case. However, one's case is unlikely to make it all the way to the U.S. Supreme Court anyway, and the U.S. Courts of Appeals, by virtue of their mission and function, are likely to give an alien's case much closer scrutiny, which can lead to a more favorable outcome for the alien. The evolution of the federal judiciary has resulted in a situation in which specific segments of an institution that has been accused of being undemocratic actually work to produce justice and widen democratic protections for one of the most politically weak and vulnerable groups in our polity, aliens.

---

[5] Gerald Rosenberg, *The Hollow Hope: Can Courts Bring About Social Change?* (Chicago, IL: University of Chicago Press, 1993).

[6] John Dinan, *Keeping the People's Liberties: Legislators, Citizens, and Judges as Guardians of Rights* (Lawrence, Kansas: University of Kansas Press, 1998), 170.

Appendix A

Further Elaboration of Case Selection Methods

CASE SELECTION

The cases in this original database were generated through a Lexis/Nexis search using the keywords "immigration" and "exclusion" or "deportation" with the relevant time constraints. These search terms generated two lists of cases, one of U.S. Supreme Court cases and the other of cases from circuit courts and from the U.S. Courts of Appeals. Any cases that were not actually immigration, exclusion, or deportation cases were not included in the sample. (These search terms occasionally picked up real estate or criminal cases having only tangential relevance to immigration.)

The immigration cases included in this study are either exclusion or deportation cases. I limited the study to these two types of immigration cases to maintain analytical consistency in the types of constitutional, other legal and political issues that arise in these cases. In an exclusion case, a court must decide if a person may enter U.S. territory; in a deportation case, a court must decide if a person may remain in the United States. Immigration scholars regard these types of entry/exit decisions as immigration policy. Exclusion and deportation cases also constitute the most common types of immigration cases and limiting the sample to these cases captures the majority of *all* immigration cases, including alienage and naturalization cases, in which the courts must decide whom to admit, symbolically, to the polity. I did not limit my search to plenary power cases, which would have skewed the sample. As I argue, any time a case is decided using plenary power as the lens, the alien almost invariably loses. An example of the kinds of cases that might be excluded using my selection criteria are cases involving the enforcement of employer sanctions against U.S. employers hiring illegal aliens, or cases involving a native-born U.S. citizen charged with selling fraudulent documents to aliens.

The database contains *all* of the circuit court cases from 1881 to 1891. In 1891, the Evarts Act created the U.S. Courts of Appeals system and the cases dating from 1891 onward were chosen from the Third, Fifth, and Ninth Circuits. By 1981, it became necessary to random-sample the cases in the Ninth Circuit because the caseload in this circuit skyrocketed. A master list of Ninth Circuit cases was created and a random sampling procedure was applied to that list to gather 10 percent of the cases on the list (650 cases total). Only Ninth Circuit cases between 1981 and 2002 were obtained through a random sampling procedure. This random sampling procedure works because presumably the influence of institutional settings on decision making is constant, stable, and empirically observable across time and cases. The cases from the circuit courts, Third Circuit, Fifth Circuit, the Supreme Court, and the Ninth Circuit from 1891 to 1980, constitute the universe of deportation and exclusion cases.

SELECTION OF TIME PERIOD

The database covers the years 1881–2002. The beginning of concerted federal efforts to regulate immigration was in 1882; prior to this, regulation of immigration was left to the individual states. Although the Naturalization Act was passed in 1790 and the Page Law in 1885, the federal government did not begin to regulate admissions in more systematic and full-scale fashion until the Chinese Exclusion Act. In addition, the broad time frame encompasses moments of restriction and non-restriction. The time periods 1883–1893, the decade following the passage of the 1921 and 1924 national origins-based laws, and the 1996 law are four time periods that are restrictionist eras in American immigration history. A watershed immigration act that is widely regarded as liberal and inclusionary was passed in 1965. The Immigration Act of 1965 was very much in the vein of the tolerance of the civil rights era. The years from 1990–1995 were also a relatively open period for immigration; another period of restriction began in 1996, marked by the passage of three pieces of legislation that were restrictionist in nature. Presumably, institutional norms as well as cognitive structures influence judicial behavior in fairly predictable ways regardless of the time period, nationality of the aliens, or the specific fact pattern of the cases.

While the initial time period for this study was 1891–2001, my concern about the potential influence of the 9/11 terrorist attacks on immigration decision making caused me to add cases from all of 2002. All cases for the Third and Fifth Circuits from 2002 were added, along with a sample of 10 percent of the 2002 immigration cases in the Ninth Circuit (included in the description of the sample above). The concern was not that there was a formal policy change flowing immediately from the terrorist attacks, or that the types of cases reaching the judges were different, but that after 9/11 a protectionist sentiment may have affected judicial decision making.

CIRCUIT SELECTION

The database includes all circuit court cases from 1881–1891, which amounted to only thirteen cases; eight of the thirteen used statutory interpretation as the mode of legal reasoning. Beginning in 1891, which marks the passage of the Evarts Act and the creation of the structure of the contemporary Courts of Appeals, the cases are limited to the Third, Fifth, and Ninth Circuits. The Fifth and Ninth Circuits were selected to maximize the number of cases in this database because these two courts, in raw numbers, adjudicated the largest number of immigration appeals. The Ninth Circuit has traditionally fielded the most immigration appeals of all the circuits. Since 2000, the Ninth Circuit alone adjudicates a little more than 50 percent of all immigration cases nationwide. Up until the late 1990s, the Fifth Circuit was responsible for the second largest number of immigration cases. By paying particular attention to these two courts, one assesses the two courts that have the most impact on immigration law. The Fifth Circuit and the Ninth Circuit experienced major surges in their immigration appeals beginning in the mid-1980s; the Third Circuit has had a much smaller but a more steady number of immigration appeals. Thus, the addition of the Third Circuit allows a comparison of the effect of rising caseloads on the adjudication of cases. These three circuits also cover different geographical regions: the northeast, south/ southwest, and western regions, thereby allowing an evaluation of any regional effects as well as a mix of nationalities of the aliens.

These three circuits were also selected to compare their institutional ideological reputation with how they have actually adjudicated immigration cases. As noted, the Ninth Circuit has a reputation among legal practitioners as the most liberal on a number of issues, most notably environmental issues and Native American law. The *Almanac of the*

Federal Judiciary, a standard legal reference manual that surveys lawyers and reports on the reputation of circuits and judges, noted of the Ninth Circuit, "while some lawyers interviewed reported that there is no single dominant legal philosophy on the court given the mix of liberal and conservative judges, others believed the court is liberal as a whole."[1] Perhaps as an inference from the general liberal reputation of the Ninth Circuit, immigration practitioners regard the Ninth as the most pro-alien circuit. Conversely, the Fifth is regarded as one of the nation's most conservative circuits, while the Third Circuit seems to lack an ideological reputation as either liberal or conservative. About the Fifth Circuit, the *Almanac* noted, "Lawyers interviewed were highly critical of the court's conservative bent." Of the Third Circuit, the *Almanac's* general assessment was that, "According to the lawyers interviewed, the Third Circuit can best be described as a moderate or centrist court. Many agree that, because of some recent appointments, it seems to be moving more to the right."[2]

---

[1] *Almanac of the Federal Judiciary,* Vol. 2 (Chicago: Aspen Law and Business Publications, 2007), 2. Some comments from lawyers about the Ninth Circuit included: "I definitely sense a liberal bias on the court"; "the decision you get really depends on who serves on the panel"; and "the circuit is still dominated by liberal judges."

[2] Ibid. at 1. Additional comments about the Fifth Circuit from attorneys included: "They are extremely conservative judges." "They seem to apply the law as they see it." "They are activist judges who do not feel constrained by precedent if they see the world differently." "[It is] one of the most conservative courts in the country." *Almanac,* 1. And a comment about the Third Circuit: "It is really a fine non-ideological court of appeals." *Almanac,* 2.

Appendix B

Further Elaboration on the Search
for Modes of Legal Reasoning

I identified the modes of legal reasoning through a close reading of the opinions to ascertain the primary (and sometimes secondary) rationale that judges used to justify the legal outcome. I did not work from a preconceived list; instead, as new modes of legal reasoning appeared, I added them to the list. To find the modes of legal reasoning, I could not simply scan for keywords, because, in many instances, judges would refer to one mode of legal reasoning by using varying rhetorical references. For example, a common mode of legal reasoning cited in Supreme Court cases was congressional plenary power over immigration and attendant judicial deference. Without ever writing the words "plenary power," numerous opinions referred to immigration as a subject that was the province of the political branches, or to the Congress or the executive (rather than the judiciary) as the "proper branch" to decide immigration issues. The use of keyword recognition software that would scan for certain words, or even a keyword search for "immigration" and "plenary power" in Lexis/Nexis, would have missed many of the plenary power cases.

In many other instances, judges ran through a list of possible legal reasoning and systematically ruled them out one by one before actually settling on one approach to justify the outcome in the case. In such an instance, a reader would have to read the opinion in its entirety to understand and identify the preferred mode of legal reasoning on which the outcome was actually based. In opinions where the decision was based on several approaches or ideas, I had to make a judgment call and narrow the field to one or two rationales that seemed to be driving the decision. Because in some instances there was more than one rationale or idea that the judges based their decision on, I included a category called "legal reasoning secondary," which, combined with "primary legal reasoning," provides a more richly textured account of the judges' method in these cases. Far and away the leading mode of legal reasoning for the "secondary mode of legal reasoning" category was doctrine. Justices and judges may have begun with one mode of legal reasoning and then followed up with doctrine as backup and further support. I acknowledge that there is a subjective element in the coding of some of the modes of legal reasoning in these cases, but note that this subjective element arises only in a minority of cases; a rough estimate would be less than a quarter of the cases in the database, where there were multiple approaches taken by the judges. In the majority of cases, the decision could be boiled down to one or two modes of legal reasoning. While tedious and time consuming, this kind of close reading and interpretative analysis was better suited to understanding how judges form preferences among competing modes of legal reasoning, which are issues that more mechanized content analysis would have missed entirely.

As far as the coding of the modes of legal reasoning was concerned, sometimes it was the overall tone and tenor, including the intensity and valence, of the opinion that was the most illuminating, and not any one particular mode of legal reasoning or even the disposition of the case. The methods of scanning for keywords or just focusing on outcomes would have simply missed much of the context of what the judges were doing in these cases. Suppose, for example, that there are two deportation cases in which aliens are challenging a provision from the 1996 Illegal Immigration Reform and Responsibility Act (IIRIRA) that would curtail federal court review of the aliens' appeals. Say that in one case, the U.S. Court of Appeals ruled in favor of the federal government, based on the doctrinal argument that there is a long-standing tradition of court deference to Congress based on Congress' plenary power to set immigration policy. In the second case, the Court of Appeals again ruled for the federal government, but decided the case on the merits, ruling that the alien had correctly been prosecuted under the tougher IIRIRA provisions and must now be expelled from the United States. A study focused only on outcomes would count both as pro-government decisions, when in fact the cases are significantly distinct. In the first case, the court is saying that Congress has primary policy making responsibility in immigration as long as it is consistently applied. In the second decision, the court preserves its policy-making role for itself even as the alien loses the case and is removed from U.S. territory.[1] In the first case, the court is recognizing the executive and congressional branches and their administrative agencies as rival policy makers; in the second case, the court is asserting judicial supremacy in having the last word on what the IIRIRA law really means. Regardless, the political significance of the two cases is very different and would require a close reading to uncover.

The analytical approach applied to the legal opinions in this book is best characterized as a combination of textual, doctrinal, and interpretative content analysis with regard to the institutional contexts of each court. This kind of thick description analysis allows one to uncover the process by which institutional attributes create incentives and disincentives for their occupants to behave in certain ways and therefore serve as "a source of distinctive political purposes, goals and purposes."[2]

[1] The example is adapted from Martin Shapiro's example of tax cases in *Law and Politics in the Supreme Court*, 39–40.
[2] Ronald Kahn, "Institutional Norms and Supreme Court Decision-Making: The Rehnquist Court on Privacy and Religion" in *Supreme Court Decision-Making: New Institutional Approaches* (Chicago: University of Chicago Press, 1999), 176.

Appendix C

Numerical Codes for Modes of Legal Reasoning

0 **Stat Interp A** Striving for a sensible construction of statute so as not to reach an absurd result.

1 **Stat Interp B** Congress would have been explicit if they wanted to deny these rights.

2 **Stat Interp C** Determining the meaning of the statute by textual analysis or deduction.

3 **Plenary Power** It is not for the courts to make changes to policy, Congress has control over this area of law.

4 **Proc Due Process** The lower court or administrative agency official made an error.

5 **Doctrine** Citing of legal doctrine and case law.

6 **Administrative Discretion** Deference to the admin agency (usually the BIA) and the court will only overturn if there was not enough substantial evidence supporting the BIA's determination.

7 **Reasonable** Decision was reasonable and supported by substantial evidence.

8 **Evidence** Decided the case based on facts and evidence.

9 **Fong Haw Tan** Standard from the case *Fong Haw Tan v. Phelan*, 333 U.S. 6 (1948): "deportation is an extreme measure; we should take care before we deport someone."

10 **National Sovereignty** The regulation of a nation's borders, including the determination of which aliens may enter and remain in the United States, is one of any sovereign nation's prerogatives.

11 **Harmony of Construction** Whenever possible, we should read statutes as not being in conflict with treaties.

12 **Foreign Policy** Immigration is closely related to Congress's foreign policy functions.

Appendix D

Interview Questions

This is the set of questions I used in the interviews with the Ninth Circuit judges. I used the same set of questions to interview the staff, but focused those interviews on having the staff describe the process and procedures by which immigration appeals are processed in the Ninth Circuit. The interviews with the judges did not cover the questions in exactly the same order nor did each of the judges provide sustained answers to the same questions. Nevertheless, the questions below provide a picture of the content covered in all of the interviews. The interviews ranged from 45 minutes to 1.5 hours in length.

I am interested in understanding how the immigration appeals to this court have affected the Ninth Circuit as an institution and you as a judge individually.

- Has the increase in the immigration appeals affected the way you perform your job? If so, how? If not, why not?
- What adjustments, if any, has the court had to make to accommodate the immigration appeals?
- Has the mix of cases at this court affected the way you do your job?
- Has your job changed from the time you were first appointed to the court until now? If so, how?
- Have you noticed any changes in the Ninth Circuit from the time you arrived on the court until now?

The immigration appeals surging into the Ninth Circuit have reportedly been a source of stress on the court. I now want to turn our discussion

to some of the proposals that have been made to lighten the Ninth
Circuit's caseload, especially its immigration caseload.

- What is your reaction to Senator Arlen Specter's proposal to route all
  the immigration appeals to the Federal Circuit Court of Appeals?
- What about a similar proposal to simply divide up all the immigra-
  tion appeals among the 12 U.S. Courts of Appeals?
- Would splitting up the Ninth Circuit assuage the caseload problem?
- In your view what is the best solution to the large number of immigra-
  tion appeals going to the Ninth Circuit?
- Do you see any benefits or drawbacks to the alien litigants and for the
  Ninth Circuit as an institution attributable to the fact that the Ninth
  Circuit handles a disproportionate number of immigration appeals
  among the 12 U.S. Courts of Appeals?

We have come to the end of my interview questions. Is there anything I
missed that you would like to add or is there anything we did not cover
today that you want scholars of immigration law and the U.S. Courts of
Appeals to know?

Index

Abel v. United States (1960), 203
abscondee removal teams,
    see National Fugitive Operations
    Program
administrative deference, in
    methodology, 47–8, 49–50
Administrative Procedure Act (APA)
    (1946), 25, 94–5
administrative state, due process and,
    204–9, 211–15
adultery, interpretation of, 120–3
aggravated felonies, 82, 223–4
agricultural workers, 76
Ah Lung, In re (Calif. Circuit 1883),
    87–8
Albright, Miller v. (1997), 9, 31
Aldisert, Ruggero J., 95
Aleinikoff, T. Alexander, 10, 30
Alien and Sedition Acts (1798), 28
aliens, 1
    criminal, 25–6, 38, 82, 212–13,
        223–4
    favorable court treatment of, 15, 16
    migration networks, 27
    Motomura on as pre-citizens, 207
    residence of, 27, 196, 204
    translation issues, 175, 180–1,
        214–15
    see also specific cases
Alito, Samuel A., Jr., 139–40

Amar, Akhil, 62
American Bar Association, 205
American Civil Liberties Union, 33
*American Power and Light Co.
    v. Securities and Exchange
    Commission* (1946), 203
Andreas, Peter, 77–8, 80–1
Anti-Federalists, 55–61, 63–5
Antiterrorism and Effective Death
    Penalty Act (AEDPA) (1996), 25,
    77, 156–7, 222–9
appeals process
    declaratory and injunctive relief, 25
    de novo review, 113, 131–2,
        139–40, 181
    vertical structure and, 141–2
    see also specific agencies and courts
appendices
    case selection methods, 237–40
    interview questions, 247–8
    modes of legal reasoning,
        numerical codes for, 245
    research methods, 241–3
apprehension practices
    Andreas on statistics for, 80–1
    Cornelius on statistics for, 80–1
    effect on caseloads, 82–3
    political expediency of statistics,
        80–1
    see also enforcement strategies

Arizona, 27
Arthur Anderson, LLP, 149
Article I (Constitution), 32
Article III (Constitution), 6, 62–3, 65
Ashcroft, John, 146–7, 149
asylum cases
    disparity of grant rates, 178
    fact/evidence in, 84
    immigration judges and, 177
    judging credibility of witnesses in,
        134
    in methodology, 37–8
    political asylum, 4
    TRAC report on, 94
    see also specific cases
Atkins, Burton, 107
Attorney General
    BIA oversight by, 23
    deportation cases and, 25–6
    Heilman on, 24
    immigration judges and, 204–5
    INS oversight by, 20
    judicial review and, 94–5
attorneys
    CLE classes for, 175–6
    government, 176
    pro bono representation by, 24–5
    quality of counsel, 174–80
    watchlist for unprofessional
        conduct, 176

*Banks v. Immigration and
    Naturalization Service*
    (9th Cir. 1979), 90
Barber, Leng May Ma v.
    (1958), 204
*Barthold v. Immigration and
    Naturalization Service* (5th Cir.
    1975), 91
Bell, Fiallo v. (1977), 7
*Beltran-Resendez v. Immigration
    and Naturalization Service*
    (5th Cir. 1999), 226–7
benefits for immigrants, 21
Berman, Sheri, 41
Board of Immigration Appeals (BIA)
    administrative hearings, 20

appeals process, 22–4, 93, 95
    due process and, 204–7
    procedural due process and,
        211–15
    writ of *habeas corpus* and, 25
    Attorney General oversight, 23
    caseloads, 23
    Circuit Court caseload surge and,
        148–55
        adjudication speed and denial
            rates, 151–2
        as catalyst for, 146
        delays in appeals process, 154–5
        streamlining rules, 148–55
        surge rates and, 152–3
    DHS and, 204–5
    EOIR and, 23, 93–4, 149
    error correction function, 23, 96–7
    exclusion of cases from in
        methodology, 35
    Heilman on backlog at, 24
    individualized review standards,
        91–2
    Justice Department and, 23, 148–9,
        151–2
    lack of confidence in, 93–4
    lack of resources for, 24
    quality control, 181–4
    on single incidence v. cumulative
        events decisions, 137–9
    summary affirmances, 150–1,
        182–3
    transmission belt model, 206–7
    see also specific U.S. Courts of
        Appeals
Board of Regents v. Roth (1971), 209
Board of Review, 22–3
    see also Board of Immigration
        Appeals
Board of Special Inquiry, 135–6
    see also Board of Immigration
        Appeals
Bobbit, Phillip, 42–3
boilerplate decisions, 91–2
Bonds, Marcello v. (1955), 94–5, 203
border enforcement, 75–83
    Andreas on politics of, 77–8

Cornelius on apprehension rates,
    80–1
illegal Mexican migration and, 76
national sovereignty views
    during 1880s-1890s, 75–6
    during 1920s-1950s, 76
    during 1960s, 76
    during 1980s, 76–7
    during 1990s, 77
    during 2000s, 77
    see also specific legislation
Border Games (Andreas), 77–8
Border Patrol, 20, 76, 78
Bracero Program, 76
Brandeis, Louis, 198
*Brea-Garcia v. Immigration
    and Naturalization Service*
    (3rd Cir. 1976), 120–3
Brewer, David J., 195–202
Browning, James R., 159–60
Brutus, 56–7, 58–60
Bureau of Citizenship and
    Immigration Services
    (BCIS), 21
Bureau of Customs and Border
    Protection (BCBP), 21
Bureau of Immigration, 20, 30
    see also Immigration and
        Naturalization Service
Bureau of Immigration and Customs
    Enforcement (BICE), 21
Bureau of Measurements and
    Weights, 176
Burns v. United States (1991), 203
Bush administration enforcement,
    81–2

Calavita, Kitty, 76, 99
California
    alien residents in, 27
    district court history, 27–9
    international ports of entry and, 27
    racism toward Chinese in, 70
Canada, 27
Carlson v. Landon (1952), 203
Carolene Products, United States v.
    (1938), 5, 6, 9

caseloads. *see specific agencies and
    courts*
*Castillo v. Immigration and
    Naturalization Service* (9th Cir.
    1991), 91–2
Catterson, Cathy, 147, 155
*Chadha, Immigration and
    Naturalization Service v.* (1983),
    188–9
Chae Chan Ping v. United States
    (1889), 11, 31, 75–6, 194,
    195–203
Chertoff, Enwonwu v. (1st Cir.
    2005), 184–5
*Chevron v. National Resource
    Defense Council* (1984), 113–14,
    174
Chinese aliens
    enforcement confusion and, 87–8
    finality clause and, 74
    history of, 27–9
    McClain on, 69, 70–1
    proof of residence, 196
    race discrimination and, 41–2, 70,
        195–202
    Salyer on, 70, 71–2
    success in lower courts, 69–74
    see also specific cases
Chinese Exclusion Act (1882)
    amendments (1892), 196
    Brewer on, 199
    district court history and, 27–9
    enforcement of, 87–8
    judging credibility and, 132
    restrictionist sentiment and, 36
Chinese exclusion case, *see Chae
    Chan Ping v. United States*
*Choe v. Immigration and
    Naturalization Service* (9th Cir.
    1979), 117
circuit courts, 64–5, 66, 87–8
    *see also specific U.S. Courts of
        Appeals*
Circuit Courts of Appeals Act,
    see Evarts Act (1891)
Civil Rights revolution, 5, 76
Cohen, Jonathan, 39

Coke, Edward, 192
Colding, Kwong Hai Chew v. (1953),
    190, 195, 203
Commerce and Labor Department,
    20
community based organizations, 24–5
Congress
    attempts to limit exercise of
        discretion, 127, 129
    on immigration regulation, 31
    legislative impact on role of courts,
        61–8
    statutes to address adultery
        interpretation, 121–3
    Supreme Court's deference to, 7, 9,
        31–2
    see also specific legislation
consistency, 7–9
Constitution
    Article I, 31
    Article III, 6, 62–3, 65
    on judicial branch, 6
    lack of provision for immigration
        regulation in, 31
    Stevens on limited judicial design
        in, 61–2
    see also framers' intent; specific
        Amendments
Constitutional Fate (Bobbit), 42–3
constitutional immigration law,
    219–21
Continuing Legal Education (CLE),
    175–6
Cornelius, Wayne, 80–1
*Cortez-Acosta v. Immigration and
    Naturalization Service* (9th Cir.
    2000), 207–9, 212–13
cost of appeals, 23, 24–5, 204–5
court reporters, 177–8
Courts of Appeals, U.S.
    on agency individualized review
        standards, 91–2
    caseloads
        BIA appeals, 93, 205
        judicialization of immigration
            policy and, 68–75
        types of, 3–4, 13–14

volume of, 3–4, 13–14, 24, 68,
    94, 114–15, 130
commitment to due process,
    188–236
    administrative state and, 207–9
    minimum procedures and, 210
    procedural due process and,
        211–17
constitutional claims review in, 26
deciding to defer, 139–41
division of labor, 83
error correction function, 13, 83
    consequences for litigants, 86–7,
        93, 174
    fact/evidence, 131–2
    ombudsman role and, 93–9
    procedural due process, 211–17
establishment of, 67
exercise of discretion, 127
as final arbiter of removal cases,
    3–4
Footnote Four and, 6
habeas corpus review, 26, 222–9
    jurisdiction and, 225–6
    retroactivity and, 226–7
    second-guessing Congress and,
        227
history of, 13, 15, 27–9, 54–61,
    63–5
individual equity, 15
individual vs. group adjudication,
    88–93
influence of, 68
innovation within immigration
    system, 173–86
as institution, 2
interstitial policy making in, 102–4
    adultery, interpretation of,
        120–3
    extreme hardship, interpretation
        of, 116–19
    ideology and, 108–9
    incentives for, 125
    judging credibility and, 131–7
    limits of positive law and,
        109–10
    opportunities for, 108–16

panel composition and, 108
purposive behavior and, 104–8,
    126–41
rise of statutory interpretation
    and, 110–12
vague statutory language and,
    112–16
vertical structure of appeals
    process and, 141–2
judges
    lack of sanctions for, 123–4, 125
    perception of roles, 96–8, 221
on judicial review of administrative
    discretion, 93–9
legislative impact on role of, 61–8
low pro-alien rates, 124–5
modes of legal reasoning
    in comparison to Supreme Court,
        85–6, 131–2, 141–2, 211–17
    fact/evidence, 85–6, 131–2, 183
    procedural due process, 211–17
    statutory interpretation, 85–6,
        110–12, 141–2
petition for review process, 25
as policy court, 86
purposive behavior in, 8, 102–3,
    104–8, 126–41
sanctions, lack of
    Cross on, 124
    Howard on, 124
    for judges, 123–4, 125
theoretical expectation of, 13
see also specific courts, cases,
    judges, and legislation
Courts of Appeals in the Federal
    Judicial System (Woodford), 83
court stripping
    consequences of, 156–7
    habeas corpus review and, 222–9
    resistance to, 222–3
    Schrag on, 23
credibility, judging of, 131–7
criminal law, 5, 7
Cross, Frank, 124
cultural insensitivity, 179–80
cumulative consequences of partial
    reforms, 54

Curran, United States ex rel.
    Schachter v. (3rd Cir. 1925),
    216–17
in custody, interpretation
    of, 119–20
Customs and Border Protection
    (CBP), 79

Daily Journal, 177
Davis, John Warren, 216–17
Davis, Zadvydas v. (2001), 9
D.C. Circuit Court of Appeals, 122
Deady, Mathew, 28–9
deciding to defer, 139–41
deep equilibria, 189
democracy, 4, 56
Denmore v. Kim (2003), 203
de novo review, 113, 131–2, 139–40,
    181
deportation cases
    Attorney General and, 25–6
    conditions for, 37
    court rationale in, 4
    deportation as punishment,
        195–204
    Legomsky on due process in, 209
    in methodology, 35–8
    petition for review process, 25
    statutory interpretation in, 84
    Supreme Court's perceived hostility
        toward, 2
    ten year return ban, 82
    vague statutory language and, 116
    see also removal cases; specific
        cases
Diaz-Resendez v. Immigration and
    Naturalization Service (1992),
    212
Dinan, John, 236
Dinnerstein, Leonard, 1
discretion
    congressional attempts to limit
        exercise of, 127, 129
    Courts of Appeals, U.S. and, 93–9,
        127
    Friendly, Henry J., on definition of,
        126–7

discretion (*cont.*)
  Kanstroom on aspects of, 126–7,
    128–9, 130
  Murphy on frequency of,
  purposive uses of, 126–41
    deciding to defer, 139–41
    judging credibility and, 131–7
    single incidence vs. cumulative
      events, 137–9
district courts, 27–9, 64–5
  see also specific courts
division of labor, 83, 86–7, 167–8
  see also Courts of Appeals, U.S.;
    Supreme Court
docket control procedures, 33–4, 66,
  148, 173
doctrine/*stare decisis*
  in Courts of Appeals, 85–6
  in methodology, 35, 47–8, 49
Doe, Phyler v. (1982), 37
*Doherty, Immigration and Natural-
  ization Service v.* (1992), 96
Dong Ah Lon v. Proctor (9th Cir.
  1940), 136
Dorsey Report (ABA), 150
Douglas, United States v. (1883), 87
due process, 7, 91, 190, 219–21
  see also procedural due process;
    substantive due process
due process and federal courts
  administrative state and, 204–9
    BIA and, 204–7, 211–15
  commitment to, 188–236
  contemporary examples of, 209–11
    minimum procedures and, 210
  deportation as punishment and,
    195–204
  due process, generally, 190–3
    Coke on law of the land, 192
    origins in Magna Carta, 191–3
  habeas corpus review, 222–9
  in immigration context, 193–4
  procedural due process
    conditions for, 211–17
    contemporary examples of,
      209–11
    landmark decisions in, 195–202

  as phantom norm, 219–21
  substantive due process vs.,
    188–236
  see also specific courts and cases

Einhorn, Bruce J., 177
Eisentrager, Johnson v. (1950), 203
elbow clerks. *see* law clerks
Eldrige, Mathews v. (1976), 209,
  210–11
elected branches
  deference to, 7, 9, 31–2
  framers intent, 4–5
  see also specific elected branches
Elements of Judicial Strategy
  (Murphy), 104–5, 110
Eleventh Circuit Court of Appeals
  on habeas corpus review, 225–6
  jurisdiction and, 225–6
  retroactivity and, 226–7
*Elting, Lloyd Sabaudo Societa
  Anonima Per Azioni v.* (1932),
  203
Ely, John Hart, 5
employers, immigration laws and, 78,
  80–1
enforcement strategies
  border vs. interior, 78
    under Bush administration, 81
    under Obama administration, 81
    personnel levels, 78
    priorities and resources for,
      78–83
  effect on caseloads, 13, 80–1, 82–3
    TRAC report on, 83
  under Homeland Security Act, 21
  by INS, 20–1
  voluntary departure option, 82–3,
    120
  worksite enforcement, 78, 80–1
  see also border enforcement
Enwonwu v. Chertoff (1st Cir. 2005),
  184–5
Epstein, Lee, 104–5
equal protection jurisprudence, 5
error correction function
  of BIA, 23, 96–7

of Fifth Circuit, 97–9
Howard on, 85–6
immigration judges and, 23
of INS, 98
under Judiciary Act (1789), 64–5
of Ninth Circuit, 14, 96–8
see also Courts of Appeals, U.S.
Evarts Act (1891), 66–7
exclusion cases
    court rationale in, 4
    habeas corpus review, 25
    in methodology, 35–8
    Supreme Court's perceived hostility
        toward, 2
    see also removal cases
executive branch, 7, 9
Executive Office for Immigration
    Review (EOIR)
    BIA and, 23, 93–4, 149
    hierarchy of, 204–5
    immigration judges and, 22, 93–4,
        178
    Justice Department and, 22, 204–5
    uniform application of laws, 178
ex rel. *see name of related party*
extreme hardship, interpretation of,
    116–19

fact/evidence
    in asylum cases, 84
    comparison among courts, 84,
        131–2
    in Courts of Appeals, 85–6, 131–2,
        183
    level of scrutiny on, 112
    in methodology, 47–8, 50
    in Supreme Court, 84, 131–2
federal courts, *see specific courts*
Federalist Papers, 6
    Federalist 81, 60
    Federalist 78, 4–5, 15–16, 57, 58,
        104
Federalists, 4–5, 15–16, 55–61, 63–5
Federal Rules of Civil Procedure, 177
Federal Rules of Evidence, 177
felonies, *see* aggravated felonies
Fiallo v. Bell (1977), 7

Field, Stephen J., 72–3, 195–202
Fifth Amendment, 190, 192
Fifth Circuit Court of Appeals
    alien residents in region, 27–8
    on aliens' right to due process, 91
    caseloads 2002 surge rates,
        152–3
    volume of, 36
    in custody, interpretation of,
        119–20
    due process violations
        BIA and, 212, 214–15
    error correction function
        BIA and, 97–8
        INS and, 98–9
    on habeas corpus review, 225–6
        retroactivity and, 226–7
        second-guessing Congress and,
            227
    on individual vs. group
        adjudication, 91, 92
    low pro-alien rates, 124–5
    modes of legal reasoning, 84
        statutory interpretation, 84
    on single incidence v. cumulative
        events decisions, 137–9
    see also Courts of Appeals, U.S.;
        specific cases
finality clause, 74
First Circuit Court of Appeals, 184–5
    see also Courts of Appeals, U.S.
Fisher, Yamataya v. (1903), 88, 190,
    202–4, 211, 217
Flores, Reno v. (1993), 203
*Flores-Miramontes v. Immigration
    and Naturalization Service* (9th
    Cir. 2000), 227
Florida, 27
*Fong Choy Yu v. Immigration and
    Naturalization Service* (9th Cir.
    1971), 117
Fong Haw Tan v. Phelan (1948), 198
Fong Yue Ting v. United States
    (1893), 11, 31, 75–6, 195–202,
    209, 217
Footnote Four, 5, 6, 9
forum shopping, 70

Fourteenth Amendment, 190, 192
framers' intent
  on judicial branch, 3, 4–5, 6, 64,
    93, 104
  on separation of powers, 64
  see also Constitution
Frankfurter, Felix, 62
Frederick, David C., 29
Friedman, Barry, 43–4, 113
Friendly, Henry J., 126–7
Fritz, Christian, 72–3, 195–6
Frymer, Paul, 14, 235
Fugitive Operations Teams (FOTs),
  79–80
Fuller, Melville, 201

Galvan v. Press (1954), 203
game theoretical studies, 103–4
Garth, Leonard I., 198
gateway cities, 27
Geertz, Clifford, 45
Geyh, Charles, 64
Goldberg v. Kelly (1970), 209
Gonzales, Alberto, 179
Gonzales, Suntharalinkam v. (9th
  Cir. 2007), 129–30
good moral character
  INS definition of, 120, 122
  interpretation of, 120–3
Gordon, Robert, 41, 51
Graber, Mark, 40–1
Graham v. Richardson (1971), 37
Grant, Edward, 151–2
Gray, Horace, 194, 197
greencard holders, 37, 162, 207
Greene v. McElroy (1959), 203
Grey, Thomas, 191
Gung You v. Nagle (9th Cir. 1929),
  133–5

habeas corpus mills, 29, 72–3
habeas corpus review
  court stripping effect on, 222–9
  exclusion cases, 25
  post IIRIRA and AEDPA, 222–9
  see also specific courts
Hamilton, Alexander, 4–5, 15–16, 104

hardship requirement, 89–90
  see also extreme hardship,
    interpretation of
Harlan, John Marshall, 202–3
Harrisiades v. Shaughnessy (1952),
  193
*Hartooni v. Immigration and
  Naturalization Service* (9th Cir.
  1994), 91–2
*Hassan v. Immigration and
  Naturalization Service* (9th Cir.
  1991), 117
Hatch, Orrin, 169–71
Heilman, Michael, 24
*Hernandez-Cordero v. Immigration
  and Naturalization Service* (5th
  Cir. 1986), 137–9
*Hernandez-Cordero v. Immigraiton
  and Naturalization Service* (5th
  Cir. 1987), 97–8
*Hernandez-Garza v. Immigration
  and Naturalization Service* (5th
  Cir. 1989), 214–15
Hess, Frederick, 151–2
hierarchy, judicial, 64–6
Hoffman, Ogden, 28–9, 72–3
Homeland Security Act (2003), 21
Homeland Security Department
  (DHS)
  administrative hearings, 20
  BIA and, 204–5
  EOIR and, 22
  NFOP and, 79–80
Hopkins, Yick Wo v. (1886), 37
Howard, J. Woodford, Jr.
  confirmation of findings of, 84,
    85–6
  on differentiated functions of
    courts, 61, 83, 85–6
  on lack of sanctions on Courts of
    Appeals, 124
Hurtado v. California (1884), 192–3

ideological politics, 33
Illegal Immigration Reform and
  Immigrant Responsibility Act
  (IIRIRA)

appeals process provisions, 25
habeas corpus review and, 222–9
impact on Circuit Court personnel, 156–7
removal case provisions, 38
restrictionist sentiment and, 77
Illinois, 27
immigrant policy, 37
Immigration Act (1965), 76
Immigration Act (IMMACT) (1990), 77
Immigration and Nationality Act (1952), 20, 25
Immigration and Nationality Act (1996)
  appeal process under, 25–6
  good moral character, definition in, 120, 122
  IIRIRA revisions to, 38
  impact on Circuit Court personnel, 156–7
  legal challenges to, 26, 188–9
  section 212c, 139–40, 212, 214–15, 223–4
Immigration and Naturalization Service (INS), 20–1, 76, 211–15
  see also Immigration Customs and Enforcement; *specific cases*
Immigration Brainstorming Session (Ninth Circuit), 163
immigration cases, *see specific cases*
Immigration Customs and Enforcement (ICE), 79–80, 81
immigration exceptionalism, 31
immigration judges (IJ)
  as accountable to Attorney General, 204–5
  agency treatment of, 24
  appeals process and, 21–2
  asylum cases and, 177
  caseloads, 22, 177–8
  cultural insensitivity by, 179–80
  decision appeal rates, 23
  disparity of asylum approval rates, 178
  EOIR and, 22, 93–4, 178

error correction function and, 23
lack of confidence in, 93–4, 177
lack of resources for, 177–8
numbers of, 24
quality of counsel as constraint on innovation, 174–80
immigration law, 9–11, 125
  see also specific legislation
immigration policy, 8, 68–75
  see also specific agencies
Immigration Reform and Control Act (IRCA) (1986), 76–7
individual vs. group adjudication, 88–93
innovation and experimentation (Ninth Circuit), 162–5
  alternating calendars option, 164
  alternative solutions, 169–73
    Hatch/Specter proposal, 169–71
    screening and level of scrutiny, 173
    splitting of Appeals Court, 171–2
  brainstorming session, 163
  grouping of cases, 165
  immigration system, constraints on, 173–86
    administrative review by BIA, 181–4
    back fill requirement, 174
    counsel, quality of, 174–80
    cultural insensitivity, 179–80
    disparity of grant rates, 178
    lack of resources for immigration judges, 177–8
    need for CLE, 175–6
    overuse of law clerks, 176
    REAL ID Act and, 184–5
  one-week option, 164
  personnel's assessment of, 167–9
  screening panels and, 163–4
  screening track, 165–6
  visitor proposal, 164
  see also Ninth Circuit Court of Appeals

institutional contexts
  ideology and, 108–9
  influence on judicial decision
    making, 2–3, 16, 73
  legislative impact on, 61–8
  political parties and, 14
  statutory interpretation and, 14
  see also due process and federal
    courts; modes of legal
    reasoning
institutional review, 85–6
institutions, 2
insular minorities. *see* minority
  groups
INS v., *see name of opposing party*
intercurrence, 12–13, 15
interpreters, 180–1, 214–15
interviews, 38–40, 247–8
  see also specific judges

Jackson, James, 63
Jackson, Robert H., 188, 190
*Jacobe v. Immigration and
  Naturalization Service* (3rd Cir.
  1978), 198
Japanese Immigration Case.
  see Yamataya v. Fisher
John (King), 191–3
Johnson v. Eisentrager (1950), 203
*Joint Fascist Anti-Refugee
  Committee v. McGrath* (1951),
  203
Jones, Edith H., 97–8
Judge A
  on BIA streamlining rules, 181–2
  on caseload surge impact, 144
  on Courts of Appeals, 102, 174,
    206
  on grouping of similar cases, 165
  on Hatch/Specter proposal, 170
  on low pro-alien decisions, 124
  on politics of splitting Court,
    171–2
  on poor quality of immigration
    bar, 174–5
  on respect for immigration judges,
    177

Judge B
  on BIA, 182–3, 186
  on cultural insensitivity, 179–80
  on mix of cases, 155
  on poor quality of immigration
    bar, 174–5, 183–4
  on substandard interpreters, 180–1
Judge C
  on BIA, 182, 183
  on caseload surge impact, 149
  on distribution of cases across
    Court, 171
  on lack of need for innovation, 162
  on poor quality of immigration
    bar, 174–5
  on psychological stress, 185
Judge D
  on BIA, 183, 186
  on caseload surge impact, 144
  on Hatch/Specter proposal, 170
  on panel composition, 108
  on screening panels, 168
  on screening system, 172–3
  on tracking procedures, 146
Judge E
  on BIA, 181, 186
  on caseload surge impact, 144, 152
  on cases with novel legal issues,
    125
  on citing Attorney General
    discretion, 129
  on Courts of Appeals as last resort,
    174
  on deference to immigration
    judges, 180
  on delays in appeals process, 155
  on disparity of grant rates, 179
  on Hatch/Specter proposal, 170
  on injustice of summary
    affirmances, 182
  on lack of confidence in
    administrative due diligence,
    130
  on mixed status family cases, 162
  on nonreview rubberstamping,
    161–2
  on overuse of law clerks, 176

on poor quality of immigration
bar, 183–4
on quality of CLE classes, 175–6
on quality of government counsel,
176
on triage of caseload surge, 146
Judge F
on administrative due diligence,
127–8
on assembly line division of labor,
167–8
on delays in appeals process, 154
on Hatch/Specter proposal, 170
on howlers/bad decisions, 180–1
on incremental approach, 165–6
on jurisdiction, 225–6
on level of scrutiny and outcomes,
129
on nonreview rubberstamping, 151
on overuse of law clerks, 176
on poor quality of immigration
bar, 174–5
on reliance on screening system, 162
on triage of caseload surge, 146
Judge G
on BIA, 186
on Courts of Appeals, 174
on grouping of similar cases, 165
on judges' attitudes, 108
on jurisdiction, 225–6
on mix of cases, 155–6
on screening system, 162, 172
Judge H, 129, 185
judges, federal
computerized selection of judge
panels, 106–7
ideology and, 108–9
lack of sanctions for, 123–4, 125
life tenure, 4, 57, 99
modes of legal reasoning and, 52
perception of roles, 96–8, 221
strategic behavior by, 14
see also immigration judges;
specific judges
judicial hierarchy, 64–6
judicialization of immigration policy,
68–75

judicial review
legislation and, 25–6, 28
purpose of, 5
Supreme Court denial of, 30
judiciary
framers' intent, 3, 4–5, 6, 64, 93,
104
hierarchy of, 64–6
history of, 3, 54–61
institutional influence on, 2–3
Judiciary Act (1789), 64–6
Judiciary Act (1801), 67
Judiciary Act (1916), 67–8
*Jung Ben Suh v. Immigration and
Naturalization Service* (5th Cir.
1979), 98–9
Justice Department
BIA and, 23, 148–9, 151–2
EOIR and, 22, 204–5
Heilman on, 24
INS and, 20
personnel levels, 24
reassignment of government
attorneys, 176
Ju Toy, United States v. (1905), 30,
31, 203

Kanstroom, Daniel
on exercise of discretion, 126–7,
128–9, 130
on *St. Cyr* case, 228–9
Katzmann, Robert A., 175
Kelly, Goldberg v. (1970), 209
Kens, Paul, 199
Kim, Denmore v. (2003), 203
King of the Hill analogy, 141–2
Klein, David, 39
*Knauff, United States ex rel. v.
Shaughnessy* (1950), 7, 194
Knight, Jack, 104–5
Kozinski, Alex, 161
Kwong Hai Chew v. Colding (1953),
190, 195, 203

Labor Department, 22–3
Lambert, Umanzor v. (5th Cir.
1986), 119–20

Landis, James, 62
Landon, Carlson v. (1952), 203
Landon v. Plascencia (1982), 190,
    195, 203
language issues. *see* translation issues;
    vague statutory language
law clerks
    immigration judges and, 177–8
    overuse of, 176
    reliance on, 146, 158, 165–6
lawyers, *see* attorneys
legal grammar, 42–3
legal institutions, democracy and, 4
legal reasoning, *see* modes of legal
    reasoning
Legomsky, Stephen, 10
    on due process in deportation
        cases, 209
    on goals of administrative process,
        150
    on immigration exceptionalism, 31
    on immigration regulation, 29–30,
        31
LeGrys, Lavita Strickland, 204–5
Leng May Ma v. Barber (1958), 204
Letterman v. Reno (11th Cir. 1999),
    226–7
Lexis/Nexis, 36
life tenure, 4, 57, 99, 204–5
*Lionel G. F. Panchevre v.
    Immigration and Naturalization
    Service* (5th Cir. 1991), 212
*Lloyd Sabaudo Societa Anonima Per
    Azioni v. Elting* (1932), 203
Los Angeles Times, 146–7, 150, 151–2
lower courts (federal), 6
Ludecke v. Watkins (1948), 203
*Lujan-Armendariz v. Immigration
    and Naturalization Service* (9th
    Cir. 2000), 225–6

Madison, Marbury v. (1803), 189
Magna Carta, 191–3
Major, Mendez v. (8th Cir. 1965), 117
*Malhi v. Immigration and
    Naturalization Service* (9th Cir.
    2003), 129–30
Marbury v. Madison (1803), 189

Marcello v. Bonds (1955), 94–5, 203
*Marcello v. Immigration and
    Naturalization Service* (5th Cir.
    1983), 207–9
Martin, David, 10
Maryland constitution, 192
Mashaw, Jerry, 94, 206, 208
Mathews v. Eldrige (1976), 209,
    210–11
*Mayer v. Immigration and
    Naturalization Service* (11th Cir.
    1999), 225–6
McCann, Michael, 41
McClain, Charles, 69, 70–1
McCloskey, Robert, 62
McElroy, Greene v. (1959), 203
*McGrath, Joint Fascist Anti-Refugee
    Committee v.* (1951), 203
McGrath, Wong Yang Sung v. (1950),
    203
mediation system, 147–8
Melnick, R. Shep
    on administrative interpretation,
        128
    on statutory interpretation, 109,
        110
    on vague legislative language, 110,
        123
memorandum dispositions, 158
Mendez v. Major (8th Cir. 1965), 117
mere judgment, 104
methodology
    administrative deference, 47–8,
        49–50
    advantages of multiple methods,
        34–5
    analytical strategies, 40–6
    construction of database
        case selection, 36, 141, 237–8
        circuit selection, 35–6, 239–40
        coding of modes of legal
            reasoning, 241–3, 245
        doctrinal analysis, 35
        time period, 238–9
    interviews, 38–40
    modes of legal reasoning, 34–5,
        40–50
    national sovereignty, 47–8, 50

overview, 32–4
preliminary findings
  legal or judicial modes of
    reasoning, 46–50
  political principles, 50
  reasonableness, 47–8, 50
  see also appendices
Mexico, 27, 76
*Mezei, United States ex rel.,
  Shaughnessy v.* (1953), 188, 190,
  203, 204
Migration Policy Institute (MPI),
  79–80
*Mikahel v. Immigration and
  Naturalization Service* (5th Cir.
  1997), 92
Miller v. Albright (1997), 9, 31
minority groups
  aliens as discrete and insular
    minorities, 5–6
  criminal law protections for, 5
  protection of, 5
    racial minorities, 5
    strict scrutiny and, 5
    Supreme Court and, 5
  see also specific groups
Minton, Sherman, 194
modes of legal reasoning, 44
  analysis of, 13
  institutional context and, 51–2
  judicial strategic behavior and, 14
  legal doctrine vs., 45–6
  see also methodology; *specific
    types and courts*
Montesquieu, 64
*Moon Ho Kim v. Immigration and
  Naturalization Service* (9th Cir.
  1975), 122
Motomura, Hiroshi, 10
  on aliens as pre-citizens, 207
  on phantom norms, 219–21, 222–3
  on procedural due process, 45,
    219–21
Mukasey, Michael, 153
Murphy, Walter, 104–5, 110

Nagle, Gung You v. (9th Cir. 1929),
  133–5

Nagle, Siu Say v. (9th Cir. 1926),
  132–3
Nagle, Young Len Gee v. (9th Cir.
  1931), 135–6
National Association of Immigration
  Judges, 162–3
National Fugitive Operations
  Program (NFOP), 79–80
  Fugitive Operations Teams (FOTs),
    79–80
  MPI report on, 79–80
  political expediency of, 80–1
nationality, exclusion based on, 73–4,
  87–8
national origins discrimination, 76
national security, 7, 8–9, 36
national sovereignty
  during 1880s-1890s, 75–6
  during 1920s-1950s, 76
  during 1960s, 76
  during 1980s, 76–7
  during 1990s, 77
  during 2000s, 77
  as justification for Court's
    deference to elected branches,
    7, 9, 31–2
  methodology definition of, 47–8,
    50
  Motomura on directives of, 219–21
  need for consistency and, 8–9
  procedural due process and,
    219–21
national vs. state power, 55–61
nativism, 30
naturalization/denaturalization cases,
  in methodology, 38
New York, 27
New York Times, 81
Ng Fung Ho v. White (1922), 198
Ninth Circuit Court of Appeals
  adultery, interpretation of, 122
  alien residents in region, 27–8
  caseloads
    Los Angeles Times on, 146–7
    merit cases and, 158
    termination rates and, 158
    2002 surge, 144–87
    volume of, 14, 28, 36, 130

Ninth Circuit Court of Appeals (*cont.*)
    computerized selection of judge
        panels, 106–7
    due process, 207–9
    due process violations
        BIA and, 212–13, 214
    error correction function, 14, 97–8
        BIA and, 96–7
        INS and, 98
    extreme hardship, interpretation
        of, 117–19
    on finality clause, 74
    on habeas corpus review, 225–6
        second-guessing Congress and,
            227
    history of, 27–9
    ideological politics and, 33
    on individual vs. group
        adjudication, 90
    influence of, 28, 29
    innovative changes in, 14
    institutional growth and
        innovation, 144–87
    see also innovation and
        experimentation
        alternative solutions, 169–73
        building on Browning era
            reforms, 158–62
        effect of caseload surge on
            personnel, 155–8
        within immigration system,
            173–86
        personnel assessment of
            experiments, 167–9
        role of BIA in, 148–55
        screening track, 165–6
    interviews, 38–40, 247–8
    on judging credibility of witnesses,
        133–5
    lack of confidence in administrative
        due diligence, 127–8
    low pro-alien rates, 124–5
    modes of legal reasoning, 84
        fact/evidence, 84, 133–5, 183
    see also Courts of Appeals, U.S.;
        specific cases and judges

Nishimura Ekiu v. United States
    (1892), 31, 194
non-argument calendar, 147–8
National Resources Defense Council,
    Chevron v. (1984), 113–14, 174

Obama Administration enforcement,
    81
Ocean Steam Navigation Company
    v. Stranahan (1909), 7
O'Connor, Sandra Day, 31
Office of Immigration Litigation, 176
Office of the Superintendent of
    Immigration, 20
order decisions, 158
Oregon, 27–9
Orren, Karen, 2–3, 12
Orth, John, 193

Palmer, John, 147
Paul v. Immigration and
    Naturalization Service (5th Cir.
    1975), 207–9
Perry, H. W., 107, 141
petition for review, 25
phantom norms, 219–21, 222–3
Phelan, Fong Haw Tan v.
    (1948), 198
Phyler v. Doe (1982), 37
Pierson, Paul, 12
Plascencia, Landon v. (1982), 190,
    195, 203
plenary power, in methodology,
    47–8, 50
plenary power doctrine
    Aleinikoff on, 30
    due process vs., 190, 219–21
    in methodology, 47–8, 50
    Motomura on, 219–21
    Scalia's opinion on cases, 9
    Supreme Court's deference to
        congressional, 1, 7, 9, 31–2
    see also Congress
political asylum cases, 4
political parties, institutional context
    and, 14

politics of immigration, opaque
statutes and, 125
positive law, limits of, 109–10
Posner, Richard A.
on caseload vs. workload, 156
on level of scrutiny and outcomes,
129
on poor quality of immigration
bar, 175
on Refugee Roulette, 179
on Seventh Circuit's caseload surge,
146
Pregerson, Harry, 89–90
preliminary findings
legal or judicial modes of
reasoning, 46–50
political principles, 50
Press, Galvan v. (1954), 203
pro bono representation, 24–5
procedural due process
conditions for, 211–17
in methodology, 47–8, 49
Motomura on, 45
as phantom norm, 219–21
substantive due process vs.,
188–236
see also due process and federal
courts; *specific courts*
Proctor, Dong Ah Lon v. (9th Cir.
1940), 136
public counsel, 24–5
published opinions, 158
Publius, 57, 58, 60
pure questions of law, 26
purposive behavior
contrary to precedent, 8
definition of, 105–6
exercise of discretion as, 126–41
deciding to defer, 139–41
judging credibility and, 131–7
single incidence vs. cumulative
events, 137–9
see also discretion; *specific
courts*

Qing dynasty law, 70

race
as basis for exclusion, 87–8
legal framework and, 9
omission of in analysis, 41–2
racial minorities, rights for, 5
racism
in California laws, 70
in Chinese exclusion era, 195–202
Fritz on equality and, 195–6
Ramji-Nogales, Jaya, 150–1, 178–9,
183
*Ramos v. Immigration and
Naturalization Service* (5th Cir.
1983), 92
*Ravancho v. Immigration and
Naturalization Service* (3rd Cir.
1981), 95
Rawlinson, Johnnie B., 129–30
In re, *see name of party*
REAL ID Act (2005), 26, 77,
184–5
reasonableness, in methodology,
47–8, 50
Refugee Roulette, 179
removal, 4
removal cases
caseloads of immigration judges,
22
Courts of Appeals, U.S. and, 3–4
due process in, 7
extreme hardship, interpretation
of, 116–19
federal courts and, 4
legislative amendments and, 25–6,
38
Supreme Court and, 3–4, 7
see also deportation cases;
exclusion cases; *specific
cases*
Reno, Janet, 148–9
Reno, Letterman v. (11th Cir. 1999),
226–7
Reno v. Flores (1993), 203
*Requena-Rodriguez v. Immigration
and Naturalization Service*
(5th Cir. 1999), 225–6, 227

*Reynoso v. Immigration and
Naturalization Service*
(9th Cir. 1981), 89–90
Richardson, Graham v. (1971), 37
*Rios-Berrios v. Immigration and
Naturalization Service*
(9th Cir. 1985), 98
role perception theory, 221
Rosenberg, Gerald, 236
Roth, Board of Regents v. (1971), 209
Rubin, Alvin B., 97–8

*St. Cyr, Immigration and
Naturalzation Service v.* (2001),
26, 228–9
St. Louis SR Co. v. Arkansas (1914),
203
Salyer, Lucy
on Chinese redress in courts, 30,
70, 71–2
on finality clause, 74
on *Ju Toy* decision, 30
San Francisco, 70
Sawyer, Lorenzo, 28–9
Scalia, Antonin, 9, 110
*Schachter, United States ex rel. v.
Curran* (3rd Cir. 1925), 216–17
Schoenholtz, Andrew, 150–1, 178–9,
183
Schrag, Philip G., 23, 150–1, 178–9,
183
Schroeder, Mary M., 163–4, 169–71
Schuck, Peter, 10
on governmental authority vs.
individual entitlement, 6–7, 190
on immigration law, 30, 32
on influence of nationhood, 7
screening track, 165–6
Second Circuit Court of Appeals
alien residents in region, 27–8
caseloads
Palmer on, 147
2002 surge, 144–5, 146, 147–8,
152–3
volume of, 36
mediation system, 147–8
non-argument calendar, 147–8
screening track, 165–6

see also Courts of Appeals, U.S.
September 11, 2001 terror attacks, 36
Seventh Circuit Court of Appeals,
129, 146
see also Courts of Appeals, U.S.
*Shah v. Immigration and
Naturalization Service* (9th Cir.
2000), 134
Shapiro, Martin, 8
Shaughnessy, Harrisiades v. (1952),
193
*Shaughnessy, United States ex rel.
Accardi v.* (1954), 209, 210
*Shaughnessy, United States ex rel.
Knauff v.* (1950), 7, 194
*Shaughnessy v. United States ex rel.
Mezei* (1953), 188, 190, 203, 204
*Sida v. Immigration and
Naturalization Service* (9th Cir.
1981), 96–7
*Singh v. Immigration and
Naturalization Service* (9th Cir.
2000), 134
single incidence vs. cumulative events,
137–9
Siu Say v. Nagle (9th Cir. 1926),
132–3
Skowronek, Stephen, 2–3, 12
social Darwinism, 76
special inquiry officers,
see immigration judges
Specter, Arlen, 169–71
stall lawyers, 175
stare decisis. *see* doctrine/*stare decisis*
state constitutions, 190, 192
Statue of Liberty, symbolism of, 1, 2,
28, 32
statutory interpretation
comparison among Circuit Courts,
84
in Courts of Appeals, 85–6,
110–12, 141–2
Howard on, 85–6
institutional context and, 14
Melnick on, 109, 110
Murphy on, 110
positive law, limits of, 109–10
Scalia on, 110

in Supreme Court, 110–12, 113–14,
141–2
see also institutional review
statutory interpretation C, in
methodology, 47–9
Stevens, John Paul, 228–9
Stevens, Richard, 61–2
*Stranahan, Ocean Steam Navigation
Company v.* (1909), 7
strategic behavior, 14, 40–1, 104–8,
173
see also purposive behavior
strict scrutiny, 5
subconstitutional immigration law,
219–21
substantive due process
origins of, 193
procedural due process vs., 45,
188–236
summary affirmances (BIA), 150–1,
182–3
Suntharalinkam v. Gonzales (9th
Cir. 2007), 129–30
Supreme Court
Brutus on power of, 58–9
caseload volume, 94, 114–15
commitment to due process,
188–236
history of, 209–11
minimum procedures and, 210
procedural due process and,
210–17
deference to plenary power
of administrative agencies, 31–2,
117–19
of Congress, 7, 9, 31–2
Dinnerstein on, 1
of Executive branch, 7, 9
denial of appeal rights, 30
division of labor, 83
docket control procedures, 33–4,
66, 148, 173
on due process for aliens, 7
on extreme hardship, 117–19
on finality clause, 74
grant rates, 209
habeas corpus review, 26, 222–9
history of, 13, 15, 54–5

Amar on stature of, 62
Federalists vs. Anti-Federalists
views, 55–61, 63–5
Frankfurter on physical location
of, 62
individual vs. group adjudication,
88–93
as institution, 2
on judicial review, 94–5, 96
legislative impact on role of, 61–8
minority groups and, 5
modes of legal reasoning
in comparison to Courts of
Appeals, 85–6, 131–2,
141–2, 211–17
fact/evidence, 84, 131–2
procedural due process, 210–17
statutory interpretation, 85–6,
110–12, 113–14, 141–2
perceived hostility toward aliens
by, 2, 29–32
as policy court, 85–6
consequences for litigants, 86–8,
93
individual equity vs., 16
removal cases and, 3–4, 7
Shapiro on roles of, 8
stature of, 62, 67, 68
on statutory interpretation, 85–6
strategic behavior in, 105
theoretical expectation of, 13
as tie-breaker for inter-circuit
conflicts, 85–8
writ of *certiorari*, 66–7, 107, 115,
141
*see also specific cases, legislation,
and justices*

"Taking Law Seriously" (Friedman),
113
Taylor, Hannis, 192–3
*Tejeda-Mata v. Immigration
and Naturalization Service*
(9th Cir. 1980), 214
Tenth Circuit Court of
Appeals, 226
see also Courts of Appeals, U.S.
Texas, 27

Third Circuit Court of Appeals
  adultery, interpretation of, 120–3
  2002 surge rates, 152–3
  volume of, 36
  deciding to defer, behavior of,
    139–40
  good moral character,
    interpretation and, 120–3
  low pro-alien rates, 124–5
  modes of legal reasoning, 84
    statutory interpretation, 84
  see also Courts of Appeals, U.S.
Tichenor, Daniel, 76
*Tipu v. Immigration and
  Naturalization Service* (3rd Cir.
  1994), 139–40
Transactional Records Access
  Clearinghouse (TRAC), 81–2,
  83, 94, 178
translation issues, 175, 180–1,
  214–15
transmission belt model, 206–7
Treasury Department, 20, 71, 74
triage of caseloads, 145–6
212c waivers (INA), 139–40, 212,
  214–15, 223–4

*Ullah v. Immigration and
  Naturalization Service* (9th Cir.
  1995), 92
Umanzor v. Lambert (5th Cir. 1986),
  119–20
U.S. ex rel. v. *see name of related
  party*
U.S. v. *see name of opposing party*

vague statutory language
  adultery, term as, 120–3
  statutes to address, 121–3
  in custody, phrase as, 119–20
  in deportation cases, 116
  extreme hardship, phrase as, 116–19
  good moral character, phrase as,
    120–3

policy making in Courts of Appeals
  and, 112–16
voluntary departure option, 82–3,
  120
voting rights, 177
vulnerable groups. *see* minority
  groups

*Wang, Immigration and
  Naturalization Service v.* (1981),
  95, 117–19, 120
Warren Court, 5, 76
Washington (state), 27–9
Watkins, Ludecke v. (1948), 203
*Watkins v. Immigration and
  Naturalization Service*
  (9th Cir. 1995), 96–7
"Well Founded Fear" (documentary),
  180–1
White, Ng Fung Ho v. (1922), 198
women's rights, 5
Wong Wing v. United States (1896),
  9, 31, 202
Wong Yang Sung v. McGrath (1950),
  203
Wong You, United States v. (1912),
  88
worksite enforcement, 78, 80–1
writ of *certiorari*, 66–7, 107,
  115, 141

Yamataya v. Fisher (1903), 88, 190,
  202–4, 211, 217
Yick Wo v. Hopkins (1886), 37
Young, William G., 184–5
Young Len Gee v. Nagle
  (9th Cir. 1931), 135–6
*Young v. Immigration and
  Naturalization Service*
  (9th Cir. 1972), 47

Zadvydas v. Davis (2001), 9
Zadvydas v. United States (2001),
  188